LATIN AMERICA

Latin America

Its Future in the Global Economy

Edited by
Patricia Gray Rich
Economic Affairs Officer of the Economic
Commission for Latin America and the
Caribbean (ECLAC)

Foreword by Sir Hans W. Singer

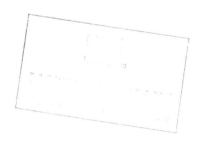

palgrave

First published 2002 by
PALGRAVE
Houndmills, Basingstoke, Hampshire RG21 6XS and
175 Fifth Avenue, New York, N.Y. 10010
Companies and representatives throughout the world

PALGRAVE is the new global academic imprint of
St. Martin's Press LLC Scholarly and Reference Division and
Palgrave Publishers Ltd (formerly Macmillan Press Ltd).

This book is printed on paper suitable for recycling and
made from fully managed and sustained forest sources.

A catalogue record for this book is available
from the British Library.

Library of Congress Cataloging-in-Publication Data
Latin America: its future in the global economy / edited by
Patricia Gray Rich.
     p. cm.
Includes bibliographical references and index.
ISBN 0–333–92901–2
1. Latin America – Foreign economic relations. 2. World Trade
    Organization – Latin America. 3. Latin America – Economic
    integration. 4. Globalization. I. Rich, Patricia Gray.
HF1480.5 .L3852 2001
337.8 – dc21   2001036100

The views expressed in this volume are solely those of the author and should in
no way be interpreted to represent the views of the United Nations or its
Member countries. The disclaimer is extensive to the rest of the authors in this
volume and their corresponding affiliations.

10   9   8   7   6   5   4   3   2   1
11   10   09   08   07   06   05   04   03   02

Printed in Great Britain by
Antony Rowe Ltd, Chippenham, Wiltshire

Contents

List of Tables

List of Figures

Foreword

The aim of policies determining the future for Latin America[1] in the global economy must be the reduction or, if possible, elimination of poverty. This definition of the aim is especially important because of the high level of inequality in Latin America. The region has almost become a symbol of inequality of income distribution within countries in almost every dimension: between sub-regions (Southern Cone versus Haiti or Central America), within countries (southern Brazil versus the north-east), rural/urban, formal/informal, skilled/unskilled, and so forth. As a realistic target, we may aim at Latin America fully participating in the internationally accepted target of reducing the incidence of poverty by one-half by 2015. Broadly speaking, the negotiations relating to regional and global trade must be conducted so that they further this aim (certainly do not obstruct it) and their success or failure must be judged by this standard. This aim must govern the domestic policies of countries as well as their position in super-national (regional and global) negotiations.

If this general objective is accepted, what follows? As long as this higher degree of inequality persists, Latin America needs higher growth rates than other developing regions to reach the same agreed goal of halving the incidence of poverty. On a per capita basis, this additional growth requirement would be increased (reduced) to the extent that the rate of population increase in Latin America is higher (lower) than in other regions. In fact, the recent (1995–2000) population growth in Latin America at 1.68 per cent p.a. is higher than in the tiger economies of East Asia and the Pacific, although lower than South Asia and sub-Saharan Africa. But any adjustment for differential population growth is insufficient to shake the basic statement that Latin America needs higher per capita income growth than any other of the major developing regions to achieve the same aim of poverty reduction – as long as the higher degree of inequality is allowed to persist. Hence, Latin America is in particular need, both in domestic policies and in regional/global negotiations, to achieve accelerated income growth. This gives added importance to the following chapters which discuss such possibilities of looking after Latin American interests in supernational negotiations over the coming 15–20 years. Yet according to World Bank projections Latin America per capita income growth at 2.37 per cent p.a. would be much lower than in East Asia (6.93 per cent) and also lower than South Asia (3.63 per cent) and Eastern Europe/former Soviet Union (4.05 per cent). Only Africa would be lower still (1.08 per cent).[2]

These projections, although by no means real forecasts but based on actual recent experience and more in the nature of extrapolations, all the same emphasize the special urgency to change the scenario and the assumptions on which they are based, including their global context. This applies in particular to the assumption of continued inequality of income distribution, both of the present income and of the nature of the additional growth over the coming 15 years or so.

What follows from all this for Latin American development and trade policies, including its stance in international trade negotiations? There is clearly no chance of meeting the poverty reduction target by growth alone, as long as growth reflects and perpetuates the existing pattern of inequality. Such growth may be defined, as in the model on which this introduction is based, as a pattern of growth where 1 per cent of overall income growth leads only to 0.5 per cent growth in the incomes of the poor. In this scenario, it would take per capita income growth of 7.0 per cent p.a. (or actual growth of over 8.5 per cent p.a.) to halve the proportion of the very poor from the 24 per cent in 1993 to 12 per cent in 2015. To the extent that actual income growth up to 2001 has evidently fallen far short of such a 'super-tiger' performance, the growth needed for the remaining years between now and 2015 would have to be even higher. Such super-tiger performance – for Latin America as a whole, not just for individual countries – is clearly utterly unthinkable. This would mean that if increased growth of this pattern is achieved by greater openness and increased, it must be accompanied by major, almost tectonic, measures of redistribution aimed directly at poverty reduction (always assuming that the internationally accepted target of halving poverty is taken seriously as a guide to development).

Nothing in international trade negotiation should be accepted that would stand in the way of such major redistribution. This would clearly have to include land reform, employment creation, effective progressive taxation, aid concentrated on the informal sector in the slum areas and in retarded regions, as well as the elimination of illegitimate rent seeking, among others. Again, such a 'tectonic' redistribution for the whole of Latin America in the 14 years now remaining is utterly utopian even for those Tinbergen 'idealists of to-day who are the reality of to-morrow'. But any international agreement must be closely examined to ensure that it is compatible with, or at least favourable in the first steps towards such a fundamental redistribution.

Even if we now relax the assumption that growth is anti-poor and underpins the exceptionally high degree of Latin American inequality, we would still be more in the realm of utopia than reality. If we assume the type of growth which Mr Dollar of the World Bank has declared to be typical for recent growth in developing countries, for example 'One-for-One' growth (where growth trickles fully down to the poor and applies equally to the poor and the better-off), it would still take 3.4 per cent per capita growth or some 5 per cent overall growth over 1993–2015 for Latin America as a whole, in order to halve poverty incidence by 2015. To this should be added at least another 1–1.5 per cent p.a. to make up for the sluggish growth during 1993–2000, so this would still require an unlikely 'tiger' performance of 6 per cent or so steady growth. So such evenly spread 'dollar growth' would still require vigorous redistribution measures and/or a trade and development policy heavily weighted towards the interest of the poor. The basic requirement of 3.4 per cent p.a. per capita growth over the whole 1993–2015 period, or 4.5–5 per cent for the remaining 2001–15 period is well beyond the World Bank projection of 2.37 per cent p.a. quoted above, although below the projection for East Asia.

The most favourable scenario for poverty reduction is pro-poor growth defined in the model used as a pattern of growth associated with an income growth for the poor of 1.5 per cent for every 1 per cent of overall growth. This is not a very radical version of pro-poor growth and could be made possible by relatively mild redistributive measures and progressive social policies combined with a trade policy (particularly agricultural and primary commodity trade) favouring the small producers and the rural areas. The required per capita growth for halving the incidence of poverty would now be 2.2 per cent for the whole period or, with population growth of 1.5 per cent p.a. something like 3.7 per cent overall. Here we are now moving from the realm of utopia to the realm of the possible. It happens to coincide almost precisely with the World Bank projection of 2.37 per cent per capita growth. It still requires a generally favourable world economic context, absence of major shocks and efficient development, trade and integration policies.

This kind of moderately pro-poor and moderately strong growth could help to achieve the objective of halving the incidence of poverty. However, we should still remind ourselves that (a) because of the steady increase in population the absolute number of extremely poor people will decline by much less than one-half and remain high, roughly equal to the total population of one of the middle-sized Latin American countries; (b) we are dealing here only with extreme poverty of the $1 per day/per person kind – much real poverty and suffering will remain just above that poverty line; and (c) we are here only dealing with income poverty, only one of the many aspects of poverty such as lack of opportunities, frustrated talent, poor health, social exclusion, denial of full human rights and so on. Thus it is only in a limited sense that we can proclaim such relatively mild pro-poor growth as sufficient to reduce poverty by one-half. Yet even this would represent a break with the recent history of development and policies in Latin America.

The objective of pro-poor growth is hardly controversial – more like 'apple-pie and motherhood'. But it is not what has happened in the globalization process so far; the devil is in the detail. This becomes clear when the contributions which follow are examined from this angle: Are liberalization, WTO rules, Uruguay Round commitments, TRIPS, and TRIMS, contributory to pro-poor growth? What domestic adjustments and policies are required to make them 'pro-poor'? Are such adjustments and policies politically and economically feasible? What are their side effects? Have the Latin American countries sufficient freedom of action to introduce such adjustments and policies?

While the change to pro-poor growth represents a trend break from recent and present patterns, it would appear at first sight that the break need not be as sharp as in many other parts of what used to be called the Third World and are now better described as the emerging economies. After all, the incidence of poverty at the beginning of the target period was 'only' 24 per cent, much lower than in South Asia (43 per cent), or sub-Saharan Africa (39 per cent) and even lower than in East Asia and the Pacific (26 per cent). Among the other regions only North Africa/Middle East and Eastern Europe/Russia had a lower incidence. Thus the required poverty reduction in Latin America to achieve the UN target of halving the incidence of poverty by 2015 requires a reduction of 'only' 12 percentage points. But any comfort derived from such a reflection that poverty reduction ought to be easier than elsewhere is rapidly dispelled by looking at trends preceding the target period. Latin America was the only one of the five regions constituting the old Third World in which the incidence of poverty increased during 1987–93 (from 22 per cent to 24 per cent). To that extent, the trend break would have to be sharper in Latin America than elsewhere – a break away from the exceptionally high income inequality (high Gini coefficients) which has become the trademark of Latin America, inequality which pervades not only incomes, but land holdings and access to opportunities. Pro-poor growth would represent a sharp break with a culture of inequality. Above all, it indicates a need to avoid a repetition of the experience of the 1980s of 'immiserizing growth' with deteriorating terms of trade.

Many – and implicitly all – of the following contributions show full awareness of the need to 'welfare weigh' the cost and benefits of regionalization and globalization and to pay special attention to the impacts on the poorer sections in defining Latin American negotiating positions. The aim of this introduction is to establish this clearly as an overarching principle applying to all the varied subjects in this volume. Greater global and domestic equality must go hand-in-hand.

SIR HANS W. SINGER

Notes

1. Always including the Caribbean Area, in line with ECLAC.
2. All these and subsequent figures are based on a study by Lucia Hammer *et al.* at the Institute of Social Studies in The Hague: 'Are the DAC Targets Achievable? Poverty and Human Development in the Year 2015' (Draft of July 1998).

Notes on the Contributors

Dieter W. Benecke is a specialist in economics and political science and author of various books and numerous articles about economic, political and cultural aspects of Latin America and Germany. He was former President of the Center of Communications Inter-Nations in Bonn and Professor of Economics and Political Science at the Catholic University in Chile. He is presently Director of the Center for Latin American Studies of the Konrad Adenauer Foundation in Buenos Aires.

Luis Fernando Jaramillo Correa has been actively involved in political and economic issues on behalf of developing countries. He was Vice President and Minister of Foreign Affairs, Public Works and Transportation, Economic Development, Mines and Energy and Interior of Colombia and participates very openly in multilateral negotiations in Geneva and New York. He was an active participant as Ambassador of his country and Chairman of the Group of 77 at the United Nations in New York. He is presently President of ODINSA Group S.A., the largest international engineering association in Colombia, and Convener of the Council of Representatives and Chairman of the Board of Directors of the South Centre in Geneva.

James R. Holbein is an international lawyer specializing in international trade, dispute resolution, NAFTA and FTAA legal issues. He was formerly the US Secretary of the NAFTA Secretariat where he actively participated with negotiators in Mexico and Canada. He is author of various articles on dispute resolution and is legal advisor at the Washington law firm Stewart and Stewart. He is also adjunct professor at the American University, the Washington College of Law, and Georgetown University Law Center.

Roberto Lavagna is actively devoted to research and previously to teaching as Professor of Economics at the University of Buenos Aires. Author of various articles on international trade, he was chief negotiator of the Argentina–Brazil common market agreement and one of the major supporters of the Mercosur Agreement. He was Director and founder of ECOLATINA, a research institution in Buenos Aires. Previous to that, he was Minister of Industry and Foreign Trade. He is presently Ambassador of Argentina in the European Union and in Geneva following closely the FTAA and WTO negotiation process.

Constantine Michalopoulos has been for many years a senior official of the World Bank and previously of USAID. He has written extensively on trade policy issues affecting developing countries and economies in transition and has taught development economics and trade at several universities. Following an assignment as Special Economic Advisor at the WTO in 1997–99, he has focused his research on issues of participation of developing countries in that organization. He is presently Senior Economic Advisor for the World Bank in Brussels.

Dennis R. Nuxoll is an international lawyer specializing in international trade, antidumping and WTO dispute settlement. He is in private practice with the Washington law firm of Stewart and Stewart. He has worked at the Office of the U.S. Trade Representative, the U.S. Department of Justice and the National Labor Relations Board.

Sarath Rajapatirana is a Visiting Scholar at the American Enterprise Institute which he joined after a long career at the World Bank where he was Division Chief of Trade, Finance and Private Sector Development in the Latin American region, Chief of the Policy Unit in Office of the Vice President of Economic Research Staff and Advisor on Operations Policy. He was the staff director and leader of the team, which wrote the 1987 World Development Report on Trade and Industrialization, and Director of a Comparative study on Macroeconomic Policies of Developing Countries. Before joining the World Bank he was the Chief of Money and Banking Research at the Central Bank of Sri Lanka. He is author of numerous articles, ranging from trade, macroeconomics to finance, in refereed journals, and of six books.

Patricia Gray Rich is actively involved in research and policy work. Her expertise is in international trade providing analytical and technical support to member countries of the United Nations. She is author of various articles in refereed journals, on international trade and macroeconomic issues, and authored various studies on trade policy and economic development. After leaving the Economic Commission for Western Asia where she specialized in the oil industry, she is presently an Economic Affairs Officer at the Economic Commission for Latin America focusing on issues related to regional integration and the WTO as well as the potential of e-commerce on developing countries.

Luis A. Riveros is a specialist in labour issues. He is author of numerous articles and papers related to labour matters, economics of education and income distribution. His research work is especially related to Latin American trade reforms and labour markets. He worked at the World Bank as an economist advising governments on structural adjustment reforms and labour issues. He has been Professor of Economics, Dean of the School of Economics and is currently the President of the University of Chile. He is Director of the Chilean-Pacific foundation and has been actively involved in public policy and economic issues.

Maryse Robert is an economist by training and a senior trade specialist in the Trade Unit of the Organization of American States (OAS). She is principally responsible for providing technical and analytical support to the investment negotiations under the Free Trade Area of the Americas (FTAA) process. She has authored numerous studies on trade and investment-related issues. Her most recent publications include a book on the NAFTA negotiations and a volume on free trade in the Americas. Before joining the OAS, she worked on trade and development issues at the World Bank and the United Nations, and was the deputy director of the Center for International Affairs at the University of Quebec in Montreal.

José-Manuel Salazar-Xirinachs is an economist and trade specialist and currently Director of the Trade Unit of the Organization of American States. As former Trade Minister of Costa Rica he chaired the FTAA process for a year and participated in the consultations leading to the San José Declaration that defines the objectives, scope and managerial structure for the FTAA negotiations. Previous to that, he founded and directed the Business Network for Hemispheric Integration. He is author of numerous articles on trade and development issues. His most recent publication includes a volume on free trade in the Americas. He also teaches at Georgetown University.

Sir Hans W. Singer is one of the pioneers of development economics and a world theorist on development issues. Author of numerous books and articles on developing countries he formulated the Prebisch–Singer theory of deteriorating terms-of-trade. He has written on almost all aspects of development but especially on development assistance, food aid, employment strategy, human resources and international trade. He was one of the founders of the UNCTAD and has worked with most of the development agencies of the United Nations system. He is professor emeritus at the Institute of Development Studies, University of Sussex, in the UK where he is actively involved in international affairs related to development economics.

Sherry M. Stephenson is a researcher and specialist in international trade and actively involved in providing technical and analytical support to the services negotiations under the FTAA process and to the participating countries. She is editor of a book on Services Trade in the Western Hemisphere, and author of various articles on aspects of trade in services. After leaving the OECD in Paris as a Principal Administrator in the Trade Directorate and acting as Advisor to the Ministry of Trade, Government of Indonesia, she is presently Deputy Director of the Trade Unit, Organization of American States.

Anabelle Ulate is Professor of Economics at the School of Economics, University of Costa Rica. She was former Director of the Institute of Economics (IICE). She has authored numerous articles on macroeconomic and structural adjustment issues and the environment especially for the Central American Region and participated very actively on international events related to the FTAA process and the WTO.

Alberto Valdés is a Chilean national and currently a consultant based in Santiago, and was until recently economist and Agriculture Adviser at the World Bank. Previous to joining the World Bank he was Program Director for International Trade and Food Security, at the International Food Policy Research Institute (IFPRI) in Washington, D.C. His publications include a comparative study on the Political Economy of Agricultural Pricing Policies, co-authored with Anne Krueger and Maurice Schiff, several studies on the impact of agricultural protection in OECD countries on the economies of developing countries, co-editor of the Proceedings of the World/Bank FAO workshops on Implementing the Uruguay Round Agreement, a book on food security for developing countries, as well as co-editor of a book on fighting rural poverty in Latin America with Palgrave.

1 Globalization and the World Trade Organization: Latin America at a Crossroads

Luis Fernando Jaramillo Correa

INTRODUCTION

Globalization, defined as an economic, political, social and cultural process that determines how societies interact and how they are structured,[1] works to the advantage of those countries that have the material and technological bases that enable them to operate within the system. Once again, it is the industrialized countries that have the upper hand. The developing world, including Latin America, is at a political and economic crossroads; its future will depend on the solutions it finds for staying afloat and laying the foundations for its development, and those solutions will also determine its integration within international organizations, which like the World Trade Organization (WTO), are the decision-making bodies that shape world economic and trade relations.

Latin America's various attempts and efforts at integration have been beset by enormous difficulties and have come up against major obstacles. Despite the best of intentions and although they may have materialized at a formal level, those efforts have not achieved the intended purpose and objectives. Deep-seated divisions exist and the political geography of Latin America is yet to be constructed. It does not act as a bloc in multilateral negotiations: there is a general lack of cohesion within groups and sub-groups and between each and the group as a whole. This separation is not only between continental America and the islands of the Caribbean: the Anglo-Saxon, Spanish-speaking, Portuguese, Central American, South American and North American segments are loose, scattered units that have not succeeded in identifying common vital interests as the basis for joint and coherent participation.

The sub-continent is not noted for its active role in the WTO. This is due not only to difficulties at the regional level in establishing effective

1

mechanisms for participation and consolidation of interests. The power structure of the Organization, which enables the economic powers to derive disproportionately high benefits as against the weakness of the developing countries, is also to blame. Moreover, the tendency to use selective negotiating mechanisms makes it even more difficult for the developing world to participate in the decision-making process. If we consider the WTO as yet another instrument of globalization, it is clear that the rules agreed for managing international trade were instituted primarily for the benefit of the industrialized countries, as will be shown later.

We must, as a matter of urgency, challenge the ethics underlying the existing world order and its bias towards the development, progress and enrichment of the capitalist and post-capitalist industrialized societies while heightening disorder and economic and social regression in the poorest and most underprivileged. However, until the governments of industrialized countries assume full responsibility and are prepared to respect the fundamental ethical values that are essential to our civilization, the system will operate to the benefit of a few communities who represent a mere fraction of the world's population. The rules today lead to a disproportionate concentration of wealth on the one hand and a steady impoverishment of the weakest economies in the world, on the other.

If Latin America is to influence the international system, action must be taken on sufficiently generic common interests in order to facilitate the adoption of coordinated policies vis-à-vis third parties. To date and despite the innumerable attempts at regional integration, this objective has not been achieved. There is an urgent need for work with respect to vital interests that transcend narrower, individual differences. Given the difficulties in acting collectively, it would be useful to 'study alternative options' which, in the long term, may promote common interests and strengthen the role of Latin America as a vital and decisive actor in the political, economic and commercial sphere.

ALTERNATIVE PATHS MUST BE SOUGHT

In this context, consideration should be given to alternative routes to those chosen in the past few years. The two scenarios outlined will probably not be the only possible outcomes. Indeed, the chances of improving the levels of well-being of developing countries may lie neither in regional integration nor in direct participation in the world system through the WTO. Hence the need to look at different scenarios that offer better prospects for enhancing the terms of Southern participation in the global system.

A Concrete Proposal: The Southern Forum

It is worth considering the option whereby a homogeneous group of countries with common vital interests and concerted strategies can defend its economic and trade policy objectives – a group that presents a united front in multilateral negotiations and which, in this difficult and inequitable scenario, can defend its vital interests over and above the isolated differences that are inevitable in any grouping. The minimum prerequisite for membership in what could be called a Southern Forum is the political will of nations that are committed to achieving development and to assume responsibility for their international role and participation.

This political and economic forum will have specific tasks and objectives, but unlike the Latin American integration groups, will not be hampered and paralyzed at every step of the way by a legal framework. Rather, it will be a forum that will use the informal experience in consultation with Asia and the Pacific. This is the idea we wish to see developed and put into effect. The principal mandate of this southern forum would be to facilitate the adoption of platforms for action which, not content with the usual *rhetoric*, direct joint efforts consistently and in a concerted manner towards the promotion of vital and fundamental interests in order to restore balance in the international economic and trading system.

A useful example for the South forum might be the Cairns Group. This group, although limited in scope, has represented a major step towards the creation of lobbies. In a scheme that breaks with the regional, continental, cultural, political and economic barriers, the Cairns Group identified an interest that was sufficiently global and generic and that enabled it to prepare a common platform for consolidating effective and efficient action in international negotiating forums. The Cairns Group was formed for the purpose of eliminating agricultural subsidies. Its members include developing as well as industrialized countries. It rallies countries of the Americas (Argentina, Brazil, Canada, Colombia, Uruguay, Paraguay and Chile), Asia and the Pacific (Australia, New Zealand, Fiji, Philippines, Indonesia, Malaysia and Thailand) as well as countries of Southern Africa. As already mentioned, its *raison d'être* centres around one vital common interest, which is to secure, through multilateral trade negotiations, the total elimination of agricultural subsidies especially those that apply in the European Union and the United States.

It should be noted that the Cairns Group has functioned because it focused on one generic and global issue, which has brought its members together. It identified one common vital interest whose strategic importance was strong enough to warrant its defence and promotion by each country, since it represented both an individual and a collective benefit – an interest that enabled developing and industrialized countries alike, nations from all continents and of all sizes to work together in international forums. This does not mean that on different issues and in other forums, these same countries will not have differences. The important point is that they can be at variance on other issues and act independently and nonetheless succeed in presenting a united front in a strategic manner to strengthen calls for the elimination of agricultural subsidies.

Three Central Issues for the Forum

In this context, three central points should be underscored. (a) The first concerns the need for more efficient and effective mechanisms for enhancing integration of Latin American countries in the international system, even though it may mean distancing themselves from the traditional concept of integration. (b) The second evaluates how WTO operates and its regional participation in this organization. (c) The third concerns the possibility of achieving greater success in fulfilling the purposes of economic and trade policy, in seeking groups for concerted action based on the global interests and objectives, vital as well as strategic, rather than individual and specific, which favour the conclusion of agreements and permit the realization of a common platform in international forums.

Latin America: A Political Geography to be Constructed

Political life in Latin America has been turbulent and complex in definition. The economic field has not escaped this reality. Assessing the future of sub-regional and regional integration; debating the advantages and complications of belonging and obeying WTO regulations; seeking new options for integration in the international system; reviving forums such as the United Nations Conference on Trade and Development (UNCTAD) for promoting Latin America's vital development interests – all of these scenarios deserve consideration, evaluation, analyzing with a view to focusing the region's attention on strengthening its social, economic and political well-being. Despite the efforts and good intentions with respect to the scenarios presented, concrete results have, in most cases, been disappointing. On the issue of integration, the lack of political will, economic and constitutional crises, border conflicts or internal weakness of countries has not facilitated the successful development of the innumerable efforts to act in a coordinated manner and to establish economic and political areas for cooperation and complementarity. The following paragraphs contain a brief presentation of the sub-regional and regional integration groups with a view to highlighting problems of *proliferation, repetition* and *rhetoric* of most of the initiatives.

Constraints and Problems of Sub-regional and Regional Integration Groups

The Group of Three includes Mexico, Venezuela and Colombia. Its distinction was to have had the idea of integrating energy interests in the market of petroleum, a product that is important for all three countries. This initiative was conceived without creating a different bureaucratic superstructure from those already established in the ministries of foreign affairs. Mexico vis-à-vis Latin America and the developing world distanced itself by entering the North American Free Trade Agreement (NAFTA) and the Organization for Economic Cooperation and Development (OECD). Its new responsibilities caused it to withdraw from the Group of 77 and to restrict its sphere of action to Latin America, with some exceptions as in the case of its bilateral relations with Cuba.

In an effort to convince its Latin American allies of its active and continued presence in the region, it signed the Free Trade Agreement with Chile and formed the Group of Three. For Venezuela and Colombia, this initiative was, at the time, an opportunity to achieve a rapprochement with NAFTA. Thus, the three nations worked out a common front vis-à-vis the Caribbean, which has been overlooked by most of the countries of the region. Irrespective of the circumstances surrounding the creation of this group and the original expectations it had generated, Venezuela, Mexico and Colombia have not behaved like a bloc in multilateral trade negotiations or acted in a coordinated and joint manner within the international system. The Group has not managed to foster concerted action in this regard, at least not for the time being.

The Association of Caribbean States (ACS), which maintains close ties with the Group of Three, is an interesting initiative and one that promotes information flows between the islands of the Caribbean and the countries of the mainland. However, this system still needs to be consolidated and is yet another example in support of our central argument. The Association has defined a number of objectives and has pledged to work in line with the principles of the WTO, and yet has not identified a common, vital and strategic interest which enables it to stand as a bloc in international forums or which promotes the fulfilment of agreements within the group.

As an entity that facilitates consultation, cooperation and concerted action, the Association seeks to build consensus in areas as diverse and as complex as: sustainable tourism and transport, developing an appropriate economic space for trade and investment, declaration and protection of the Caribbean Sea as a natural reserve, cooperation in science and technology, linguistic integration programmes, respect for democracy and the rule of law, political pluralism and coordination of meetings with the European Union. To date, this exceedingly ambitious project has gone no further than to organize ministerial meetings and listen to rhetorical pronouncements by heads of state or government.

The Central American Common Market (CACM) was one of the first attempts at political and economic development through integration. Its major achievement was the establishment of the Central American Bank. However, ideological divisions that had built up over the decades and the remoteness of political agendas caused setbacks in the realization and fulfilment of its declared strategies. The civil wars in El Salvador and Guatemala, the Sandinista revolution, the border conflicts between Honduras and El Salvador and recent problems between Honduras and Nicaragua have delayed the achievement of its initial objectives. Despite all the efforts made at presidential, ministerial and expert meetings, Central America has not succeeded in establishing itself as an economic and negotiating bloc representative of the interests of the subregion in world forums. It remains dependent and weak.

The Caribbean Community, or Caricom, which has existed for 27 years, is one of the attempts at integration that has functioned best in the region. Nevertheless, much remains to be achieved in terms of concerted action and coordination. In managing political crises in Caribbean countries (Grenada, to be precise), the group has lacked unity. Although the objective is not to compare Latin America and Caribbean integration efforts with those of the European Union, the latter can serve as a point of reference. Admittedly, the European Union has disagreements and will need to resolve the issues on which it has not managed to build consensus; nevertheless, as a group, it presents a united front to third parties in the majority of cases. It is not a matter of repeating the experiences of others, but rather of understanding what an integration process must seek and in which areas compromises must be made in order to achieve common objectives.

The Andean Community, originally known as the Andean Group, included Peru, Chile, Venezuela, Bolivia, Ecuador and Colombia. Today, Chile is no longer a member, while Bolivia is leaning more towards the Southern Common Market, Mercosur (Mercado Común del Sur) than the Community, and Peru's membership has been difficult to define on many occasions. The Community, however, despite its inertia and weakness, has been the framework for strengthening commercial ties between Colombia,

Venezuela and Ecuador. Although trade between these countries declined sharply in 1999, 2000 and 2001 as a result of economic and political crises in these countries, it is important to recognize the useful role that the Andean Community has played over the years. This recognition does not deny the deep deficiencies and the crises it has passed through.

Although it is formed by neighbouring countries, the Andean Community has weak commercial ties, and notwithstanding the objectives consigned in presidential or ministerial declarations, bilateral conflicts and economic competitiveness have prevailed rather than complementarity of action. The Andean Community maintains commercial links mainly with the United States. Colombia is the third trading partner for Venezuela and Ecuador but these countries account for a much lower percentage than the United States.[2]

The political evolution of the Andean countries has not allowed fulfilment of the initial objectives. The Community's economic and trade aspirations were thwarted by a series of problems including: the dictatorship in Chile in the 1970s and that country's withdrawal from the group in 1976 following the dispute over its neo-liberal policies and the protectionist stance adopted by the Andean group; Peru's disenchantment with the group's restrictions and policies; the border disputes between Peru and Ecuador, which were finally resolved in 1999 thanks to the mediation of the Guarantor Countries; and Colombia's problems with its neighbuors – Ecuador and Venezuela – due to the civil war and its temporary transfer to the border zones. The proliferation of bureaucratic and legal mechanisms has created a white elephant that has proven difficult to reactivate or modernize.

As of 1985, Mercosur generated great expectations of bringing together important countries like Brazil and Argentina, which were at the forefront of this initiative, and Uruguay and Paraguay, which joined in 1991, with the establishment of the Treaty of Asunción. The objectives of Mercosur are to promote the free circulation of goods, services, capital and labour, to establish a common external tariff, to coordinate macroeconomic and sectoral policies and to harmonize national legislations. Bolivia (which also belongs to the Andean Community) has been an associate member since 1997. Although more concrete results have been seen than in other efforts at integration, macroeconomic policies and policies relating to the automobile industry are uncoordinated, as demonstrated by the financial crisis of the late 1990s. From 1995, integration has existed and the common external tariff applies to 85 per cent of trade relations with third parties. Despite the asymmetry among members, trade has grown within the group, admittedly with the gigantic Brazilian economy – the eighth largest in the world – clearly in the lead.

Political and economic relations and their coordination by the members of Mercosur highlight a central issue on the agenda. The fact that these nations are moving towards the deepening of a customs union or members of the Cairns Group does not prevent them from disagreeing on other issues of vital interest. In the case of Brazil and Argentina, for example, working together and in a coordinated way in forums and on common issues has not been incompatible with their positions, on occasion, regarding reform of the United Nations Security Council. Just as they defend different positions and viewpoints on this issue, they may equally well be united on other issues of national interest. This element is fundamental to an understanding of the need to create groups or forums that enable them to defend vital interests over and above the natural differences existing between the states in the international arena.

The system Latin American Free Trade Association/Latin American Integration Association (LAFTA/LAIA) sought to become the pioneers in a Latin American customs union but was unsuccessful in achieving the more limited objective of setting up a free trade area. The lists of concessions and products never materialized. In 1960, LAFTA served as a regional focus of agreement and disagreement. Given the stalemate in their relations, members regrouped and the new project that succeeded LAFTA was named the Latin American Integration Association (LAIA). It entered into force in 1980 and has its headquarters in Montevideo, Uruguay. Efforts were made to overcome the obstacles and review the prospects of consolidating a Latin American bloc for trade, economic and integration issues. However, the LAFTA/LAIA system is falling into oblivion given the failure of its concrete objectives and the challenges to integration in the global economy and trade, which are overwhelming for the countries of the region.

The Enterprise for the Americas Initiative proposed by President George Bush in June 1990 launched a United States proposal for the creation of a Free Trade Area of the Americas (FTAA). The Summit of the Americas held in Miami in 1994 culminated in a new rhetorical declaration strewn with good intentions. The innumerable statements made over the years show how little importance is attached to such words, since everyone knows in advance that these routine statements are insignificant and will remain unfulfilled as time passes. Rhetoric has become one of the chief ills of sub-regional, regional and, of course, multilateral integration.

In 1994, 34 heads of state and government from all over the Americas, with the exception of Cuba, met in Miami. In the declaration signed at the outcome of the meeting,[3] these leaders reaffirmed the general principles of their political and economic systems. They reiterated that democracy was 'the sole political system which guarantees respect for human rights and the rule of law'. Access to justice; the fight against corruption; the recognition of the harmful effects of organized crime, illegal drugs and money laundering on economies and on ethical values; public health and social structure; the fight against terrorism and trafficking in arms; the promotion of free trade and economic integration; the eradication of poverty and discrimination; the environment and sustainable development – each of these issues was treated to its usual paragraph which is reiterated in successive declarations in different regional and multilateral forums. Are there any of these challenges that can used by countries of the hemisphere as the basis for joint action which reflects a shared and vital strategic interest as defined by all?

The IDB/OAS/ECLAC Triad

It should be noted that the different declarations of principles and plans of action have not identified the vital interests that enable coordinated participation in any area of possible agreement. Neither the nine FTAA working and negotiating groups nor the annual ministerial meetings have managed to truly push forward the proposals for eliminating trade barriers and investment in a free trade area that might enter into force in 2005. The triad of the Organization of American States (OAS), the Inter-American Development Bank (IDB) and the Economic Commission for Latin America and the Caribbean (ECLAC) provide valuable and necessary technical support to groups, agencies and governments, but these have not achieved the expected results for reasons which have more to do with the lack of political will than with technical limitations.

One Redeemable Area is the Link with the Private Sector

One redeemable area is the private sector link with this intergovernmental initiative, which has already held four meetings to strengthen ties among businesses in the Americas. Another important element is the participation of academia, business associations, labour unions, and other organizations interested through the Civil Society Committee.

LATIN AMERICAN ISSUES HAVE BECOME
BOGGED DOWN IN RHETORIC

Although some advances have been made, there is a great deal of uncertainty with respect to hemispheric dialogue. While some prefer to speak of human rights and consolidation of democracy, others seek to discuss more pressing trade issues. Major strides have been made on issues of interest to the United States, owing to the pressure on human rights issues or institution-building and strengthening democracy. However, Latin American issues, which reflect a real deterioration in the economic and social situation in the countries, remain bogged down in rhetoric. It must be recognized that social and economic development at the national level, in this case the Latin American countries, will advance the cause of human rights. The reverse has rarely been seen.

The punitive approach to the issue makes it difficult for states and experts to work towards a common objective on the issue of human rights. No one is unaware of the urgent need to foster respect for human rights in the world and, within these, it is urgent to mention the right to development and to ensure that cooperation and international resources are redirected towards such rights on which all others depend. There are various approaches to this end and the same major issues are different but not necessarily contrary.

In this hemispheric context, it is necessary to consider the unequal effects of globalization and economic and trade integration and the priority that the actors and issues have received. Following the Seattle debacle, the United States will probably seek to strengthen other groups in order to rein-force its position on the pedestal of the global economy. One such group is FTAA. However, the benefits seem to be biased in one way only. While the United States maintained a per capita income of approximately US$30,000 in the 1990s, Latin American countries have lagged far behind. Per capita income levels ranged from US$9,000 in Argentina, US$5,000 in Brazil, US$4,300 in Mexico and US$2,000 in Colombia. In February 2000, unem-ployment varied between 2 per cent and slightly over 20 per cent compared with 4 per cent in the United States. The rate in Mexico was 2 per cent, in Chile, 9 per cent, Argentina, 14 per cent and Colombia, 18 per cent.[4]

Lack of competitiveness in Latin America, among other factors, has restrained the progress of FTAA. In this context, Brazil took the lead by proposing the South American Free Trade Area (SAFTA) with the objec-tive of strengthening the economies of the region vis-à-vis the North American multinationals. SAFTA also seeks to be a forum for coordinat-ing Latin American participation in negotiations with FTAA and WTO. The Seattle dynamic has demonstrated that groups from the developing world and Latin America still lack coordination and play no part in the decision-making process in WTO.

The Rio Group is another example of the practical deficiencies of efforts to achieve integration and concerted action among Latin American countries.[5] Its 13 summit meetings have been ineffectual in achieving Latin American integration within the international system; the duties of

interim secretariat rotate among member countries, with Colombia's turn
having taken place in 2000; but all these efforts, however convincing they
may appear, never seem to produce any concrete programmes. It is difficult to discern what role, if any, it has played in WTO or in connection
with FTAA, although it does seem interested in negotiating in a concerted
and consistent manner.

This Group is not an integration organization in the same vein as those
mentioned to date; its status as a forum for consultation and ongoing
political consultation points to an evolution in the traditional concept of
integration. Notwithstanding its nature, the same flaws have been detected
as in other groups. The oversight, disregard or neglect in identifying viable
and feasible common interests that may enable member countries to arrive
at international forums with a united platform, remains evident in this
forum, which periodically brings together the leaders of Latin American
countries.

The Summit of Heads of State and Government of the Rio Group and the
European Union in Brazil in June 1999 had similar shortcomings to those
observed in meetings relating to the FTAA. This forum has been meeting
since 1990 in a desperate attempt to identify common interests, but without
success. While some wish to focus on development issues, others consider
terrorism or human rights to be priority areas of common interest. These
two regions will have great difficulty in the short and medium term in identifying common interests, especially since Latin America accounts for less
than 4 per cent of total trade conducted by the European Union.

The United Nations Conference on Trade and Development (UNCTAD),
held in Rio, established a bi-regional group, and reaffirmed its commitment
to democratic principles, education for peace, the Treaty on the Non-
Proliferation of Nuclear Weapons and to the control of international crime.
It underscored economic cooperation and the importance of the WTO as the
principal forum for establishing the basic rules and guidelines governing
the system of international trade.[6] It is relevant to compare this statement
with the criticisms made by Latin American countries at the conference in
Seattle concerning the inherent imbalances in the structure of the WTO
and in the implementation of its agreements. It should be pointed out that
Latin America also affirmed its interest in working on trade issues within
the organization although it maintained a critical stance.

Depreciation of the Word

The various declarations made along the path to integration and concerted
action at the sub-regional, regional, hemispheric or inter-regional level

reiterate the main issues on the international agenda defined by the developing world, including of course Latin America. In the final analysis, few new ideas have emerged from these meetings and, in this regard, specific commitments to join forces to work in a particular area have been scant. Countries and groups have still not identified the vital common interests that might enable them to put into practice and implement these rhetorical declarations. The word is becoming devalued, since as pointed out, it is known in advance that all these texts will remain a dead letter.

Owing to their economic and political fragility, developing countries do not always comply with the goals established in international forums. Latin America's track record with integration projects has resulted in more disappointments than successes. Therefore, it is time to seek world integration through alternative strategies.

WTO: A NEW SCENARIO FOR EXCLUSION?

In order to understand more clearly the reasons why a mechanism for concerted action such as has been proposed is necessary, it is useful to make a brief assessment of WTO negotiating procedures. The revival by the current director Michael Moore of closed or 'green-room' consultations, as they are called, among a few privileged specially invited members, is a disturbing practice, which affects the transparency of negotiations. Moore, a New Zealander, has been criticized not only for his working methods but also, on occasion, for his closeness to the developed world.

In noting the inefficient and confused management that has prevailed in WTO in recent months, one may well wonder if it was not a mistake to block the application of the Thai candidate, Supachai Panitchpakdi.[7] As Deputy Prime Minister of his country, he demonstrated his capacity as a conciliator at the last meeting of UNCTAD in Bangkok in February 2000, in promoting a rapprochement between North and South following the farce that was Seattle.

The deep-seated disagreements[8] that have prevented the United States and the European Union from reaching agreements under the Millennium Round have opened up new opportunities for developing countries. An unexpected, favourable context has arisen without direct interference in the negotiating process of WTO during preparation of the third Ministerial Conference and during its meetings in Seattle. Within this new range of possibilities, UNCTAD and its revival as a viable alternative for facing up to this thorny trade and development issue, can provide the chance to move beyond the stage of impassioned complaints to concrete action through multilateral mechanisms for concerted action.

HYPOCRISY AND 'PHARISAISM'

While, in Bangkok, Michael Moore considered it a moral responsibility and an economic imperative to open up the markets of the rich countries to the poor countries, in Seattle, he attempted to exclude poor countries from decision-making that would have an impact on all countries. Similar displays of hypocrisy and pharisaism were made by Michel Camdessus, the former director of the International Monetary Fund (IMF), in his languid farewell speech in Bangkok. Camdessus has now become an advocate for the poor after the structural adjustment programmes presided over by the IMF have successfully generated the century's worst crisis of absolute poverty and development in Africa, Asia and Latin America, with the resulting state incapacity to make the social investment needed to solve the deficiencies in housing, education and health.

Secret consultations create an atmosphere of distrust which makes it difficult to accept a shared agenda. They alienate the marginalized countries from so-called agreements, irrespective of their degree of vulnerability. Moreover, the lack of transparency inherent in the secret consultations is not a respectable practice in any type of organization, much less in those which pride themselves in being entities, governed by democratic principles. Boutros Boutros-Ghali during his stint as Secretary General of the United Nations (1992–96) resorted to similar practices to obtain support for his initiatives and projects for peace and security. Thus were concluded the negotiations which led to the military operations for peace-keeping. Such practices are not the norm now under the administration of Kofi Annan, who lacks the arrogance of his predecessor.

Moore has attempted to exclude the developing world by reviving selective practices involving in-camera study of issues for presentation at plenary sessions in the search of approval without prior open and transparent negotiation. In the WTO, as in other multilateral organizations, alongside other informal open-ended consultations, secret, selective consultations are conducted in camera. This practice is a hindrance to the legitimate channels for decision-making within the multilateral system and operates to the detriment of the interests of the African, Asian and Latin American countries, who, for the most part, are absent from the clandestine consultations.

Closed consultations occurred once again in the lobbies of Seattle. Although there are constant participants such as the United States, the European Union, Australia, Canada, Japan, New Zealand and Switzerland, participants from the developing world are handpicked to participate depending on the issue of the day. Countries such as Argentina, Brazil, Mexico, India, Egypt, Pakistan, Dominican Republic, Republic of Korea, Hong Kong-China, Singapore or Malaysia have had their turn to sit in on some of the secret consultations.[9] Others have been invited sporadically and most developing countries have been systematically excluded.

Weak Countries Now Appear More Vulnerable Than Ever

The few developing countries invited to the secret consultations are likely to be manipulated by the industrialized countries. By not functioning within the structure of WTO, the Group of 77 (G-77) weakens concerted action and coordination in the developing world on crucial issues on its agenda and among its vital interests. In this context, weak countries now appear more vulnerable than ever. All the attempts to bring the G-77 into WTO were torpedoed and sabotaged by the developed countries, probably in order to prevent the developing countries from entering this organization with a united voice.

The non-existence of coordination mechanisms that operate within the WTO is another reason for promoting the creation of a group of like-minded countries capable of exerting pressure and of presenting a united platform on vital issues which enable them to act in a coordinated way with a single voice and purpose. A select and well-defined list can advance this cause more than the enthusiasm that oppresses each meeting and where participants strive to justify their presence by outdoing each other with good intentions.

The Central Issue of Interest for the Developing World

The obscure procedure for handling negotiations is accompanied by a discriminatory treatment of issues to the detriment of the developing world. The major issues of interest to the developing world at Seattle and at preparatory ministerial meetings in Geneva and Singapore included: the imbalance; discrimination in the way market regulations and conditions are applied, especially as regards access to markets by products such as agricultural products and textiles, which are vital for the developing world; new protectionism in the guise of concern for labour and environmental issues; the lack of an equitable and effective system for regulating free trade; the problems of implementing WTO provisions which create obstacles to the development of the countries that are economically most vulnerable. Of course, by the same token, they are persistently excluded from the agenda of negotiations.

The deep imbalance in world trade relations is not merely a matter of rhetoric. Ten countries dominate the world export and import markets. The United States for example accounts for 12.6 per cent of world exports and

16.8 per cent of imports. Next comes Germany with 10 per cent of exports and 8.3 per cent of imports.[10]

Different Agreements Imply Organizational and Implementation Difficulties

The Agricultural Agreement, the Trade-Related Investment Measures (TRIMS), Trade-Related Aspects of Intellectual Property Rights (TRIPS) and/or the efforts to incorporate environmental and labour issues in WTO have extremely grave implications for the countries of the South.

The Agricultural Agreement would mean that most developing countries, except for the least developed countries (LDCs), would have to reduce domestic subsidies to their farmers and convert non-tariff controls on agricultural products to tariffs for future dismantling. The lack of competitiveness will wipe out these farmers thus aggravating the rural problems in the developing countries, with all that this implies in terms of unemployment, rural–urban migration, food shortages and violence. These issues were already raised by the developing world with respect to the crucial issue of application of the WTO agreements in an effort to make the industrialized world, which is technologically advanced and competitive as regards food production, realize that its ambitions in this area are out of proportion. No constructive responses have been received in this regard.

The TRIMS will prevent the implementation of economic policies to promote the development of local firms in developing countries by restricting their regulatory capacity related to foreign investment leaving their balance of payments vulnerable. Once again, the lack of competitiveness and industrialization of the developing world means that implementation of TRIMS will bring deterioration rather than an improvement in well-being and progress. Some of these countries have called for greater flexibility by the WTO in order to continue with investment measures that promote local development in accordance with national objectives. Today, another multilateral investment agreement is being promoted which would leave complete sectors of the developing economies open to the unlimited greed of the countless multinational companies from the strongest economies in the world.

Extended Protection Will Hamper Development of 'Local Technologies'

The TRIPS agreement implies the adoption of intellectual property legislation in the countries of the North. Although the right to ownership in the countries and entities that have invested in research and development should be respected, extended protection will hamper development of local technologies and must be reviewed. The industrialized countries could do it without this type of restrictive legislation; the developing world is caught in a straitjacket which leaves it lagging far behind. For some, TRIPS is not just a trade issue but an instrument of protectionism that has no place in an organization that claims to defend free trade. Its application, as it stands, implies remaining in the hands of the multinationals, which are the owners of the majority of patents, and having further grounds for imposing trade conditions.

There is no question of not complying with international trade regulations that have been adopted. It is rather a matter of amending them by common agreement. The developing world knows that disregard for any decision or any agreement of the WTO would have devastating effects in terms of reprisals on those who might be affected. Another very different reality is that faced by countries, such as the United States or the European Union, which take the liberty of ignoring the decisions of this organization, safe in the knowledge that they will receive no response to prejudice their position. Anyone who states that the system is equitable and democratic should re-examine the definition of these concepts and the way they have been applied over the years since the inception of this organization.

The countries of Latin America reiterated[11] their commitment to free trade and the regulating activities of the WTO in Seattle. However, they felt the flaws in the system needed to be corrected as a matter of urgency and, as the Venezuelan minister put it, to satisfy the economic, social and political needs of their societies. Most delegations were emphatic in their demand for an end to the imbalances in existing rights and benefits in the inappropriate and discriminatory treatment reserved for products from their countries. The Minister of Foreign Trade of Colombia[12] compared the treatment given to products with that meted out to some delegates in Seattle. Like the ministers, the products had been the target of all kinds of hostilities, setbacks, barriers and attacks, which had impeded their free access to international markets. The corollary of the so-called peaceful demonstrations was the phyto-sanitary measures, anti-dumping regulations or new regulatory frameworks for labour.

Latin American countries agreed on the need for fair trade, the need to strengthen WTO by correcting distortions and the need to combat protectionism of the industrialized countries. Countries like the United States and the European Union countries wish to have the organization take on issues such as the environment, investment and labour, despite the existence of specialized multilateral forums and organizations for dealing with each of those issues. By including them on the WTO agenda, those issues would become new instruments of conditionality and would prejudice even further the southern countries' chances of development. It is not irrelevant to recall that the industrialized countries today have not suffered any constraint on their progress such as those that they would have to apply to the developing countries.

The Agriculture agreement and the elimination of subsidies are of special importance for all countries in the region and this was stressed by Brazil and Argentina, which are members of the Cairns Group. Agricultural and livestock exports from Argentina account for 50 per cent of that country's exports to external markets, hence the future treatment of this category is of vital interest to it. Chile has linked the problem of poverty to the conditions governing world agriculture markets. For Mexico, a major beneficiary of free trade agreements, protectionism and implementation are crucial issues.

The Minister of Brazil pronounced an eloquent and accurate warning against the harmful trends emerging within the WTO:

> We all know that the world is no level playing field, but it is imperative that, at the very least, all players can trust that there are rules which apply to all alike, rules which are not written to protect the strong from their own weaknesses and to prevent the weak from taking advantage of their own strengths.[13]

The Lack of an Outcome at Seattle is an Opportunity

Strategies can be reassessed, issues reopened and work undertaken for an organization that acts for the benefit of all and not just for a few at the expense of the majority of the inhabitants of the world. The reorientation of WTO calls for a consistent and concerted strategy. The proposed South forum would be well-suited to start the discussion and give new form to this organization with headquarters in Switzerland, given its neutrality.

Manipulation and secrecy did not obtain the desired results in Seattle. The profound difference of interests between the United States and the European Union with respect to subsidies, investment, competition or foodstuffs cancelled out the efforts by Moore and the then United States Representative Charlene Barshefsky to have adopted, at all costs, a declaration on a new mandate, which lacked the necessary consensus for its approval. Similarly the demonstrations by trade unions and non-governmental organizations of the industrialized countries finally worked to the benefit of the weakest and most marginalized members of the World Trade Organization, the developing countries, notwithstanding the fact that their intention had been to obtain even greater privileges than those currently held.

Various participants declared their opposition to irregularities in negotiations. African, Latin American and Caribbean countries expressed their dissatisfaction with the working procedures of Moore in Seattle in press releases. They spoke out against the lack of transparency and the exclusion of their delegations in negotiating the text of the final document, which Barshefsky, in her capacity as Chairperson of the third Ministerial Meeting of the WTO, was intent on pushing through.[14]

The issue of implementation is of special importance for the developing countries. There are proposals to modify the rules of the game. The powers that be have refused to discuss these issues, preferring to focus on those they consider of absolute priority for their interests. As occurs in other forums, WTO is engaged in a dialogue of the deaf with agendas and projects that do not coincide. The lack of cooperation in the pursuit of a collective benefit in which everyone wins can paralyze negotiations on the issue of global trade. A longer-term vision would facilitate the return to equitable negotiations.

In 1918, Woodrow Wilson, the then President of the United States, prefaced his 14-point proposal by stating that there was a need for transparency in international relations and in order to overcome the policy of secret alliances which culminated in a world war. Transparency is as relevant today as it was 80 years ago and is a requirement if the member countries of an organization are to undertake to fulfil its policies and objectives. The majority of WTO members, developing countries, must not ratify agreements that have been made without their participation and whose clear purpose is to achieve an even greater concentration of world output, to the detriment of four-fifths of the total population. It is precisely to avoid future manipulative ploys of this kind, which are becoming more and more frequent, that it is necessary to form a unified group with common interests and consisting of Latin American, African and Asian countries committed to their own development and to balanced integration in the international system. Faced with the dilemma of strengthening regional organizations or participating in the globalizing trend favoured by WTO, Latin America must seek creative solutions that leave aside hollow rhetoric. The status quo on both fronts will keep them marginalized from the decision-making centres.

In the quest for alternative and independent routes, Malaysia's experience is an interesting example. Against the background of the economic crisis of South East Asia, the government of Prime Minister Datuk Seri Mahathir Mohamad adopted exchange control measures in September 1998 to regulate international trade in local currency and foreign currency movements in order to reduce the country's vulncrability to financial speculation and better manage the effects of the crisis in the region. Malaysia was one of the first countries in the region which experienced an economic upturn. This success won Mahathir the admiration and support of his countrymen.

The Malaysian experience shows the benefits obtained in seeking alternative routes within the global system which defend national interests against models imposed from abroad. To quote Mahathir:

> they [IMF] see our troubles as a means to get us to accept certain regimes, to open our market to foreign companies to do business without any conditions. It says it will give you money if you open up your economy, but doing so will cause all our banks, companies and industries to belong to foreigners.[15]

UNION BASED ON SIMILAR INTERESTS: NEW ALLIANCES (OBSERVATIONS)

Latin America both in its attempts at subregional, regional or hemispheric integration and in its participation in the WTO, is facing structural and policy design failures. These scenarios would serve to promote greater integration in the world economic system if they responded to fundamental interests that enjoyed full political backing with a view to advancing projects that would benefit the development of the subcontinent. As explained earlier, the vast majority of initiatives and agreements are the product of tradition without any competitive element or else are merely imposed by the multilateral system. In this context, creativity is of the essence in the search for options that permit development and economic growth.

The proposal for establishing a 'Southern Forum' which would promote common interests in multilateral and regional international mechanisms will be a first step towards the formation of a united transcontinental bloc, that will strengthen the participation of Latin America and the rest of the developing world in international organizations, especially in the WTO. In this context, the countries of Latin America must meet the challenge of looking beyond their geographic boundaries for strategic alliances with nations from other continents in order to move forward with integration in the international system and increase their participation in the global economy.

The consolidation of new mechanisms is part of the globalization process. This does not have the same effect for different peoples of the world. Whereas some have enjoyed greater prosperity and greater freedom, others have sustained economic losses with catastrophic social effects. Some peoples who are not in a position to compete have been suffering greater socio-economic losses than the apparent benefits of maintaining their economies open to the competition of industrialized and technologically advanced countries, as was pointed out briefly with reference to some of the agreements that developing countries have been forced to observe, such as the agricultural agreement, TRIMS and TRIPS.

Globalization has opened up great opportunities for economic and social progress and has also led to disruptions such as the financial instability experienced in Asia in 1998 and marginalization of countries and of persons ill-prepared to take advantage of its benefits. An intelligent, long-term management of this trend could reduce overall costs to avoid the development of endemic, permanent syndromes of backwardness, exclusion and global destabilization.[16]

In this difficult context, the developing world, including Latin America, is unprotected, divided and in too vulnerable a position to confront the challenges of globalization and the dominance of a small number of industrialized countries, intent on pursuing their policies of concentration of wealth and prosperity. The Group of 77 and the Movement of Non-Aligned Countries have become forums where declarations are repeated without identifying any specific joint action. These groups draft dense, lengthy documents containing reams of multiple, varied objectives. However, they have not succeeded in focusing on a *joint*, *clear* and *decisive* action, with respect to their vital, strategic and pressing interests.

The reasons for inaction and lack of agreement are numerous: the diversity of countries with at times opposing interests; political, social, cultural and economic differences within groups; failure to identify sufficiently generic common interests that would enable them to overcome their differences and focus action on fundamental priority responsibilities. Given this lack, pages and pages of agreements will be drafted without any prospect of their ever being implemented. The Bali Plan of Action of December 1998 relating to regional and subregional economic cooperation between developing countries identified as a priority the need to 'establish and strengthen regular mechanisms of consultations, communication and the sharing of information, experience and expertise among regional and subregional groupings/communities as well as the identification and implementation of joint projects and activities'.

It is high time for the developing world to move beyond the stage of criticizing the international system, which has all the structural failures referred to above, and to adopt a responsible attitude by generating new options that promote and favour the development and well-being of its peoples.

This proposal can start on a small scale and gain momentum in terms of concrete and vital interests, shared by all concerned, and which transcend the inevitable differences that exist. In other words, a small scale which can be a stepping-stone to something larger can be a good start for enabling developing countries to make their presence felt on the multilateral stage and to defend their vital interests in a joint, concerted and coordinated manner. To date, no regular effective cooperation mechanisms have been promoted for implementing the proposals contained in political declarations. After each of the meetings and once the final document has been distributed in all the official languages, member countries return to everyday politics. In order to establish mechanisms that favour concerted policies, different procedures must be adopted in order to facilitate regular exchanges.

RECOMMENDATIONS AND CONCLUSIONS

The following are some ideas on how an action group representing the developing world should be set up to satisfy the minimum requirement of having a fundamental strategic interest as a common denominator for collective and coordinated action:

- Define urgent, vital and strategic interests which unite and bring them together in spite of possible differences between member countries in other areas.
- Involve private sector companies linked to competitive export industries (natural resources, manufacturing, industry, technology) in member countries.
- Develop informal high-level consultation mechanisms with the participation of competent, experienced technocrats. Whereas high-level participation is necessary to guarantee the political will of the state, the contribution of experts who deal on a daily basis with issues is fundamental for overcoming the *rhetoric* and declarations written in '*invisible ink*'.
- Use informal mechanisms for consultation to identify the interests that make for a united front on different regional and multilateral issues for presentation in international forums. Secure agreements and prepare proposals for achieving greater participation in forums, traditionally controlled by industrialized countries.
- Be realistic about the agreements that are reached. In other words, develop policies that correspond to *feasible* rather than *ideal* objectives. This attitude reflects maturity and seriousness. It is easy to secure agreements on utopian proposals, but, in a sense, everyone knows that they will never be implemented. Assuming a responsible approach by adopting concrete actions that can or will definitely be realized not

only demands national political will but also a real group coordination and a sincere determination to carry through an objective that goes beyond temporary and specific differences.

This is probably not the developing world's only alternative for improving its bargaining position in multilateral forums such as the WTO. However, it may mean an efficient, inexpensive way out and one that can be implemented in the short and medium term. Just as no one will pay the external debt for the developing world, in the same way no one will pave the way towards establishing a balance in world economic trade. Failure to pursue fundamental interests that are feasible will condemn developing countries to remain on the list of the system's underprivileged and marginalized.

A group of countries, few in number, that can join forces on the basis of the proposed criteria is a good start as an example of what can be achieved by working around realistic and specific interests that are sufficiently generic to encompass all, a group of countries from all the regions in the world committed to improving the terms of their integration in the international system, a group of countries that is representative and aware of the power of consistent, coordinated and joint action.

A handful of developing countries, based on their relative regional status, the characteristics of their economies, their participation in multilateral forums, their pursuit of autonomy or their contribution to strengthening the 'Southern Forum' which will enable them to achieve an effective and efficient joint and coordinated action, would be the natural members of this informal group for consultation and negotiation with third parties. The political will is, without doubt, the fundamental criterion. Thus, the commitment to implementing concerted strategies is an essential requirement, if one wishes to overcome the rhetorical imperative that has characterized groups based on integration, consultation and coordination in Latin America and the developing world. For the above reasons, Latin America and the developing world as a whole, have the responsibility to define, organize, orient and conduct their policies for economic and social development beyond all the difficulties and obstacles that the international system imposes. Creativity and courage are necessary as are the political will and intelligent action geared towards a clear and coherent purpose.

There are indeed opportunities and challenges that emerge for Latin America and the rest of the developing world from the events in Seattle. The revival of existing forums, such as UNCTAD, which can act as a counterbalance to WTO, the review and, in some cases, the dissolution of inoperative, anachronistic integration groups and the creation of pragmatic and flexible forums that will facilitate concerted action and participation in multilateral forums, are all options open for developing countries. Failure to recognize them at this particular juncture means only a few will decide in the designing of the future world economic order and trading system. It is time to move from *rhetoric* to *action*.

Notes

1. Garay, *Globalización y Crisis*.
2. In 1998, 38 per cent of Ecuadorian imports originated in the United States and 22 per cent in other countries. Only 5 per cent were from Colombia. Exports to Colombia accounted for 10 per cent of Ecuador's total exports compared with 30 per cent to the United States. In 1998, Venezuela obtained 6 per cent of its imports from Colombia and 44 per cent from the United States and those trading partners absorbed 50 per cent of its total exports.
3. See the Declaration of Principles: Partnership for Development and Prosperity: Democracy, Free Trade and Sustainable Development in the Americas and the Plan of Action of the Summit of the Americas, December 1994.
4. The figures come from national statistical databases and from the United Nations and are approximate only.
5. Established in 1986 with a membership of 20: Argentina, Bolivia, Brazil, Colombia, Chile, Ecuador, Mexico, Panama, Paraguay, Peru, Uruguay, Venezuela, Panama, Costa Rica, Nicaragua, Honduras, Guatemala, El Salvador, Dominican Republic and Guyana (as representative of the Caribbean States).
6. Communiqué of the Summit of the European Union, Latin America and the Caribbean, Rio de Janeiro, 29 June 1999.
7. It is important to note that Supachai will assume the reins of WTO in September 2002 and will then also hold the chair of the UNCTAD. The Bangkok Declaration seeks to ensure that the right to development is included as a fundamental part of the new rounds of negotiations within the WTO.
8. Genetic engineering and agricultural subsidies being the most controversial issues.
9. Raghavan, 'The Return of the "Green Room"', *Third World Economics: Trends and Analysis*, Malaysia, 1–15 December 1999, pp. 2–7.
10. *Bilan du Monde, Bilan Economique et Social, edition Janvier 2000*, On the list of exporters, the United States and Germany are followed by Japan (7.2 per cent), France (5.6 per cent), United Kingdom (5 per cent), Italy (4.5 per cent), Canada (4 per cent), Netherlands (3.7 per cent), China (3.4 per cent) and Belgium-Luxembourg (3 per cent).
11. Taken from the statements of the ministers of these nations in Seattle, 1999.
12. Statement by Martha Lucía Ramírez, Minister of Foreign Trade, 1 December 1999, third WTO Ministerial Meeting in Seattle.

13.   Words of Dr Luiz Felipe Lampreia, Minister of Foreign Affairs. Statement of 1 December 1999 to the Third Ministerial Meeting of the World Trade Organization in Seattle.
14.   Tetteh Hormeku, 'Dirty Tactics in Seattle', *Third World Resurgence*, Penang, Malaysia, December 1999–January 2000, No. 112/113, pp. 19–21. This point of view is echoed by Abid Aslam in his article in the same publication on 'Developing Countries Assail WTO "Dictatorship" ', pp. 22–3.
15.   Martin Khor, 'Why Capital Controls and International Debt Restructuring Mechanisms Are Necessary to Prevent and Manage Financial Crises' (essay distributed by *Third World Network*).
16.   Dani Rodrik, in his book entitled *The New Global Economy and Developing Countries: Making Openness Work*, makes an interesting contribution to this issue.

Bibliography

BECK, ULRICH (1998) *¿Qué es la globalización?: Falacias del globalismo, respuestas a la globalización.* (Barcelona: Ediciones Paidós Ibérica, S.A.).
CHOMSKY, NOAM (1993) *The Prosperous Few and The Restless Many* (Berkeley, California: Odonian Press, The Real Story Series).
GARAY, LUIS JORGE (1999) *Globalización y Crisis: '¿Hegemonía o corresponsabilidad'?* (Bogotá: Colciencias y Tercer Mundo Editores).
JARAMILLO, LUIS FERNANDO (1994) *El Grupo de los 77: hacia una estrategia colectiva*, Compendio de las intervenciones realizadas por Colombia durante su Presidencia del Grupo de los 77 (Nueva York: Misión de Colombia ante las Naciones Unidas) Enero.
KHOR, MARTIN (1999–2000) 'The Revolt of the Developing Nations' 'The Seattle Debacle: What Happened and What Next?', *Third World Resurgence*, issue Nos. 112–113, Penang, Malaysia: Third World Network, in *The Seattle Debacle: What Happened and What Next?* Issue nos. 112/113, Penang, Malaysia: *Third World Network*, December/ January.
KHOUDOUR-CASTÉRAS, DAVID (1999) *¿Una moneda única para América Latina?*, Las lecciones de la construcción monetaria europea para América Latina (Bogotá: Colección Pretextos, No. 11, Facultad de Finanzas, Gobierno y Relaciones Internacionales, Universidad Externado de Colombia).
RAGHAVAN, CHAKRAVARTHI (1999) 'The Return of the "Green Room" ', *Third World Economics: Trends and Analysis*, Malaysia, 1–15 December.
RODRIK, DANI (1999) *The New Global Economy and Developing Countries: Making Openness Work*, Policy Essay No. 24 (Washington, D.C.: Overseas Development Council and Johns Hopkins University Press).
ROITMAN, MARCOS and CARLOS CASTRO-GIL (coordinadores) (1990) *América Latina: Entre los Mitos y la Utopía* (Madrid: Universidad Complutense de Madrid).
TALBOTT, STROBE (1997) 'Globalization and Diplomacy: A Practitioner's Perspective', *Foreign Policy*, Washington: Carnegie Endowment for International Peace, Fall 1997, pp. 69–83.

2 Latin America in the WTO

Constantine Michalopoulos[*]

INTRODUCTION

Throughout the 1960s and 1970s, countries in Latin America and the Caribbean (LAC) preferred to use the United Nations Conference on Trade and Development (UNCTAD), the Economic Commission for Latin America and the Caribbean (ECLAC) and other regional and sub-regional forums rather than the General Agreement on Tariff and Trade (GATT) to promote their international trade agenda. Many Latin American and Caribbean (LAC) countries were not contracting parties of GATT. Those that were, participated only passively in GATT multilateral trade negotiations prior to the Uruguay Round (UR), meaning that they did not engage in a significant way in the mutual exchange of concessions on a reciprocal basis.

Beginning with the Uruguay Round, attitudes in LAC towards participation in the GATT and, subsequently, in the World Trade Organization (WTO) changed significantly. Many countries played a very active role in the Uruguay Round negotiations; and practically all LAC countries which were not members of GATT/WTO decided to accede. This attitude change reflects a number of complex and interrelated developments: developing countries, in general, and LAC countries, in particular, have become more effectively integrated in the international trading system, and several have become exporters of manufactures. Trade policies in many countries have been liberalized, favouring an outward orientation and lower protection. There has been a growing appreciation of the importance of observing international rules in the conduct of trade as well as the need to safeguard trading interests through effective participation in the activities of the new organization. LAC countries were especially active at the launch and during the UR negotiations.

The establishment of the WTO has resulted in further changes which place additional demands on LAC countries for their effective participation.

---

[*] The author wishes to thank Esperanza Duran of AITIC and Sylvia Saborio of ODC for providing him with insights and material regarding Latin America trade policies and policy-making which were very helpful in the preparation of the chapter.

First, the WTO covers a variety of new areas, such as services, standards, and intellectual property rights, all of which require additional institutional capacity in member governments for more effective representation both in Geneva and in their home capitals. Second, the WTO, unlike GATT, has been engaging in a number of ongoing negotiations in the liberalization of different sectors which require continuous active involvement by member countries. Three such negotiations, on Basic Telecommunications, Information Technology Products and Financial Services, were concluded in 1997 and more are in store on Agriculture and Services starting in 2000, as part of the built-in agenda of the Uruguay Round.[1] Third, the new Dispute Settlement Mechanism offers increased opportunities for developing countries to address grievances but poses tremendous challenges because of their limited institutional capacity in the area of international trade law.

A key question, which has concerned developing countries more broadly, is whether the WTO processes of decision-making, especially in the context of multilateral trade negotiations, permit an effective participation of developing country interests. Another question that concerns especially the smaller LAC countries is how to ensure effective participation in the activities of the Organization and, through it, the promotion of their interests in the expanding range of issues being addressed. This issue is of special importance because the WTO, like the GATT before it, is a member-driven organization, meaning that the bulk of the analytical work, the development of proposals as well as the negotiation of agreements and handling of disputes, falls on the member countries and their representatives. The Secretariat of the WTO performs primarily support functions for the effective consideration of topics at the different meetings. It does not normally initiate proposals or ideas for new agreements.

This chapter analyses participation of LAC countries at the WTO as of mid-2000. The focus is on three main issues: (a) participation in the affairs of the WTO, with respect to the formal and the informal processes that characterize WTO governance and decision-making on day-to-day issues as well as in the context of WTO Ministerial Meetings and the preparations and conduct of multilateral trade negotiations; and what it requires in terms of institutional capacity at home and representation in Geneva; (b) participation in the Dispute Settlement Mechanism (DSM) and (c) LAC country positions on multilateral trade negotiations, those that are ongoing, and the potential new Round. Based on this analysis, the last part of the chapter draws a number of conclusions and recommendations for the more effective participation of LAC countries in the WTO.

MEMBERSHIP AND PARTICIPATION

LAC participation in the WTO now numbers 32 countries, with almost all countries and territories represented.[2] This was not always the case. Brazil, Chile and Cuba were charter members of GATT. But many LAC countries did not become members until much later. This includes the Central American countries (except Nicaragua) and Mexico. Seventeen countries, or more than half of the present membership, have acceded since 1982. The most recent were Ecuador, Granada and Panama. Ten Caribbean countries which were former colonial dependencies of GATT contracting parties, came into the GATT upon acquiring independence through the simplified Article XXVI: 5(c) procedures. The rest went through the GATT/WTO accession process (Duran, 2000).

Once becoming members, LAC countries have been quite active participants of the organization. This is reflected in the number of leadership positions they hold, their involvement in the formal and informal processes of decision-making, as well as their involvement in the Dispute Settlement Mechanism (DSM). In all these aspects their participation in the WTO is far greater and probably more effective than on average for the developing countries as a whole. But as is the case with all developing countries, there is a great divide between the involvement and effectiveness of participation of the larger countries and those of the smaller economies, especially those in the Caribbean and Central America.

Decision-Making

Any institution such as the WTO, and the GATT before it, which is based on consensus must develop a variety of processes, both formal and informal, in order to reach decisions. In principle, any single member of the institution can block a decision by casting a negative vote.[3] It was clear, even in the context of the GATT where the developing countries had a majority of the votes but played a decidedly lesser role, that it would be futile to attempt to exercise voting strength either to block major progress or to force developed countries to implement obligations not freely accepted (Evans, 1968). In practice there is rarely, if ever, any voting. This puts a premium on consultation, both formal and informal, that builds consensus.

As the WTO now has more than 140 members, it is very difficult to conduct consultations, or for that matter any kind of business activity, when everybody has to be consulted about everything. Thus, while the General Council, the ultimate decision-making body where all members are represented, as well as all the various subsidiary bodies and committees, meet frequently, informal consultations take place even more often.

Leadership Positions

The analysis of leadership positions focuses on the country distribution of chairs in various GATT/WTO bodies and Committees. Chairs have traditionally had the opportunity to play a somewhat active role in forging consensus in the GATT and the WTO – their role has not been purely cosmetic. An organization like the WTO which works with consensus despite the fact that the countries represented are very different in their economic size, presents complex challenges in designing decision-making structures that result in an equitable representation of the interests of all participants. Chairs play a role in this effort both to forge consensus and to maintain a reasonable balance of interests. Thus, the share of chairs and other offices held by developing countries could shed some light on their involvement and potential influence in the organization, especially over time. Over the last two decades, developing countries increased substantially the absolute number of chairs they hold, in particular, 'important' chairs of the main bodies of GATT and WTO and Committees reporting to them. Indeed, starting with 1987, developing countries held, in absolute terms, more chairs than developed countries (Michalopoulos, 1999). In all cases, their proportion of chairs has been lower than their share of the total membership of the institution, but higher than their share of international trade.

LAC countries hold a significant proportion of these positions. In 2000, LAC countries held seven chairs or one-third of the twenty-one leadership positions in WTO Bodies and Committees held by developing countries; and one of the top leadership positions, Chair of the Council on Goods by Uruguay. The implications of this analysis should not be exaggerated. They do suggest that the WTO, as an institution, is formally flexible enough to accommodate an increasing interest on the part of developing countries. Whether this translates into moving forward issues of importance to the agenda of the developing countries is a more complex issue, however. Preparation and presentation of issues does not hinge primarily on the holding of chairs or leadership positions. It is based on a lot of preparatory work and institutional capability in capitals. It is also based on the development of points of common interest with similarly minded countries and delegations.

Informal Consultations

When issues of importance to the WTO as a whole require consultations, these usually involve the Director General and a smaller group of members, that include the major trading countries, both developed and developing, and others who are judged to be representative of the views of the remaining membership. The actual composition of this group (called the 'Green Room Group' because it meets at the Director General's green conference room) tends to vary by issue. But on issues of general importance to the organization it could consist upwards of thirty members. Often, five or more of these countries are from LAC, including almost always Argentina, Brazil and Mexico, one country from the Caribbean and one from Central America, plus one or more countries from the rest of Latin America. There is little doubt that LAC countries have an important voice in these consultations. However, they often do not have a common position on major issues before the WTO. As a result, like other developing countries, they participate in a variety of groups, some of mixed composition with developed countries, others only with developing country participation, to try to forge consensus on various issues.

There is a Developing Country Group in the WTO that holds consultations from time to time. However, the establishment of common positions, that will encompass all the developing countries' members of the WTO as a group, is becoming a rarity as there are growing disparities in their income levels, their trading interests, their integration in the international economy, their institutional capacities and their participation in WTO affairs. There is a regional caucus for LAC countries, known by its initials as GRULAG (Grupo Latinoaméricano y del Caribe), which meets regularly, chaired by an Ambassador from the Geneva LAC Missions on a rotating basis. Despite the frequency of meetings, there is little effort to forge consensus in the group and most of the discussion focuses on exchange of views on the different positions. Sub-regional groups, like Mercosur (the Southern Common Market), do coordinate positions and speak with one voice – articulated by one of the national delegations, members of the group.

The 'Cairns Group' is the one other major group to which a number of the larger LAC countries belong and which represents both developed and developing countries with important exporting interests in agriculture. Nine of the 15 members of the Group are LAC countries, Argentina, Bolivia Brazil, Chile, Colombia, Costa Rica, Guatemala, Uruguay and Paraguay. They coordinate positions on agricultural trade very closely, in the context of the group, which speaks with one voice in the negotiations on agriculture.

Another sectorally oriented body is the International Textiles and Clothing Bureau, with more than 20 developing country members. It provides a forum for collaboration among textile and clothing exporters and counts almost half of its membership from LAC. But unlike Cairns, it is not clear whether membership in the Group results in identical positions on all issues: for example, the textile exporters from LAC tend to be more high-cost than their Asian competitors and hold somewhat different views on specific issues of trade liberalization in the sector.

Several other informal groups of mixed membership are worth noting: the so-called 'Invisible Group' consists of about twenty officials from trade ministries of major trading countries, balanced between both developed and developing countries, including the 'Quad' – Canada, the European Commission, Japan and the US, but also Argentina and Brazil, India and Korea. It meets in Geneva (or nearby) perhaps twice a year, with the participation of the Director General to discuss, usually in general terms, up-coming issues of importance to the WTO.

In advance of the Seattle Ministerial a number of other country groups emerged – as has been customary during the preparatory processes before (and during) a multilateral Round. Three such groups may be noted: first, the 'Friends of the Round' consisting of fifteen countries with liberal trade policies, including five from LAC of the ten developing countries (Argentina, Chile, Costa Rica, Korea, Mexico, Morocco, Singapore, Thailand, Uruguay and Hong Kong, China). Second, a 'Like Minded Group' consisting of six developing countries, with somewhat more protectionist policies and confrontational stance (Dominican Republic, Egypt, India, Pakistan, Indonesia and Malaysia). It has emphasized the importance of ensuring 'implementation' especially of the special and differential (S&D) provisions of the UR, before agreeing to a new Round. A third group of Central American countries (including Panama) and the Dominican Republic – the so-called 'Paradiso Group' – also came into existence with somewhat similar views to the 'like minded' but with special concerns for maintaining S&D provisions for export subsidies.

In addition to these groups, the development of a consensus involves numerous other meetings in formal or informal settings. For example, developing countries consult in other regional groupings, such as the Africa group or the Association of South East Asian Nations (ASEAN) as well as in the context of groups with a wider agenda such the G-15, or in smaller caucuses among like-minded countries whose composition sometimes includes both developed and developing countries.[4]

Agenda Setting and the Ministerial Meetings

In advance of and during the recent Seattle Ministerial Meeting of the WTO, developing countries voiced two sets of complaints regarding their capacity to influence the issues addressed by the WTO and to ensure that the Agenda of future multilateral trade negotiations reflects their interests.

First, there were concerns that, partly because of their own institutional weaknesses and partly because of the absence of an international institution – such as the one provided by OECD for the developed countries – they are unable to undertake research and analyses as well as develop proposals that reflect developing country interests, which can then be presented at the WTO for consideration by its full membership.[5] As it turned out, these sets of concerns may not have been justified because developing countries submitted perhaps the bulk of the proposals for inclusion in the Seattle agenda.

But the second set of concerns, which had to do with their perception that the processes used in Seattle (and in Singapore) to develop consensus tended to ignore the interests of many developing countries, has proved to be a serious and lasting problem for the WTO as an organization. The problems derive fundamentally from the fact that WTO Ministerial Conferences which take place at least once every two years, such as the one in Seattle which was expected to launch a new round of multilateral trade negotiations, put an especially heavy burden on processes to build consensus. This is because such Conferences attempt to deal with a large range of issues in a very short period of time. In the absence of adequate preparation and development of consensus in advance of the Conference, devising procedures that would permit both effective negotiation and full participation at the Conference itself is extremely difficult, if not impossible.

Consensus decision-making is essential for any actions that affect the legal rights and obligations of governments as they do under the WTO. No government will cede to others this right. On the other hand serious negotiations are simply not practicable if every issue must be discussed in a body as large as the General Council. 'Green Room' style meetings need to be kept small enough to allow effective negotiations to take place, but at the same time the major developed and developing countries need to be present, if the results are to command consensus support. (LAC presence in the 'Green Room' discussions in Seattle was substantial.) However, this meant that very few of the many small developing countries – including many in the Caribbean – are ever included in such consultations, prompting many to complain that their interests are not being taken into account.

In the aftermath of the failure of the Seattle Ministerial a variety of proposals have circulated aimed at making the decision-making processes more fair, transparent and inclusive. Some countries advocated an UNCTAD type system with regional groupings. Others proposed variants on the World Bank/IMF constituency groupings. Still others focused on proposals aimed at opening up the WTO deliberations and increasing transparency in the proceedings.

Following consideration of many of these proposals, it appears that
WTO members are moving towards agreement involving a range of
reforms which would tend to help the participation of the smaller developing countries in decision-making while increasing the information flow to
all. The central principle of reaching decisions by consensus will be
retained, as would the practice of smaller negotiating groups. But an effort
would be made to ensure that participation is more truly representative
of the whole membership and the range of subjects to be discussed.
Moreover, it is intended that the deliberations in the smaller group be
promptly reported to an open meeting of the whole membership, giving an
opportunity for countries to participate and express views; and that more
information about the deliberations of the organization be made promptly
available to the public in order to increase transparency. Implementation
of these procedures would be left to the Director General. The challenge
would be to put these procedures in practice during the pressure-packed
Ministerial meetings. These are unlikely to make significant progress
unless they are better prepared in the sense that there is more consensus on
the issues under consideration in advance of the actual meeting.

Representation

Membership in the WTO does not automatically imply effectiveness in the
representation of a country's interests in the organization. For this, it is
necessary to have the appropriate representation in Geneva and the needed
institutional capacity at home.

There are severe limitations and constraints to representing a country's
interests effectively in a 'member' driven organization such as the WTO
without a significant presence in the seat of the Organization in Geneva.
Today, ten of the 32 LAC countries or almost a third do not maintain WTO
Missions in Geneva. These are primarily the smaller island economies of
the Caribbean that have very few representatives abroad and simply cannot
afford many separate Missions. Until very recently, many of these countries have considered their main international trade policy issues to involve
relations with the European Union, rather than the WTO, and thus have
located their representatives in Brussels, from where they also are supposed to follow WTO issues.[6]

There is little doubt that representation from Brussels or another
Mission in Europe can cause difficulties, delays and sometimes confusion
in the participation of the activities of WTO in Geneva. The limitations

and constraints to effective participation in the WTO that derive from lack of representation in Geneva have been noted many times and they have been documented in the case of Sierra Leone, a least-developed country with representation to the WTO from Brussels.[7]

Effective representation to the many bodies of the WTO also requires a Mission of a certain size. Discussions with representatives of Missions from both developed and developing countries suggest that they are all hard-pressed to cope with the increased number of meetings and activities of the WTO. According to one estimate (Blackhurst, 1997), there were approximately 40–45 scheduled WTO meetings in the average working week in 1995–96. To this one must add all the other informal gatherings for consultations that occur among delegations outside formal settings to develop consensus discussed earlier.

During 1997–2000, there was a very sizable increase (18 per cent) in the number of staff devoted to WTO matters by both developed and developing countries represented in Geneva. This reflects both the increasing complexity of the issues and the desire of developing countries to increase the effectiveness of their representation at the WTO.

Based on informal estimates developed in consultation with a number of Missions, just to follow the topics of the various WTO bodies and attend their meetings requires a staff of at least four to five people, and the average is increasing.[8] If one uses this yardstick, it is clear that, as of mid-2000, many LAC countries did not meet it. Assuming for example, that effective representation in the WTO requires a Mission in Geneva of a size of at least four staff (including the head of Mission), ten LAC countries did not meet this requirement because they did not have a Mission in Geneva; another six had a Mission, but with less than four staff (including the head of Mission) assigned to WTO tasks. Thus, fully half of the LAC country delegations to the WTO were below the minimum required for effective participation.

The problem obviously is most critical for the smaller economies in the Caribbean. If we exclude these countries, the average size of the LAC Missions in Geneva is six staff, or close to the average for developed countries and much higher than the average for all developing countries. Including the small Caribbean economies, however, brings the average for LAC as a whole very close to that for all developing countries (Table 2.1). A duality has thus emerged in LAC much as in the representation of developing countries as a whole: on the one hand there are a 'few countries, mostly larger middle and higher income countries' with effective representation; and many others with 'weak or totally absent' representation.

Table 2.1   Country* membership and representation GATT/WTO 1982–2000, by location and number of mission staff

(a)

Countries/ territories	1982 Geneva		Europe		Capitals		1987 Geneva		Europe		Capitals	
	No.	Staff	No.	Staff	No.	Staff	No.	Staff	No.	Staff	No.	Staff
Developed	24	99					24	120				
Developing	40	120	14	15	4	5	45	147	15	21	5	5
LAC	*12*	*36*	*3*	*3*			*13*	*43*	*4*	*4*	*1*	*1*
Transition	6	16					6	18				
Total	70	235	14	15	4	5	75	285	15	21	5	5

Countries/ territories	1997 Geneva		Europe		Capitals		2000 Geneva		Europe		Capitals	
	No.	Staff	No.	Staff	No.	Staff	No.	Staff	No.	Staff	No.	Staff
Developed	24	166		1	1	2	25	179		1		2
Developing	64	277	26	60	7	7	72*	331	24	73	3	4
LAC	*21*	*99*	*8*	*18*	*2*	*2*	*22*	*118*	*9*	*19*	*1*	*1*
Transition	9	25					12	40				
Total	97	468	26	61	8	9	109	550	24	74	3	6

* In countries for which there is representation both in Geneva and in European Missions and/or capitals (Barbados, Central African Republic, Mauritania and Mozambique) only the Geneva representative is shown but all staff working on WTO matters have been included.

Capacity Constraints

The increasing range and complexity of issues handled by the WTO, some of which are very technical, implies that the capacity of developing countries to participate effectively in the work of the WTO will depend very heavily on the analytical capacity and strength of governments and other institutions handling the range of WTO issues in capitals. This is all the more so in the WTO, a member-driven organization, with a very small Secretariat, and as mentioned before, a great deal of the analysis of issues and development of positions is done by members. There is no point in trying to strengthen the representation in Geneva without improving institutional capacity in the home country.

(b)

Table 2.1 Country membership and representation GATT/WTO 1982–2000, staff per country

Countries/ territories	1982			1987			1997			2000		
	No.	Staff	Staff/ country	No.	Staff	Staff/ country	No.	Staff	Staff/ country	No.	Staff	Staff/ country
Developed	24	99	4.1	24	120	5.0	25	169	6.8	25	182	7.3
Developing	58	140	2.4	65	173	2.7	97	345	3.6	99	408	4.1
LAC	*14*	*36*	*2.6*	*17*	*48*	*2.8*	*31*	*119*	*3.8*	*32*	*138*	*4.3*
Transition	6	16	2.7	6	18	3.0	9	25	2.8	12	40	3.3
Developing (Geneva)	*40*	*120*	*3.0*	*45*	*147*	*3.3*	*64*	*280*	*4.4*	*72*	*320*	*4.4*
Total	88	255	2.9	95	311	3.3	131	539	4.1	136	630	4.6

Source: Compiled by author from figures derived from GATT/WTO, *Directory* 1982, 1987, 1997, 2000.

Developing countries face a variety of challenges in this regard: the drafting of appropriate legislation and regulations, the meeting of procedural notification requirements, the staffing of government institutions with technical personnel able to implement the policies and commitments undertaken and the monitoring of trading partners' implementation of WTO obligations to assess whether market access has been unfairly denied or trade rights infringed – as well as to prepare an appropriate response (UNCTAD and WTO, 1996). In addition there are the institutions related to the 'New Areas'. These include Customs as well as the institutions which ensure that products entering trade meet technical and sanitary and phytosanitary standards, those that deal with the implementation of the Trade-Related Aspects of Intellectual Property Rights (TRIPS) agreement and so on.

In several of these new areas the UR agreements have resulted in such onerous obligations that it is difficult for many developing countries to implement them, especially in the time frames provided–which themselves were arbitrarily set (Michalopoulos, 2000).

Weaknesses in trade-related developing country institutions have been clear for some time, especially in Sub-Saharan Africa (Oyejide, 1990). But they have become an even greater constraint, in the light of the heavy burden of reporting and implementation entailed by the UR Agreements. These weaknesses are amply documented in the assessment of needs for technical assistance of the least-developed countries (LDCs). But they are also present in a number of the smaller and lower-income countries of LAC.

Indeed some of the institution building is quite costly and may not deserve as high a priority in these countries' development efforts. This is a general problem for the smaller and lower-income developing countries, but it also affects many countries in LAC.

Strengthening the institutional capacity at home through international assistance is essential to effective representation of a country's interests in Geneva. But much of the international community's assistance effort has focused on the least-developed countries and on Africa, with very little assistance directed to the smaller and low-income countries in LAC.

At the same time, it is worth noting that the international community has established a number of initiatives with a special focus of assisting low-income countries' overall representation in the WTO. Most notable of these is the Agency for International Trade Information and Co-operation (AITIC) established in Geneva in 1998 to help-low-income and least-developed countries in WTO participation through seminars, and other information and training activities. The focus of the Agency's activities is in both the Geneva delegations and in Brussels.

DISPUTE SETTLEMENT

An effective dispute settlement mechanism has been touted as one of the main achievements of the UR.[9] Such a mechanism is of special importance for developing countries with smaller clout in international trade. Both developed and developing country members have utilized the new WTO Dispute Settlement Mechanism (DSM) far more actively than the GATT mechanism for settling disputes. As of August 2000, developing countries had made 43 requests for consultations on 37 separate matters. Roughly half of these were against developed countries. Developing countries were the respondents to 67 complaints by developed countries on 53 different matters. Developing countries also joined developed countries in raising complaints against developed countries in another ten cases involving four distinct matters (see Table 2.2).[10]

The experience so far suggests that an asymmetry may be emerging in the use of DSM between developed and developing countries. Developing countries have been the target of complaints through the DSM much more than their relative share in developed country exports would suggest. Table 2.2 shows that fully 46 per cent of developed country complaints have been raised against developing countries' WTO members, while the latter account for only about 25 per cent of developed country trade. Developing countries on the other hand had raised slightly more than half of their total complaints against developed countries, which is considerably less than the latter account of developing country WTO member trade.

LAC countries have been active users of the DSM, probably on average more so than other developing countries. Countries like Argentina, Brazil, Chile and Mexico have been involved both as complainants and as respondents to complaints. But although the DSM has been used actively by some developing countries, the overall number using the mechanism (either as a respondent or complainant) has so far been only around 20, about half of whom have been from LAC.

Developing countries seem to fare reasonably well in cases which have been completed. Of the 38 cases where legal action has been completed, in the sense that Panel and or Appellate Body reports were adopted by decisions of the Dispute Settlement Body (DSB), 13 involved complaints by developed countries against developing countries, seven were complaints

Table 2.2   WTO disputes[*] (in number of cases)

Complaint by	Respondent					
	Developed		Developing		Total	
	Distinct matter	Consultation request	Distinct matter	Consultation request	Distinct matter	Consultation request
Development	64	79	53	67	117	146
Developing	19	23	18	20	37	43
Mixed[**]	4	10	0	0	4	10
Total	87	112	71	87	158	199

Source: WTO.
Notes: [*]As of 22 July, 2000. [**]Combined developed and developing country complaints.

by developing countries against developed, three were between developing countries, and one by a combination of developed and developing countries against a developed country.[11]

There is no point in attempting to reach conclusions regarding who 'won' these cases. In any case, the complex rulings adopted frequently made it possible for all sides to claim victory. The record shows, however, that in the context of cases decided so far, a fair number of legal points were decided in favour of LAC countries (either as complainants or as defendants), and both developed and developing countries have taken actions to implement the decisions or to deal with issues that gave rise to the complaints – that is, that the DSM is in fact working. For example, the US announced implementation of the recommendations of the DSB in a complaint by Venezuela and Brazil in the gasoline standards case.

Some of the disputes have involved LAC countries themselves: for example a complaint by Mexico against Guatemala's use of anti-dumping measures on cement imports from Mexico. Perhaps the most famous case, however, which has pitted LAC countries against each other, is the famous 'banana split' in which a number of Latin American exporters of bananas – at various times nine countries (Costa Rica, Colombia, Guatemala, Ecuador, Honduras, Mexico, Nicaragua, Panama and Venezuela) – have complained together with the US against the EU over the preferential access it provides to smaller Caribbean banana exporters.

It is beyond the scope of this chapter to discuss the complexities of the case (see Duran, 2000). While it has been often portrayed as an issue of the big Central and South American exporters against the little exporters from the small Caribbean economies, in practice it has been more a battle between major US and EU multinationals over how to apportion the rents that are generated from the EU restrictions. The bottom line is that everybody seems to have lost. The EU arrangements have been found inconsistent with the WTO on two occasions. The EU measures have not changed the system much and have been judged by the US as inadequate remedies. In turn the US has imposed additional tariffs on EU products which are supposed to hurt EU producers, but of course hurt US consumers at least as much.

Latin America's Experience

The Latin American experience would suggest that active developing country participation in the DSM would provide them with the kind of opportunity to address trade issues of concern to them. But so far, this opportunity has been seized by only relatively few countries. Perhaps in no other area are the institutional weakness so glaring as in international legal matters involving the use of the DSM. The legal issues underlying the WTO agreements are very complex, requiring legal expertise in international law which in most developing countries is absent in the private sector and the government. Governments also often lack the expertise necessary to make the initial case assessment or direct the case during its preparation whether in defence or as complainant.

Hiring international law firms that do possess the necessary expertise is an extremely expensive proposition with costs ranging from 250 to 1,000 dollars an hour, raising the total costs of prosecuting a case to levels that cannot be supported by many developing country government budgets. Trying to pass on these costs to the industries affected is also a problem. A legal system which relies totally or predominantly on the participants' capacity to pay for the legal costs involved introduces inequities and distortions and may result in situations, such as the banana case, where the DSM is seen primarily as a locus of adjudication of interests of large and/or wealthy companies and countries.

Providing assistance to developing countries in the legal area raises complex issues. Many governments find it difficult to provide bilateral assistance to developing countries, which could be used to do legal battle with the commercial interests or the trade ministry of the same government. The WTO is required by Article 27.2 of the Dispute Settlement Understanding (DSU) to provide legal advice and assistance to developing countries. Accordingly, the WTO Secretariat has engaged the services of two legal experts as consultants, who are available to assist developing countries in their cases. But the support they can offer is extremely limited: their services are available for a total of roughly 400 hours a year – which is usually not enough to deal with one case.

Raising the capacity of the WTO Secretariat in a significant way to assist developing countries presents a fundamental problem. Staff or consultants to an impartial international Secretariat who are supposed to be neutral would have to take sides in a legal dispute between two members. While the Secretariat could use additional resources, its staff or consultants are better able to focus on providing basic technical assistance, such as training courses on DSB procedures and general advice on the meaning of legal provisions.

Case level assistance, which is very much needed, is the main mandate of a new entity, the Advisory Centre on WTO Law, legally separate from the WTO itself, which has been established recently, notably under an initiative from Colombia. It is funded partly by donors and partly by developing country users, with current membership of 32 countries, of which 23 are developing, including nine from LAC.

THE CHALLENGES OF A NEW ROUND OF
MULTILATERAL TRADE NEGOTIATIONS

Why Did Seattle Fail?

LAC countries worked hard and successfully to develop a coherent view on the major issues in the UR. Collaboration during this period was helped both by the fact that they were all being faced by new issues on which there was little experience, and because they wanted to work together and learn from each other. It was also supported by the analytical effort of Sistema Económico Latinoamericano (SELA) which produced a number of technical studies on the topics under negotiation.[12] It was a standard of collaboration that may be difficult to match in the future except in particular sectors, such as agriculture.

In contrast, in the Seattle Ministerial, there was little convergence of views among LAC countries on the general scope of the negotiations. A number of delegations with relatively open economies such as those in the 'Friends of the Round' group were generally supportive of a new Round. Many of the smaller Caribbean and Central American countries were much less favourably disposed. These countries tended to emphasize implementation issues and special and differential measures to be taken up-front before negotiations took place. These included the small islands in the Caribbean as well as the Paradiso group. The latter, as noted, had made a special point of seeking greater flexibility in providing export subsidies. Interestingly enough, this group did not include Costa Rica, which had extensively used export subsidies in the past but grew disillusioned with them as a means of promoting exports because of the budget burden they created and because the benefits from them tended to accrue to a few producers/exporters.

Another reason why the Seattle Ministerial failed to reach agreement on launching a new Round was that the developed countries tried to overload the Agenda. Even the developing countries which were reasonably supportive of launching a new Round – many of whom were from LAC – were unwilling to take on all the various subjects being proposed for possible negotiation. This was partly because of capacity constraints and an inability to absorb a new set of rules on more new topics when the UR had not yet been digested; and partly because they felt that some of the new topics such as 'labour standards' and 'environment' were motivated by protectionism by developed countries.

On specific topics, LAC positions on agriculture have been and are going to be dominated by the views of LAC members of the Cairns Group. This happened in Seattle and is happening again in the ongoing negotiations in Geneva. LAC countries are likely to be strong opponents of export subsidies, multi-functionality, and the 'precautionary' principle as applied to sanitary and phytosanitary related measures.[13]

There are a few slightly dissenting voices emanating from a group that includes Cuba, the Dominican Republic, Honduras and El Salvador who have associated themselves with a number of Asian net-food-importing developing countries to develop a proposal that focuses primarily on improving developing country market access by targeting developed country tariff peaks and dirty tariffication, while keeping developing countries flexibility to impose controls that favour agriculture (WTO, 2000b).

On services, many developing countries in LAC have come to view an efficient service sector as essential to future integration in the world economy. As a consequence, they are likely to participate quite actively in the negotiations, with many of them asking for further developed country commitments on, for instance, liberalization of services provided by natural persons (mode four).

It is unclear what other topics will be included in a new Round, or even if there is one. Should there be a Round, industrial tariffs are likely to be among the topics – as it seemed to have been agreed at Seattle. In this area, LAC countries will be facing demands to liberalize further through reducing both ceiling and applied rates. It is unlikely that their reaction will be uniform, as different countries will try to preserve different degrees of flexibility regarding the maintenance of ceiling bindings. Conversely, LAC countries may not be as forceful as other developing countries in demanding a reduction of tariff peaks in textiles, especially in the US, where they are likely to continue to enjoy preferences – which would be reduced to the extent the tariff peaks in the sector are reduced on the basis of formula cuts.

With respect to other topics, such as investment, competition, environment, labour standards or TRIPS, there was no unanimity before or at Seattle and it is difficult to see more consensus emerging soon. For many of these topics, developing countries in other parts of the world tend to be stronger opponents for their inclusion in the agenda of future negotiations than LAC countries. In this fashion, LAC countries, especially the larger trading nations, may find themselves in the position of mediators in efforts to forge a consensus – a role which they played well in the Uruguay Round and which they may be called upon to play again in a new Round.

One of the new elements in the international scene since the UR whose impact is difficult to gauge at this time, is the emerging regional integration commitments of the LAC countries. There have always been regional integration efforts in LAC. But the deeper and wider integration which is becoming a reality in NAFTA and Mercosur did not exist during the UR. Also, the pledge to unite Mercosur with the Andean Group in an FTA starting with January 2002 as outlined in the 'Brasilia Communiqué' in addition to the commitment to a potential Free Trade Area of the Americas (FTAA) in 2005, is bound to have an impact on regional attitudes as well as the degree of coordination in the context of the WTO.

Past regional integration efforts have not necessarily impeded multilateral trade negotiations; and there are arguments that such efforts in certain conditions may contribute to multilateral trade liberalization. Clearly the formation of an LAC group of twelve countries is likely to have a bearing in the bargaining position that these countries have in a new Round. At the same time it raises questions about the implications of this grouping for the smaller countries in the Caribbean, both in terms of its direct economic impact and in terms of its implication for their participation in the WTO where the smaller countries already feel marginalized in the decision-making.

How the FTAA plays out in this context is also unclear. Will it happen? is the first question. And what it will involve is also uncertain. But if it does happen, it may move the LAC countries closer to the US and Canada on a number of issues. More generally, will the regional agenda occupy the attention of policy-makers so much that the WTO negotiations will be given a much lower priority? It would be a mistake if that happens.

Because then the multilateral trading system would run the danger of splintering into major blocs which may detract rather than contribute to worldwide economic integration.

CONCLUSIONS AND RECOMMENDATIONS

LAC participation in WTO formal and informal decision-making processes is substantial, although countries frequently do not speak with one voice, as their interests, depending on the issue, may diverge and result in the forming of different coalitions. While there is a regional caucus, it is used primarily to exchange views rather than to forge consensus.

The analysis suggests the emergence of a duality in the participation of LAC countries in the WTO. On the one hand, there are many countries which have increased significantly their capacity to participate in WTO activities in the aftermath of the Uruguay Round and whose representatives are playing an active role in the decisions of the organization. On the other hand, there is a large group of primarily smaller and lower-income countries, which account for perhaps half the LAC/WTO country membership, for which effective representation and participation in the Organization's activities is still a serious problem. Many are not represented in Geneva and hence cannot effectively participate in the consultations leading to the development of consensus on which the WTO is based. Their staffing has not increased significantly, while the complexity of the issues and the number of meetings and obligations in the WTO has multiplied tremendously.

For many of the smaller LAC countries and especially some of the smaller island economies, institutional weaknesses are the major constraints both in meeting their obligations under the WTO and in effective participation in the Organization and representation of their interests. But it must be recognized that institutional development is a complex process that takes a great deal of time. As a consequence, the solution to the problems of representation of these countries in the WTO is not going to be easy and is not often amenable to quick, stroke-of-the-pen changes in policies or rules. This being said, there are a number of things that can be done, some of which should start now, although their payoff may be long-term.

First, the matter of effective participation through Geneva Missions of the appropriate size is a complex issue for which there are no general solutions. For some countries with very small international representation in general, it may not be an optimal use of scarce human and material resources to set up such Missions. In such cases, the main objective should be twofold: (a) to ensure that they have adequate information flow on the issues handled by the WTO and how they affect their interests; and (b) to

identify like-minded countries or groups which do have effective representation, develop a process of consultation with them and thereby obtain
some assurance that their interests are reflected on an ongoing basis. Some
of the alternatives that countries need to explore in this connection are,
first, whether they can pool their resources and representation in Geneva in
the context of regional groupings to which they belong; and second, to
determine whether they can transfer one or more staff to already established Missions in Geneva of like-minded countries.

For all countries, measures to increase effective representation in
Geneva should be taken *pari passu* with measures to strengthen their institutional capacity at home, as part of a broader decision to become more
effectively integrated in the international trading system. Adequate information flow to the appropriate ministries or other decision-making bodies
in capitals is essential and should be addressed at the earliest. At the same
time, developing countries need to initiate efforts as well to strengthen the
policy-making and implementation capacity of these institutions as well as
to seek assistance for this purpose from international donors and the WTO
itself. Greater use should also be made of the services offered by AITIC
and the Advisory Centre on WTO Law on the use of the DSM mechanism
and overall assistance to WTO missions.

Institution building in the 'New Areas' is costly, time-consuming and
possibly not even the highest priority for many smaller countries. For
many of these countries, it is important to join with other developing
countries in seeking extension of some of the transition periods for implementation of certain WTO obligations which have already expired (for
example on TRIPS). It is also important to start thinking about how to
meet some of these obligations on a cooperative basis at the sub-regional
level. For example, the Andean Community has done this in the context of
implementing TRIPS. The example can be replicated by other groups in
other sectors. There is absolutely no reason that every Caribbean country
has to have a separate TRIPS regime or a separate institution dealing with
WTO's sanitary and phytosanitary provisions.

In terms of forging a LAC view, it is natural that the bigger countries
play a leadership role. Several LAC countries already play such a role
among developing countries in the WTO. And as their position is frequently in between those of developed countries and several of the developing countries, they can play an important role in bridging differences
among various groups, such as on the scope and content of a new Round
of multilateral trade negotiations.

The influence of the major LAC countries is exercised, in most
instances, individually. This is because of the divergence of interests

among them. To the extent that integration efforts within the region deepen, this will help forge greater consensus of views in dealing with the rest of world, including in the WTO. But as this happens, countries in the region must not forget one of the key lessons of the 1990s, namely that they need to pursue an 'open' regional integration. The place in which to pursue such open integration is in the multilateral WTO context which should be used as a vehicle for worldwide trade liberalization. In doing so, they must also keep in mind the interests of the many smaller countries in LAC, which have weaker capacities to participate in the WTO and more generally in international trade.

Notes

1.   The participation of the developing countries in the Uruguay Round has been discussed extensively elsewhere (see especially Croome, 1995; Martin and Winters, 1996; and UNCTAD and WTO, 1996), and is not going to be addressed in this chapter.
2.   The Bahamas is one of these exceptions. Membership in the WTO is defined according to the existence of a separate 'customs' territory. Thus both Hong Kong, China and Macau, China are separate members, though they are not 'countries'. This chapter ignores the distinction and uses the term 'country' irrespective of the sovereign status of the member involved.
3.   This became abundantly clear when St. Lucia blocked consensus in a General Council discussion related to the banana dispute (see below).
4.   One such group active in the late 1990s was called the 'Beau-Rivage Group', which included the Geneva-based representatives of a number of smaller countries both developed and developing, that shared an active participation in WTO affairs and a commitment to the multilateral trading system. It was similar in composition and orientation with the 'De la Paix Group' active during the Uruguay Round. The composition of these groups sometimes is supposed to be secret and is frequently unstable, changing when a particular Ambassador leaves Geneva.
5.   Many developing countries continue to look to UNCTAD as an institution in which such analyses and positions can be developed. UNCTAD has also provided a forum for discussion of broader aspects of a trade policy agenda for developing countries (see e.g. UNCTAD, 1997).
6.   The basic information used for the analysis of representation as well as leadership positions is based on GATT/WTO Directories issued in 1982, 1987, 1997 and 2000. A detailed discussion of the limitations of these can be found in Michalopoulos (1998). The annex to that study contains a detailed listing of the location and size of each WTO Mission as of mid-1997.
7.   See Chaytor and Hindley (1997).
8.   This is consistent with the estimate for a minimum size Mission presented in Blackhurst (1997).

9.   Martin and Winters (1996).
10.   The banana issue brought by several Latin American countries and the US
      against the EU is an example of such a case and is discussed below.
11.   WTO (2000a).
12.   Duran (2000).
13.   Otteman (1999).

Bibliography

BLACKHURST, RICHARD (1997) 'The Capacity of the WTO to Fulfill Its
    Mandate', in A.O Krueger (ed.), *The WTO as an International Organization*
    (University of Chicago Press).
CHAYTOR, BEATRICE and MICHAEL, HINDLEY (1997) *A Case Study of
    Sierra Leone's Participation in the World Trade Organization* (Cameron).
CROOME, JOHN (1995) *Reshaping the World Trade System* (Geneva: WTO).
DURAN, ESPERANZA (2000) 'The Participation of LAC Countries in the
    Multilateral Trading System', Agency for International Trade Information and
    Co-operation (AITIC), Geneva.
EVANS, JOHN (1968) 'The General Agreement on Tariffs and Trade',
    International Organization, vol. XXII, no. 1.
GATT, *Directory*, 1982, 1987.
MARTIN, WILL and L. ALAN, WINTERS (1996) *The Uruguay Round and the
    Developing Countries* (Washington DC: World Bank).
MICHALOPOULOS, CONSTANTINE (1998) 'Developing Countries'
    Participation in the WTO', World Bank, Policy Research Discussion Paper, No.
    1906, March, Washington DC.
MICHALOPOULOS, CONSTANTINE (1999) 'The Developing Countries in the
    WTO', *The World Economy*, vol. 22, no. 1, January.
MICHALOPOULOS, CONSTANTINE (2000) 'The Role of Special and
    Differential Treatment for Developing Countries in GATT and the WTO', World
    Bank, Policy Research Working Paper no. 2388, July, Washington DC.
OTTEMAN, SCOTT (1999) 'The United States and Latin America and the
    Caribbean: Co-Operation or Conflict in the New WTO Round?', *Trade and
    Investment in the Americas*, September.
OYEJIDE, ADEMOLA T. (1990) 'Africa and the Uruguay Round', *The World
    Economy*, vol. 13, no. 3, September.
UNCTAD (1997) *The Uruguay Round and Its Follow-up: Building a Positive
    Development Agenda* (Geneva: United Nations).
UNCTAD and WTO (1996) 'Strengthening the Participation of Developing
    Countries in World Trade and the Multilateral Trading System', UNCTAD,
    TD/375.
WTO, *Directory*, 1997, 2000.
WTO (2000a) 'Disputes Status Report', 22 July, Geneva.
WTO (2000b) Committee on Agriculture, G/AG/NG/W/37, September.

3 Different Paths towards Integration

Roberto Lavagna

INTRODUCTION

Few areas of economic theory are viewed more favourably than those relating to international trade and its central role in efficient resource allocation. Nevertheless, the traditional paradoxes that exist between the concrete forms of specialization found in the real world and those that should emerge in theory have not yet been sufficiently clarified. Beyond the purely theoretical, countries and policy-makers are constantly faced with the need to define policies within a framework in which tariff and non-tariff barriers as well as subsidies determine specialization patterns that are very often far removed from the factors of production available.

In this intrinsically dynamic world, opening an economy (particularly a developing economy) offers the alternative of pursuing different *paths* that have different implications in terms of production and employment structures, and this is obviously also the case for the integration of the economy into the international market.

In the following section, two basic hypotheses are assumed in the analysis of these paths from the perspective of developing countries:

1. Market opening leads to positive changes in resource allocation;
2. There is a clear-cut correlation between trade and development, whereby *sequences* and *time frames* play a central role in the results obtained.

THE COMMERCIAL VERSUS THE PRODUCTION APPROACH

Economic 'opening' tends to be regarded as involving measures that modify trade flows to a greater or lesser extent. The commercial bias is so strong that it is very often easy to lose sight of the key fact that market opening leads to changes in relative prices in the economy. In turn, these changes produce modifications in decisions governing production and

47

investment. At the end, all of the above define and condition a country's production and occupational structure.

Few economic instruments have a more decisive effect than tariffs and non-tariff mechanisms. Modifying these mechanisms automatically alters trade flows but this is only the most obvious and superficial effect. The underlying effects include all material modifications that constitute and determine a country's 'production model' and that stem from changes in relative prices.

In view of the interdependence of trade and production, two potential relationships exist in terms of dominant causality and, thus, the following economic policy approaches are possible:

- Open the market and allow this process to trigger the ensuing changes in the production structure. This structure is thus the result of commercial factors and of the impact exerted by these factors on prices;
- Establish objectives in terms of production and occupational structure, and design a compatible trade policy based on these objectives. The causal relationship is the exact opposite of the previous approach and, in this case, the (dependent variable) is trade.

For many years, under the import substitution model, the explicit or implicit objective consisted in achieving the maximum degree of expansion (both widening and deepening) of the 'production structure'. Of the instruments employed, the key instrument was the level of trade protection and this level varied between the infinite and the very high. Despite the benefits obtained from the import substitution strategy (IS), particularly in the 1960s and 1970s, it is clear that this strategy should not have been understood as anything more than a single phase in the overall development process. When import substitution became a pure and permanent strategy, it entered a phase of diminishing returns, and this occurred towards the end of the 1960s or in the early 1970s at the latest. Growth strategy must now be defined in a more open commercial context, and this is precisely what has led to the current situation in which economic policy-makers and governments are faced with the need to 'open' their economies.

What is the Main Objective of Economic Integration?

The basic objective is to create conditions that enable the more efficient use of production factors, for example increasing average economic productivity, while rendering the effects of the accompanying structural changes socially and politically acceptable. When this is done in closed economies, two conditions are required to achieve the desired effect:

- The domestic production structure must be exposed to stiffer competition, so as to induce higher productivity and remove purely vested interests;
- The preferential market[1] must be expanded in order to achieve scales of production that are more in line with optimal international standards.

In the light of these objectives and requirements involved, the above alternatives may be evaluated with a view to drawing conclusions on economic policy and international strategy.

HOW AND WHEN

The new international framework thus makes it necessary to ask new questions, such as how and to what extent to proceed with market opening. It is worth undertaking a synthetic review of possible responses, particularly from the perspective of developing countries.

1. Comprehensive Unilateral Opening

This response addresses the idea that, regardless of other countries' trade policies, a country that opens its economy will be in a position to specialize in products in which it enjoys comparative advantages in relative terms, while purchasing all other (probably higher-quality) goods abroad at lower prices. In practice, this type of policy has been implemented rapidly in a single operation, or via a programme of scaled and predetermined reductions over short periods. This strategy was first implemented in Chile, at least in the industrial sector,[2] with a low uniform tariff of 9 per cent (value added is not differentiated), and there are plans to further reduce tariffs to a level of 6 per cent. Argentine initiated this policy in the period 1976–82.

It must be noted that, in both countries, this strategy was pursued by highly authoritarian military governments acting outside the framework of policies based on broad consensus. The difference is that in Chile it was possible to achieve a controlled political transition accompanied by growth. Without making value judgments on these events, the economic effect of a decision of this type is to concentrate specialization on relatively few economic sectors (generally primary sector activities such as agriculture or mining), and perhaps on certain industries engaged in processing raw materials produced by these sectors.

2. Negotiated Reciprocal Opening

This alternative generally predominates nowadays and features four main models based on the following integration 'types':

(a)   Integration with smaller or similar sized countries with smaller or similar average productivity;
(b)   Integration with countries featuring very high average productivity approaching international productivity thresholds;
(c)   Integration of similar medium-sized countries with medium productivity levels and 'dense' production structures as a result of sectoral linkages;
(d)   Integration with countries with medium-productivity levels (developing economies) that exceed domestic productivity levels.

Alternative 'a' relating to market opening agreements negotiated with similar-sized countries with low average productivity levels tends to retain an import substitution model. However, the number of countries party to the agreement now increases the scale of this model. Unless the potential scales of production are substantially broadened immediately (for example not over long implementation periods), and unless the regional business community is very active, the effect of this strategy may be very limited or have a very slow impact on a rapidly changing world.

This case scenario involves negotiations between relatively small developing countries with production structures that are not particularly 'dense' in terms of their forward and backward linkages, and average productivity that is far below international levels and relatively uniform among all countries involved in the negotiation process. In Latin America, the Andean Community structure tends to fall roughly under this category, in which market opening resulting from the negotiation process does not produce the effects indicated above.

Alternative 'b' relating to market opening agreements negotiated with much more highly developed countries places the domestic economy in competition with large countries boasting high productivity. The results are largely similar to the effect of opening the economy unilaterally, and the ensuing specialization will be concentrated in only a few (mainly primary sector) activities. Moreover, this specialization will be of the type that stems from static comparative advantages.

This case scenario deals with negotiations conducted between developed and developing countries, with the exception of the case in which the developed country grants the developing country decidedly preferential treatment for non-economic reasons, such as geopolitical considerations, security, and so forth, like the United States and Mexico. In this case, there is a possible alternative consequence, in that the agreement may have the economic effect of rapidly integrating only the border areas of the developing country into the larger economy and thus exacerbating regional differences within the developing country (Mexico once again serves as a suitable example and this effect had already occurred before it joined the North American Free Trade Area (NAFTA), and was reinforced after the signing of the agreement).

Alternative 'c' involving negotiations between relatively large countries at an intermediate stage of development is the best way of ensuring that the above-mentioned conditions are met. These consist in a large-scale regional market, a substantial critical mass in terms of entrepreneurs, and 'dense' production structures that make it possible to develop intra-industrial specialization. An agreement of this nature guarantees that the domestic effect on competition will be considerable, due to the significant increase in the number of suppliers.

The importance of intra-industrial as opposed to inter-sectoral specialization may be argued in many ways but the most obvious and conclusive argument is that, in the last 50 years, growth in international trade has been specifically based on intra-industrial specialization. The Argentina–Brazil–Mercosur format featuring 'regulated' market opening that is nevertheless relevant due to its structural effects may be cited as an example of this alternative.

Alternative 'd' involves negotiations between unequally sized developing countries, and the effect should be similar to the previous case; beneficial in terms of increased productivity. Although this alternative obliges the less developed country (countries) to implement structural adjustment in their search for a more efficient use of production resources, these adjustments will be much less pronounced than would be the case if negotiations were conducted with highly developed countries. In other words, there will be a considerable increase in the 'number' of sectors in which the less developed county (countries) may compete, and the sector 'type' (according to the level of value-added incorporated) will also be denser in terms of linkages.

The Mercosur–Andean Community negotiations are an example of this category. In terms of structural adjustment, this process is demanding for all involved. The relative size and productivity of Argentina and Brazil imply major changes in the smaller economies (Andean Community).

However, the resulting structural adjustment is potentially more conducive to the development of dynamic comparative advantages and thus to the establishment of a broader degree of specialization and a wider definition of production structures than would be the case if negotiations were conducted with much more highly developed countries.

STRUCTURAL CONSEQUENCES

As indicated in Figure 3.1 there is a clear relation between the 'number' and 'types' of sectors requiring specialization and the characteristics of trade negotiations. The upward curve shows that the more closed an economy is, the higher the number of sectors displaying national production will be.

However, this involves a 'cost' in terms of efficiency (as observed in Figure 3.2), in that the more closed the economy is, the lower the degree of efficiency in the use of production resources within that economy. At one extreme, we find closed economies or agreements involving small countries. These feature a high 'cost' in terms of economic efficiency and, consequently, in terms of economic well-being. At the other extreme, unilateral market opening or agreements with large countries guarantee higher efficiency.

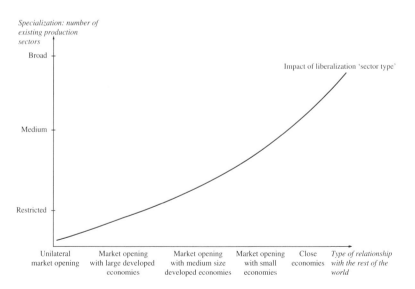

Figure 3.1   Relation: production structure/market opening

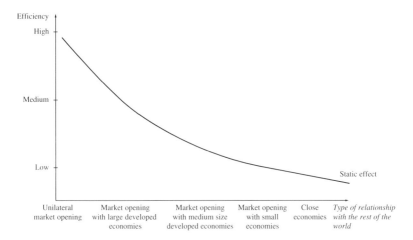

Figure 3.2 Relation: economic efficiency/market opening: static effect

Nonetheless, this involves major structural adjustment and restricts specialization, as a result of a static interpretation of comparative advantages. It is only possible to combine interesting levels of specialization and efficiency in medium-sized regional groupings that, in addition to displaying intermediate levels of development, also boast broad-scale markets and a production capacity that exceeds certain minimum production thresholds.

The concept of interesting levels of specialization and efficiency requires further consideration. If the immediate (static) effect is that indicated in Figure 3.2, the question remains as to the nature of the foreseeable dynamic impact, as indicated in Figures 3.3 and 3.4. The dynamic effects in the production structure as indicated in Figure 3.3 shows higher levels of specialization following trade liberalization allowing for broader market scale and in the medium to longer run for increases in productivity.

In Figure 3.4 there is a displacement to the right (upward) of the systemic efficiency curve in sections 1 and 2, and a downward displacement in section 3. There is an *increase* in efficiency in the first two sections, section 2 displaying a higher increase than section 1. The potential for increased efficiency is greater given the higher density of forward and backward production linkages generated by regional integration. At the same time, this development occurs in conditions that are equal or at least tend to close the gap with current conditions at international levels.

The incentive in terms of attracting foreign investment is high given the size of the local market. The fact that a certain degree of protection remains and discriminates (albeit only moderately) against imported goods

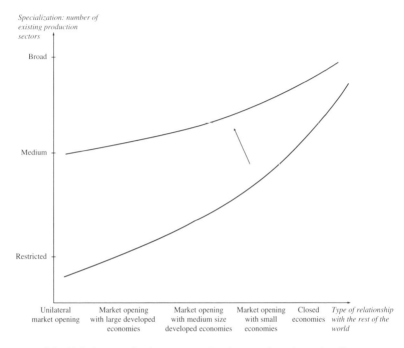

Figure 3.3　Relation: production structure/market opening: dynamic effect

guarantees this effect. In turn, the possibility of exporting goods to the global market based on the combination of natural resources and intermediate-level human resources at below international market cost presents an additional advantage.

Although section 1 reflects an increase in efficiency, the dynamic impact is lower, and there is less intersectoral 'spillover'. This is due to the fact that we are dealing with the integration of developed economies with more 'open' trade structures and high scales of production that existed even before the signing of the integration agreement. This is further emphasized by the high level of technological availability and the (more competitive) internal market structure displayed by these economies.

In contrast, by maintaining a high level of protection on a domestic (or more broadly) on a regional scale that is nevertheless small compared to international levels, section 3 produces what may be termed a 'growth trap'. Even if integration on a limited regional scale were to have a positive impact on production structures, the effect would be minor and take a long time to materialize. This implies relative retrogression vis-à-vis other processes employed in the search for efficiency worldwide, and this relative retrogression tends to divert investment to other geographical regions.

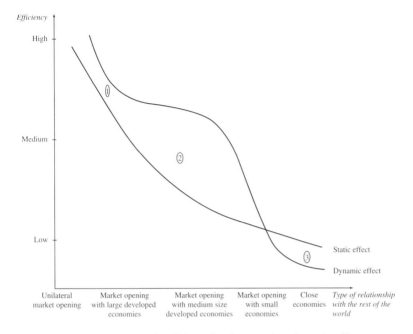

Figure 3.4   Relation: economic efficiency/market opening: dynamic effect

The latter regional agreements fall short of constituting an attractive format for investment. In this case, investment only tends to be maintained when vested interests play a role in decision-making (like in subsidized privatization of public utilities aimed at the domestic market).

OVERLAPPING ALTERNATIVES

The decisions that countries will be required to take have been complicated as a result of the number of integration alternatives available. Many of these alternatives involve simultaneous negotiations, and some clearly overlap, while others do so indirectly. While nothing is more certain than Baghwati's description of regional treaties as a *spaghetti bowl*, his criticism should not be applied to this approach to free trade.

When working with preferences or discrimination, such as those outside the framework of the Most-Favoured-Nation-clause, all new agreements tend to 'dilute' or even 'nullify' previous agreements. If negotiators lapse into casuistic talks that end up with the simple (albeit bureaucratically complex) process of 'exchanging concessions and lists', they will have adopted the static criterion of allowing their decisions to be governed by the conditions imposed by prevailing trade patterns and the current pro-duction structure. The analysis of how to develop dynamic comparative and competitive advantages ceases to be relevant to the point that, in some cases, the decision is taken to abandon or disregard certain negotiations.

If the static approach and the influence of pre-established trade flows had been adopted as the predominant criteria, the low level of trade existing between Argentina and Brazil prior to the decision to integrate in 1986 would not have produced any form of preferential trade agreement. It was precisely the decision to adopt the inverse causal relation in which strategic and dynamic *production development* components predominate over *trade* that led to the agreement. The results are plain to see: strong growth in investment and trade in new product groups and a clear commercial interdependence between both member countries to the point that Argentina is Brazil's second largest market and the leading consumer of Brazilian industrial goods, while Brazil is Argentina's main market for all product groups. Obviously, the above does not consider other benefits of a political nature, those linked to international politics (like the mutual recognition of nuclear programmes), the joint attraction of foreign investment (like the automotive sector), and all other external economies stemming from integration. The underlying idea is that this type of regional or sub-regional integration maximizes economic well-being when the criterion of considering trade as the resultant rather than the explanatory variable is adopted, for example when strategic criteria are adopted. When applied to multiple negotiations, these criteria result in a logical 'sequence' that maximizes the strategic-dynamic approach and 'time frames' that make it possible to achieve optimal results.

The real issue consists in confronting the 'spaghetti bowl' phenomenon without rejecting the multiple negotiation formats, while ensuring that the implementation stages are adapted to the time frames required for the basic project. Thus, the first issue in the sequence of priorities and time frames consists in 'deepening' the Mercosur regional market and, if the political will to do so is forthcoming, possibly by creating a South American Free Trade Area (SAFTA) (with the Andean Community), and subsequently pursuing possibilities of the type envisaged in the FTAA or the European Union–Mercosur negotiations.

Any process involving structural change awakens doubts and sparks resistance. However, perhaps it is worth remembering the question that was asked to Argentina in 1986: If Argentina does not feel capable of competing with Brazil, with whom else could it compete? If these negotiations had not taken place, Argentina would have been condemned to remain a closed economy or, at the other extreme, to become an open economy driven by the international environment and characterized by specialization based on static comparative advantages. The same question must have been asked in Brazil at the time, the only difference being in terms of 'degree'. To judge by events over the last fifteen years, both countries came up with the same answer. The same question can be asked concerning other regional integration projects involving developing countries.

THE ARGENTINA–BRAZIL–MERCOSUR EXPERIENCE

The alternatives facing Mercosur member countries may be seen in the context of the issues discussed above. The Mercosur model can easily be qualified as the integration of medium-sized developing economies. The presence of Brazil and Argentina, which alone account for 90 per cent of Mercosur gross domestic product (GDP) (Uruguay and Paraguay contribute the remaining 10 per cent), lends this regional agreement considerable stature within the developing world. Moreover, Mercosur is relevant at a global level, in that it constitutes the ninth largest global economy, although its share in the overall global economy is limited.

When the two 'founding' members (Argentina and Brazil) signed their trade agreement in 1986 and the agreement launching a ten-year Common Market in 1987, this was done within the framework of clear strategic policy. 1986 was not exactly a year in which regional initiatives were well received. We need only remember that the GATT Round of Multilateral Trade Negotiations was launched in Punta del Este (Uruguay) in that year, and that, within the region itself, multilateral negotiations were conducted by the 11 members of LAIA (Latin American Integration Association). Furthermore, the NAFTA agreements did not yet exist, and the bilateral agreement between the United States and Canada had not even been negotiated.

In other words, it could be said that the project was launched against the prevailing wisdom. The political and academic justification of regional agreements as building blocks rather than stumbling blocks in the global trade liberalization process only emerged later as a result of the regional agreements promoted by the United States. This would prove the fact that the initiative undertaken in the Southern Cone, which superficially appeared to run against the current, was actually a precursor of events that would soon follow.

Argentine and Brazilian strategic policy consisted precisely in searching for a way of opening two closed economies, and this process involved injecting competition by increasing the number of suppliers, boosting efficiency and augmenting market scale, creating complementarity and critical mass in technology, and so forth. However, at the same time, it was necessary to avoid unleashing violent structural adjustment processes that, in addition, would not have been viable in the context of two 'young' democracies recently established after long years of military regimes (1983 in Argentina and 1985 in Brazil).

The guarantee that no violent structural adjustments would be unleashed was based on two established facts:

1. 'relative' productivity between both countries was not substantially different; and
2. trade liberalization conformed to a methodology that combined the generalized lowering of tariffs with sectoral agreements on industrial reconversion (automotive, iron and steel, capital goods, and so forth) and joint industrial development in relatively new sectors like aeronautics industry, biotechnology, communications, among others.

In the first case, these agreements were directed at regulating the effects of structural adjustment induced by the liberalization process (at least in terms of time frames), while in the second case, they were aimed at searching for new types of development without duplicating investments, promoting complementation via intrasectoral specialization and combining the critical mass of human resources required. The objective was not to settle for a market-opening format that repeated the import substitution model on a broader scale, but rather to actively search for market opening on a generalized basis.

Consequently, a process of comprehensive market opening via the removal of non-tariff barriers vis-à-vis the rest of the world has been in place (primarily) in Argentina since 1986 and in Brazil since 1991. This involved the progressive elimination of the sworn declarations on import needs employed in Argentina, and a similar process was applied, with a certain lag, to the even more complex and obscure non-tariff instruments that existed in Brazil.

The importance of establishing and at the same time regulating market opening does not only stem from the political fact that Argentina and Brazil are 'young democracies' but also from common and individual circumstances affecting both countries. The common denominator was that, at the time, both countries were facing the 'external debt crisis', as well as an extremely low availability of foreign investment for emerging economies, a state of affairs that predominated until the early 1990s. The situation peculiar to each country was connected to the past events that had occurred in both countries.

During the military regime, Argentina implemented a vigorous policy of 'unilateral market opening' that was characterized not only by a substantial trade deficit-financing requirement but also by a marked fragmentation of the Argentine industrial structure. Many production links were lost during this process, creating negative external economies. In the case of Brazil (possibly due to its relatively better performance during the 1970s and its larger market scale), there was still a higher level of confidence in the possibility of maintaining a semi-closed economy. It was not until the early 1990s that a conceptual shift and the ability to impose these ideas on specific vested interests became evident in Brazil.

CURRENT CHALLENGES

In addition to the basic need for deepening, Mercosur currently faces the dilemma of the *sequences* and *time frames* governing the following alternatives:

1. Free Trade Area of the Americas (FTAA) negotiations
2. Possible creation of a South American Free Trade Area (SAFTA)
3. Negotiation of an interregional association agreement with the European Union
4. Global WTO negotiations
5. Other bilateral negotiations of lesser magnitude and somewhat less specific as to their objectives (Mexico, South Africa, Australia/New Zealand)

The arguments presented in this chapter should serve to dispel any doubts that Mercosur should be the '*nucleus*' of all strategy for Argentina and Brazil. By way of digression, it may be useful to point out that in 1991 the new governments in Argentina and Brazil ratified the strategic agreements concluded in 1986. However, they adopted an integration methodology that merely concentrated on generalized and progressive trade liberalization, instead of combining across-the-board liberalization with sectoral agreements on reconversion and development. As a result of its powerful and concentrated lobby, the automotive agreement was the only sectoral agreement to remain in force, and it is precisely in this sector that success was achieved in attracting major investment, in implementing the technological modernization of processes and products, and in maintaining a notable balance within the group. All other agreements were substituted by a more automatic approach that led to growing internal conflicts once the phase of inverted economic cycles had run its course in Argentina and Brazil (1991–94 and 1994–98 respectively).

The ratification of these agreements was conducted within a methodological framework that stripped the integration process of policy instruments. The intra-zone zero tariff (with few exceptions) and the common external tariff (with many exceptions) are not sufficient to sustain a deep and balanced integration process between partners, and this is one of the challenges that Mercosur must meet at this time.

(1) The FTAA process must be regarded as a necessary condition for market opening, in as much as changing internal competitive conditions, broadening market scale, consolidating human resources for technological purposes, pooling government purchasing power, among others, create conditions for productivity and competitiveness that make it possible to achieve broader market opening with fewer structural imbalances.

(2) The second link could (but need not necessarily) be the South American Free Trade Area, insofar as this would do no more than reinforce some of the arguments mentioned above with regard to scales of production and a higher level of internal competition. The impact could be particularly considerable especially for value-added sectors, in that by obtaining preferential conditions for access to a broader South American market, these sectors could acquire a higher degree of economic viability. It must not be ignored that several other Latin American countries have a significant level of trade with the United States and even with Central America and Mexico, as well as protectionist agricultural policies (Chile), and this could lead to a lengthy negotiation process. These negotiations could be so slow that other negotiations must not be subordinated to progress in this area, as the cost/benefit ratio tends to rise over time if a higher degree of global integration is not achieved.

If we regard the previous option as an appendage of intra-Mercosur affairs, the second option is clearly that of pursuing multilateral negotiations within the World Trade Organization. In principle, as importers of high-value-added goods, Mercosur member countries gain no advantage from granting preferential access to any one major developed country producing these goods, be it the United States, the European Union or Japan. Any option of this type would result in possibly having to buy from a less than optimal source. Nevertheless, this assessment may change under certain conditions and consideration should be given to the following scenarios:

(3) Cases in which interregional negotiations grant Mercosur exports significantly higher access to the other market: Here, the advantages would clearly favour the European Union, since this market imposes the highest number of restrictions on Mercosur agricultural and agro-industrial products. In this connection, it should be noted that the United States is a natural competitor in agricultural production, and thus any opening of this market would have a much lesser impact than opening the agricultural and agro-industrial market of an inefficient producer such as the European Union.

However, the theoretical advantage the EU would gain by signing an association agreement with Mercosur and assuring itself of an import market
for high-value-added goods (no less than US$ 35 billion per annum) in
exchange for market access, would seem to be a complex issue at the
moment in terms of implementation. The political and social inflexibility
displayed by the EU when it comes to opening its agricultural markets
hampers its ability to obtain preferential treatment in the industrial and services sectors in exchange for increased market access for food commodities. This applies even more to Japan, where protection of the domestic
agricultural industry far surpasses European Union levels.

(4) Cases in which WTO negotiations are totally blocked or seriously
delayed: The agricultural question is not the only issue but it does constitute a major hurdle. Under these circumstances, regional agreements may
provide a means of achieving at least a few advantages in terms of market
access. In this scenario, the United States and ultimately the FTAA (Free
Trade Area of the Americas) project are likely to provide some form of
concrete advantage vis-à-vis the other alternatives. As was the case during
the Uruguay Round, the US would once more use the regional alternative
in combination with specific comprehensive agreements for some sectors.

(5) Cases in which the impact on trade is merely secondary to the political
or financial effects expected from broad interregional agreements: The political impact is reflected in what has come to be referred to as the 'anchoring'
of Latin American economies in the American democratic model and its
capacity to discipline any attempt to stray from these forms of political organization. The financial impact stems from the capacity to obtain direct
financing or the ability to influence the major international credit organizations (IMF, World Bank, IBRD, Inter-American Development Bank) to meet
the emergency needs of member countries. In this case, the FTAA project
again holds advantages given the recent rescue packages for Mexico, Brazil
and (more recently) Argentina, while there was clear evidence of European
reluctance to participate and Japan was very conspicuous by its absence.

(6) Cases in which the availability of foreign direct investment flows
and/or technology transfer via joint ventures and local supplier networks
to major foreign investors play a key role: In this respect, both the United
States and the European Union (but not Japan) would be on equal footing
in terms of their ability to implement an integration project. In view of the
criteria governing investment decisions and the pattern of foreign direct
investment flows in recent years, the EU might even have a certain advantage. We need only remember the strong European involvement in Latin
American privatizations in general and privatizations in Mercosur member
countries in particular.

However, at some point in the future, European investors may find themselves less able and less willing to invest if they simply concentrate on serving internal markets characterized by unsatisfied demand and contractually guaranteed high profit rates. This is precisely the case in markets that have undergone privatization, as a large number of privatization projects have already been almost completed. If European investors do not modify their investment decisions, they may find themselves powerless against investors with a greater capacity to take business risks.

The scenarios described above remain valid even in the absence of problems in the global WTO negotiations. If WTO negotiations were to advance and prove to be successful, there is still room for WTO-plus agreements with both Europe and the United States, and Mercosur should adopt an '*a priori* stance' of remaining receptive to obtaining a higher level of 'quid pro quo' without making prior judgments.

SUMMARY AND CONCLUSIONS

These comments attempt to draw attention to some unassailable facts in dealing with different paths towards economic integration. First, the impact in terms of higher productivity and, by extension, in well-being is more pronounced in the case of economic integration involving medium-sized developing economies that are relatively large within the context of non-developed countries as a whole, than is the case for regional agreements among small developing countries or among developed countries.

Second, 'open' regional agreements are compatible with the globalization process and WTO negotiations, and may in fact be regarded as an alternative instrument in the same liberalization process. Even in the light of successful multilateral negotiations, regional agreements are justified, in that they make it possible to regulate market opening by introducing free trade, while at the same time lowering the social and political cost of structural adjustment. In view of the fact that all forms of open regionalism are ultimately aimed at achieving global liberalization, the main focus switches to determining the sequence of the various market opening projects involved and the time frames followed in the implementation of the different phases of these integration projects. Based on these criteria, Mercosur must become the *nucleus* of market opening in South America, while simultaneously accepting multilateral negotiations and possible interregional agreements.

Third, the two most important interregional agreements currently being negotiated by Mercosur (FTAA and European Union) have alternative prospects, depending on which of the following elements predominate in these negotiations:

- Advantages in terms of access for industrial and agro-industrial products;
- Whether progress is or is not forthcoming in multilateral negotiations;
- Whether political or financial considerations take precedence over economic and trade considerations;
- Whether foreign direct investment flows play the dominant role.

Consequently, there is no single *path* but rather a set of alternatives which policy-makers must prioritize in line with their objectives and with the criteria required to achieve these objectives. The only path to be avoided is that of engaging in simultaneous negotiations without setting priorities beforehand, as this could result in the most inefficient response. This equally applies to achieving global liberalization objectives and national objectives aimed at developing dynamic advantages within a framework of structural adjustment that is capable of producing social and political consensus.

Notes

1. Chile is notably protectionist concerning traditional agriculture.
2. It should be borne in mind that, by definition, all regional and subregional agreements fall outside the Most-Favoured-Nation Clause, and are therefore 'discriminatory' in that they grant 'preferential treatment'.

4 Exceptional Protection the Way Ahead: A Developing Country Perspective

Sarath Rajapatirana

INTRODUCTION

Although the Uruguay Round agreement has been signed and most of its provisions are now being implemented, there is not only a remaining agenda which the Round either did not address at all or addressed inadequately, but also a new agenda that has emerged in response to development in world trade since 1994. The issue of exceptional protection straddles both aspects of an area which was not dealt with satisfactorily during the Uruguay Round and in which loopholes have consequently been left open that permit protection levels to be maintained or even increased in some sectors in the aftermath of the Round.

As commonly understood and agreed upon by trade 'aficionados', the term 'exceptional protection' refers to antidumping duties, safeguards and countervailing duties. Developing countries have followed the example of traditional users of exceptional protection such as Australia, Canada and the United States by increasingly resorting to antidumping duties in particular and, to a lesser extent, countervailing duties and safeguard measures. By the same token, developing countries as a group have been on the receiving end of new exceptional protection measures which the developed countries are employing, now that they have reduced their tariffs and eliminated subsidies (except for the few that are permitted under the Uruguay Round agreements).

Exceptional protection figures very prominently on the reform agenda at the multilateral level, the plurilateral level (since the use of exceptional protection measures is growing the fastest among regional trading partners), and at the level of individual developing countries as they strive to increase the efficiency of domestic resources and tap into new resources and technology in the rest of the world. In this chapter I will seek to address some of the issues that have arisen in this area as viewed, in particular, within the context of a new round of multilateral trade negotiations.

The chapter is structured as follows. The introduction contained in section 1 is followed, in section 2, by a general description of exceptional protection measures which explains what they are and how they tie in with one another and with other protection measures. The overview includes an extensive evaluation of antidumping duties, as they are the most commonly used and abused form of exceptional protection. Safeguards – a form of exceptional protection which offers the greatest hope for doing away with the abuses of such measures – and countervailing or 'antisubsidy' measures are then assessed as well. Section 3 concludes the chapter with a discussion of the way ahead.

This chapter identifies antidumping duties as the most egregious form of exceptional protection because they have a very low threshold for abuse and have, in fact, been protectionist forces' weapon of choice in the wake of the Uruguay Round. Limiting the use of antidumping duties by replacing them with safeguards is one strategy that can work for the time being. The long-run solution is to bring all exceptional protection under competition law.[1] Although this is not something that can be accomplished overnight. Competition policies could be considered in a new round of negotiations if some of the major players in international trade were to agree to this. Even if they were, developing countries are still far from arriving at that point. The reform of antidumping provisions is not a satisfactory solution because they can be so easily abused and turned into protectionist measures. Hence, from the point of view of developing countries, the most practical solution is to substitute safeguards for antidumping measures and to make the imposition of countervailing duties more transparent and to regulate it more stringently. Increasing recourse to the WTO Dispute Settlement Body is a new development that may discourage the use of exceptional protection in ways harmful to the international trading system and, more to the point, to the countries that impose such measures themselves.

GENERAL CONSIDERATIONS

Exceptional protection measures – antidumping duties, safeguards and countervailing duties – are exceptions in two important senses. From a multilateral trade perspective, exceptional protection constitutes a major departure from the most-favoured-nation principle in that it is applied with the aim of having differential impacts on trading partners.[2] Hence, it is a negotiated exception to the standard trade rules agreed upon in multilateral trade forums. It is also an exception to the general provisions of the trade regime, as the application of such measures depends on the given circumstances in each case. Accordingly, exceptional protection is also referred to as 'contingent protection'. In this chapter, the term 'exceptional protection' has been preferred, since the 'contingency' can be created by the party that has resource to exceptional protection.

One important reason for the existence of exceptional protection is that it provides a useful safety valve for letting off protectionist 'steam'. Without such a safety valve, producers seeking to redress an import surcharge might well lobby to change the trade regime on a permanent basis. Exceptional protection permits a departure from the existing trade regime precisely for the purpose of discouraging lobbies from seeking permanent protection in order to stifle competition from imports on a long-term basis. Therefore, a third feature of exceptional protection is that it is time-bound and, at least in theory, gives domestic activities affected by a surge in imports time to 'adjust' to the competition by restructuring, cost-cutting, changing their product mix, developing better advertising or finding other way to face up to the competition.

The use of exceptional protection has evolved in an interesting manner. During the initial stage, when countries still had significant trade barriers, the use of exceptional protection was somewhat limited. However, as the negotiations have progressed (the Kennedy, Tokyo and then Uruguay Rounds) and as traditional means of protection are reduced and domestic producers find themselves facing greater competition, there has been an increasing tendency to resort to antidumping measures, safeguards and countervailing duties. In the wake of the Tokyo Round, many of the leading trading nations began to use 'grey area measures' such as voluntary export restraints (VERs), orderly marketing arrangements (OMAs) and special quota arrangements such as the Multi-Fibre Arrangement (MFA). Under the Uruguay Round, grey-area measures such as VERs and OMAs were prohibited while the MFA was brought under GATT/WTO disciplines and is to be discontinued in 2005.

Developing countries themselves have begun to use exceptional protection measures on a wider scale following their participation in the Uruguay Round and the adoption of formal legislation that allows them to use such measures.[3] It is ironic that the developing countries began to use exceptional protection measures after signing on to international rules. In the past, under the Tokyo Round, countries could opt to sign on to some rather than all trade rule provisions, but under the Uruguay Round such exceptions were no longer allowed. As a result, all the developing countries that belong to the WTO are legally entitled to use exceptional protection.

One common use of exceptional protection has been within regional integration groups. This practice has emerged as the countries in such regional groups approach free trade status and is illustrated by the fact that the largest number of antidumping actions among developing countries has been between Argentina and Brazil (both members of Mercosur). Developing countries have been reluctant to apply exceptional protection measures to their major trading partners for fear of retaliation.

Antidumping

Dumping is said to occur when the export price of a good is below the exporter's home-market price or, if the home-market price cannot be determined, when the export price is below the export price in a third market or lower than the cost of production in the exporting country. It is this third type of test that has become the most common parameter for defining dumping. The difference between the price and cost must cause 'material injury' in order for an antidumping duty to be imposed. Thus, GATT/WTO rules allow the imposition of antidumping duties only when there is both dumping and injury. The definition of dumping used in GATT/WTO rules and by industrial countries does not make a great deal of economic sense, however. Injury is difficult to show since, in the sense of national welfare, there is no actual injury but rather a loss of expected profits by producers in the importing country, which may, in the meantime, have lost their comparative advantage in producing the good in question, if they ever had one. As protection is removed, the production structure may be responding to newly created incentives and becoming more efficient. Given the lax enforcement of this law, it is no wonder that antidumping duties have become protectionists' instrument of choice, as it serves as a ready-made tool for limiting foreign competition.

Other instruments such as safeguards, which either allow domestic industries to adjust to temporary surges in imports or give them time to make a permanent shift, are rarely if ever used. Antidumping measures have increased steeply since the Uruguay Round. When the figures are corrected for the per dollar value of imports restricted by antidumping measures, it turns out that developing countries have actually initiated more antidumping actions than industrial countries have (see Tables 4.1 and 4.2). These tables, in which the initiation of antidumping cases (per dollar of United States imports) is measured using a standardized index, indicate that antidumping actions brought by developing countries have increased 10 or 20 fold over the United States' use of this instrument.

68

Table 4.1 Antidumping initiations per US dollar of imports, by economy, 1995–99

Country/ economy initiating	Against all economies	
	No. of antidumping initiations	Initiations per US dollar, index (USA=100)
Argentina	89	2125
South Africa	89	2014
Peru	21	1634
India	83	1382
New Zealand	28	1292
Trinidad & Tobago	5	1257
Venezuela	22	1174
Nicaragua	2	988
Australia	89	941
Colombia	15	659
Brazil	56	596
Panama	2	431
Israel	19	418
Chile	10	376
Indonesia	20	33
Mexico	46	290
Egypt	6	278
Turkey	14	204
Korea	37	185
Canada	50	172
Guatemala	1	168
Costa Rica	1	144
Ecuador	1	140
European Union	160	130
Philippines	6	113
United States	136	100
Malaysia	11	97
Slovenia	1	66
Poland	4	65
Czech Republic	2	45
Singapore	2	10
Thailand	1	10

Source: J. Michael Finger, Francis Ng and Sonam Wangchuk (2000). 'Antidumping as Safeguard Policy' (mimeo).

Table 4.2   Antidumping initiations per US dollar of imports,
by country group, 1995–99

Against by	All economies	
	No. of antidumping initiations	**Initiations per US dollar, index (USA=100)**
Industrial economies	463	116
Developing economies	559	184
Transition economies	7	23
All economies	1029	140

Source: J. Michael Finger, Francis Ng and Sonam Wangchuk
(2000), 'Antidumping as Safeguard Policy' (mimeo).

Many analysts have viewed the pattern of antidumping complaints as denoting the use of a protective, anti-competitive instrument whose use has increased as tariffs and quantitative restrictions (QRs) have been reduced in industrial countries. While the original intent of antidumping laws in countries such as the United States was to discourage predatory or anti-competitive behaviour by a foreign importer in the domestic market, that rationale has since been superseded by the new law, under which the only requirement for determining that dumping is taking place is that export prices are lower than average domestic production costs as constructed by the importing country. Accordingly, the 1921 Antidumping Act and its successors, such as the Trade Reform Act of 1974 and the Trade Agreements Act of 1979, stipulate that if export prices are lower than domestic production costs in the exporting country, then dumping is purportedly occurring, even though actual dumping – in the economic sense of predatory pricing – could not have taken place. Antidumping measures generate greater uncertainty in international trade; the threat itself is harmful, since it can lead to collusion and recourse to anti-competitive behaviour in general, as is the case of VERs.

First, from a normative point of view, the mere existence of a lower export price may not necessarily imply any national welfare loss on the part of an importing country. It could, on the contrary, reflect the presence of monopoly power or a lack of competition in the exporting country and nothing more than price discrimination by the producer in that country. Another possibility is that it may simply be a reflection of an industry's adjustment to a reduction in global demand, with no intent to injure the importing country's domestic industry. If there is no motive of predation, the availability of imported goods at lower prices increases consumer welfare. While there would indeed be a reduction in the profits of domestic producers, this would be the result of nothing more than the normal vagaries of changing demand conditions in different markets. In his original work on the subject, Viner believed that industries that enjoy strong economies of scale sell at lower prices during slack periods.[4] It is true, however, that alleged dumping practices have involved various types of goods and not necessarily those that are subject to economies of scale and/or are sensitive to business cycles.

Second, the application of actual dumping policies in industrial countries and in Latin America has given these countries a great deal of discretionary power in determining the presence of dumping and in estimating dumping margins. GATT rules in this area were also permissive, as will be discussed below. The Uruguay Round revisions did not improve the situation much. For example, the use of antidumping measures by Latin American countries suffers from the same shortcomings as in industrial countries, and this situation is compounded by the fact that they have much less technical expertise and weak institutions with respect to trade remedies in general. The comparison between the cost of production in the importing country and the price charged in an exporting country is central to the determination of dumping. Values for the exporting country's average production cost can be imputed or constructed.[5] Even in a situation where there is no difference in price between the export market and the exporter's home market, dumping can be said to occur if the constructed cost is higher in the domestic market than in the export market. This construction entails arbitrary elements, such as the method of averaging costs in imputing reasonable sales and administrative costs.[6] Often in the construction of domestic costs, sales that are undertaken below average costs (when marginal costs are below average costs as output expands) are not included in the construction of total average costs, this leads to the appearance of high average costs compared to the export price and provides ammunition to institute antidumping actions.

Third, average production costs are not an economically meaningful concept if in the short run firms continue to produce when they can recover variable costs. It is good business practice to ride out periods of slack demand by covering variable costs, even if fixed costs are not recovered throughout the life of a capital asset. Moreover, when a new product is brought into the market, there may be high start-up costs that have to be spread over the product–cycle. The construction of average costs would ignore this factor, however, and lead to a determination of dumping. In addition, with more imports being offered at lower prices to an importing country, and with such a wide range of discretion in constructing average costs, countries can impose antidumping duties under these conditions, as they have in fact done. For example, the more efficient exporters to the US may be penalized and face antidumping actions just because the prescribed profit margins and administrative expenses used in estimating average production costs have been calculated incorrectly.

Fourth, macroeconomic crises, capital flight and related adjustments in exchange rates make it difficult to estimate production costs in developing countries and have complicated the construction of average costs of production. Paradoxically, exchange rate depreciations aimed at restoring developing country producers' competitive position can lead to antidumping actions in industrial countries when in fact such exchange rate adjustments and trade liberalization measures have made developing countries' markets more accessible to industrial countries' exports. Thus, from the standpoint of resource allocation, antidumping measures stand in the way of policies that would benefit both importing and exporting countries. In other words, in efficiency and national-welfare terms, both parties stand to lose when antidumping actions are instituted.

Fifth, following a finding that the constructed production costs are lower than the export price, the way in which injury is determined is arbitrary in several respects. In the US, the International Trade Commission uses a number of indicators to determine injury. These indicators include penetration ratios, changes in employment, capacity utilization in the industry concerned and profit levels, among others. Changes in these variables can and do occur regardless of whether dumping is or is not taking place. The basis upon which changes in a domestic industry may be attributed to dumping constitutes a very serious issue. Changes in these indicators can be caused by many factors unconnected to foreign competition.[7] This is true for the US as well as for developing countries. Antidumping represents the path of least resistance for protectionist interests, even in situations where a competition law exists to prevent predation and the consequent monopolization of the domestic market (as in the 1890 Sherman Act in the US).[8] Thus, it is no surprise that in developing countries – where competition laws are often weak, not strictly enforced or lacking altogether – antidumping measures have proliferated.

Using the definition whereby dumping is equated with a price below production cost, and defining cost as average cost, it is clear that dumping can be a rational, profit-maximizing, non-predatory course of action for a firm in the short run (as long as it covers its marginal cost during periods of slack demand). This type of dumping may also occur in a situation where the cost structure is different for exporters than it is for domestic firms. For example, foreign exporters may classify a larger proportion of their costs as being fixed (for example, a Japanese firm may regard labour as a fixed cost whereas a US firm may view it as a variable cost), and in periods of diminished demand in the domestic economy prices may quickly fall below the marginal costs of domestic firms, which will then exit the industry, while remaining above foreign exporters' lower marginal cost levels. Under these circumstances, exports will displace domestic production, but only because of the higher fixed costs of exports.

There are also other reasons why firms may price below marginal costs as part of an interim profit maximization strategy. Slapping antidumping duties on these products provides domestic firms with protection, but it may be costly in terms of national and consumer welfare. The argument for antidumping duties is that firms may be dumping products in a predatory manner to eliminate competition and then raise prices once the competition has been crowded out of the market. This is a controversial issue, and if this argument is to be made successfully, it requires the assumption of the existence of sunk costs and the expectation by potential entrants that the same behaviour by the dumping firm would occur were they to enter the market. In addition, dumping and subsidies can be justified from the exporter's point of view if the firm or home country derives significant externalities from the production of the goods or if there are scale effects. Scale effects can justify pricing below the average domestic price, since in that case the marginal cost is lower than the average cost.

Another explanation for pricing below marginal cost, if indeed this is the case, may be that the firm's objective is not profit maximization but rather sales maximization and the expansion of market share. In the former case, it is argued that managers of firms are not primarily maximizing shareholder profits because they are actually rewarded according to the firm's growth rate (for example, scale of operations/sales maximization). The excess output depresses price, harming competitors and expanding consumer surplus. In the latter case, the firm's objective may be to capture market share by reducing prices, as in the case of 'experience goods'. A producer of such goods will sell to its export market at a dumped price while its product is new and unfamiliar to the market and will then raise the price once a preference for it has been developed. This, however, is not only a common practise used by firms that are introducing new products in a country, but it is also pro-competitive and should not be penalized.

Another undesirable side-effect of antidumping measures is their potential use as an instrument of collusion. The EU experience demonstrates that antidumping actions have in some cases come to be used as a means of price collusion. It has often been the case that domestic prices have stabilized after a decrease in antidumping actions and foreign prices have risen. Clearly, then, there are tradeoffs. Obviously, the elimination of antidumping measures could result in a more competitive domestic market albeit at the risk, however small, of the potential long-term consequences of predation.

The overall social costs to consumers of antidumping laws, including wasteful rent-seeking activities on the part of producers to protect their industries from foreign competitors and other deadweight costs, generally outweigh the benefits to producers (in the form of reduced competition) and to the government (in the form of the duties collected), to say nothing of the significant costs of litigation and dispute settlement proceedings. As the above discussion would lead one to expect, most antidumping cases are consistently being challenged by the 'injuring' party. This has been the case with both NAFTA and Mercosur. The costs associated with the dispute process include government resources devoted to such proceedings. Here again, this is a deadweight welfare loss that can and should be avoided by doing away with antidumping duties.

The imposition of antidumping duties on a particular product originating from a given country may lead an exporter to engage in 'country hopping' or 'product shifting' in an attempt to avoid the duties. The offending country may move production to the jurisdiction that imposed the antidumping duty or to a third country. It may also differentiate the product slightly in order to elude the duty.

Different countries interpret GATT articles differently (for example, the definition of 'like' products discussed above). There are also different levels of discretion allowed in different countries. Under the US system, which is considered to represent the most 'mechanical' approach, duties equal to the calculated dumping margin are automatically applied, whereas other systems may confidentially indicate minimum prices under which duties would be imposed. The foregoing shows that antidumping provisions pose a serious threat to the open trading system, as they encourage departures from the basic principles of the multilateral trading system. They are more harmful than other measures of exceptional protection, are easier to deploy and have become more widespread than was anticipated at the Uruguay Round. In fact, it has been found that among new users of antidumping measures (particularly some developing countries), the rate at which antidumping actions are being initiated – as measured against per dollar value of imports – is on the rise. Thus, antidumping duties are not only the most pernicious form of exceptional protection but have also become the weapon of choice for protectionists.

Safeguards

Safeguards are based on GATT Article XIX and are used to shelter countries from surges in imports that may injure domestic industry, presumably in order to give the industry breathing space to adjust. By virtue of its nature, safeguard protection may help to maintain an open trade regime in a country. In practice, however, safeguards have proved difficult to implement. If they are used too readily, they may damage the cause of free trade. If they are used too sparingly, they may allow protectionist forces to establish a lasting foothold in the trade regime. The Uruguay Round incorporated an amended safeguard provision into the WTO agreement which addresses some of the problems that arose with the earlier GATT rules on safeguards (the earlier provision did not clearly define what constitutes serious injury or threat thereof, did not establish a time limit to indicate how long safeguards could be in effect and did not set clear rules regarding the application of safeguards on a selective basis).[9]

From a national welfare and efficiency perspective, safeguards are superior to antidumping duties. Yet safeguards have been used very sparingly by industrial countries and even less by Latin American nations. The major industrial countries did, of course, have recourse to various 'grey area' measures such as VERs and OMAs, but these mechanisms were prohibited by the Uruguay agreement. Nonetheless, antidumping duties, rather than safeguards, are more likely to be used by both industrial and Latin American countries.[10]

The Uruguay Round allowed the application of transitional safeguard measures to agricultural goods, textiles and clothing as the price that was paid to the developing countries for their acceptance of multilateral trade rules as applied to these sectors. The good news is that they are limited in time (hence the description 'transitional measures'). These transitional measures are provided for by the Agreement on Textiles and Clothing (ATC) and differ from normal safeguard measures in that they can be invoked only during the MFA transition period, which will end in 2005, and refer to so-called 'non-integrated' items, which are those that fall outside the scope of normal (or integrated) safeguards. Certain textiles are excluded, such as handloom fabrics, traditional folklore handicrafts and historically traded textile products, such as carpets, bags, sacks, luggage, mats or items made from fibres such as jute, coir, sisal and the like. Pure silk is also exempted from the transitional safeguards. The United States, Brazil and Colombia have been the main users of the transitional safeguard arrangements under the ATC.

Very few safeguard actions have been initiated in connection with agricultural goods. This is because there has been little or no change in the levels of protection for agriculture since the Uruguay Round. There has consequently been no need to make a great deal of use of the transitional arrangements for agriculture, and they have indeed been few and far between. Some of the safeguards that have been used have dealt with fresh tomatoes (United States), dairy products (South Korea) and pork (Australia and Slovenia).

Safeguards are less attractive to protectionists for a number of reasons. First, a higher threshold is required for safeguards than for antidumping duties in showing 'serious injury'. In addition, in determining whether or not safeguards are called for, consideration must be given to the benefits accruing to *consumers* as well as the costs, whereas with antidumping duties only the costs to domestic *producers* of lower priced imports are taken into account.

Second, safeguards have to be imposed on a most-favoured-nation (MFN) basis, whereas antidumping duties are applied selectively and may be restricted to one or a few exporters. In the case of safeguards, if compensation were to be offered to the exporting countries, this could be construed as constituting a departure from the MFN principle.

Third, some interest groups may find it appealing to refer to dumping as an 'unfair trade practice' and thereby garner more domestic support for antidumping measures than for safeguards – which do not have the former mechanism's emotional impact or xenophobic content – rather than having domestic producers accept the responsibility of making an adjustment.

Finally, when a country uses safeguards, it must offer compensation after a specified time period or remove the restraints it has imposed on the basis of the safeguard action; if it fails to do so, it becomes subject to legally sanctioned retaliation. The combination of these provisions makes for a higher threshold for safeguard measures than for antidumping duties. Moreover, using their superior market power, industrial countries could institute 'grey area' measures. The threat of antidumping duties is what induced exporting countries to acquiesce to 'grey area' measures, and it is developing countries that have been at the receiving end of such mechanisms.

The Uruguay Round reaffirmed the MFN basis for safeguards. It also provided a more precise definition of the concept of 'serious injury', which has a higher threshold of proof than the material injury requirement for antidumping duties. In addition, it stipulated that safeguards were to be applied for a four-year period, with provision being made for their continuation if the injury persisted and for a ten-year limit for developing countries (versus a period of eight years for developed countries). Safeguard action by developed countries against developing countries is allowed only if the latter's imports exceed 3 per cent of all imports and those from all developing countries amount to 9 per cent. Finally, as opposed to the earlier provision, compensation is voluntary rather than mandatory, but the affected exporters may retaliate after three years' time.[11]

In sum, safeguards have been used more sparingly than antidumping measures because they require a higher threshold and, ironically, when antidumping action is an option there is no reason to pursue a more stringent process. Finally, within the framework of the transitional arrangements, many developing countries have used safeguards under the ATC rather than for agriculture. While safeguards are a more reliable means of maintaining an open world trade environment, they have not been found to be either politically feasible or strategically expedient.[12]

Countervailing Duties or Anti-Subsidies

Like antidumping duties, countervailing duties are imposed to offset the adverse effects of a foreign country's trade policies on a domestic industry or activity. Unlike antidumping duties, however, countervailing duties requires the involvement of a foreign government in the subsidization of exports from that country. Thus, unlike both antidumping and safeguard measures, which are a governmental response to private sector activity, countervailing duties are a *government-to-government* form of exceptional protection. As stated in GATT Article VI:3 these duties are 'for the purpose of offsetting any bounty or subsidy bestowed, directly or indirectly, upon the manufacture, production or export of any merchandise' by a foreign government. Yet subsidies have been widely used by governments to achieve a number of goals by various means. Such subsidies have included grants, tax exemptions, low interest financing, and investment in particular activities, among others.

As in the case of antidumping measures, an injury test is a prerequisite for the imposition of countervailing duties. According to John Jackson (2000), this is the result of a decision reached by the negotiators at the Tokyo Round to bring antidumping test into line with the test required for countervailing duties, even though there was no persuasive reason for doing so.[13] A distinction is made between subsidies to domestic producers and subsidies to exporters or exports. The GATT/WTO system regards the latter as being particularly pernicious, since they 'export' a distortion. An example of distortions in the world market brought about by agricultural subsidies is provided by the European Union, even though they have not been designated as export subsidies. In other words, subsidies given to domestic producers can end up in the export market and distort world prices as European Agricultural subsidies have done for decades. This causes domestic and world prices to diverge and resource allocation to depart from the optimum; which happens when domestic marginal rates of transformation in production is equal to domestic (marginal rates of) consumption and equal to the foreign rate of marginal transformation. Of course, subsidies are superior instruments compared with tariffs for promoting certain activities.[14]

The theoretical literature of the 1970s speaks of an optimal subsidy that can be targeted for a particular purpose. More generally, the literature of that time recognized the use of export subsidies to offset the export bias created by import duties. During and since the Uruguay Round, however, this tolerant attitude towards export subsidies has waned. All the industrial countries were given five years to eliminate export subsidies, while developing countries have been given eight years to do so. There is, however, no such restriction on the least developed countries. There is some question as to whether countervailing action should be taken against each and every export subsidy, since in some cases they can be viewed as a 'gift' from an exporting country. In fact, many economists have argued that countervailing laws should be abolished. The mainstream view, however, is that they can be harmful because a foreign government's subsidy can discourage production of certain goods in other countries that actually have a comparative advantage in that area. In such case, subsidies can be seen as having much the same effect as the predatory pricing which serves as grounds for antidumping duties.

Subsidies can be countervailed at any time, since importing countries are not required to allow any grace period to expire before taking such action. Thus, countervailing duties can indeed serve as a powerful instrument of exceptional protection. The United States has been the most active user of this instrument of all the member countries of the WTO. This may be due to the fact that the United States has a more extensive legal basis for the use of countervailing measures than other countries.

During the Uruguay Round, the subsidies code was revised and a more specific definition was established of the circumstances under which countervailing duties can be imposed. The problems involved in defining what constitutes 'injury' and in estimating the appropriate duty had yet to be resolved. This was done in the Agreement on Subsidies and Countervailing Measures, where subsidies were divided into two broad categories: specific and non-specific subsidies. The category of specific subsidies was divided into two sub-categories: prohibited (red light) and actionable subsidies. Prohibited subsidies include export subsidies and subsidies that are contingent upon the use of domestic goods. Actionable (Yellow or amber light) specific subsidies may be countervailable. Non-actionable (green light) subsidies include R&D development and environmental subsidies that meet given criteria. This category also includes non-specific – and non-countervailable – subsidies. The Uruguay Round thus defined the various types of subsidies more accurately than before and permitted some of them (such as R&D, environmental and regional development subsidies). While this is an improvement over the earlier subsidies code, it has still left many of the ambiguities of the earlier system in place.

The experience with the use of safeguards under GATT/WTO has been analyzed by Finger, who draws three main conclusions. First, GATT/WTO provisions are fungible in the sense that antidumping and safeguard actions can be substituted for one another, since imports can be restricted by means of antidumping provisions under Article VI or through the use of safeguards under Article XIX. Developing countries have used an infant industry argument (Article XVIII.C) or a balance of payments based argument (Article XVIII.B). As mentioned earlier, antidumping duties have been the preferred mechanism because of their ease of use.

Second, GATT/WTO rules have not provided the discipline needed to make the system work well. There have been many instances in which the original intentions of GATT rules have been flouted. The use of VERs and other non-transparent measures not based on bilateral agreements has contravened both the spirit and the letter of the principles of multilateral free trade. In the absence of adequate enforcement mechanisms, the powerful countries have held sway over the system. Prior to the Uruguay Round, developing countries sat out and attempted to free-ride the MFN-based multilateral liberalization process. With the advent of the Uruguay Round, developing countries began to participate in negotiations and pursue their interests. In addition, the creation of a much stronger dispute settlement mechanism has provided a new form of discipline to some extent.

Finally, none of the provisions relating to exceptional protection make a clear, valid distinction between the import restrictions that are sometimes necessary to prevent a permanent rupture in the free trade system and those that are in neither the national or international interest in the long run. In other words, the original intention of creating exceptional protection mechanisms to serve as a safety valve has not been realized. Hence the need to reform exceptional protection provisions in order to establish greater discipline in the future.

CONCLUSION: THE WAY AHEAD

The above discussion demonstrates that exceptional protection has not served the purposes for which it was created. Rather than serving as a safety valve, exceptional protection has become an important instrument of protection itself, whereas the intent was to prevent protection from becoming a permanent feature. This was the case throughout GATT's existence, and it has remained true since the creation of the WTO. While significant efforts were made to address some of the shortcomings of the various instruments during the Uruguay Round, they have had no more than a marginal effect. In fact, the use of antidumping provisions has actually been increasing. This is because of antidumping provisions' substitutability vis-à-vis safeguards and countervailing duties, on the one hand, and their substitutability vis-à-vis traditional protectionist devices such as tariffs and QRs, on the other. It should be acknowledged, however, that some progress was made in reforming these measures during the Uruguay Round that has helped to limit, if not eliminate, more hidden forms of protection, such as 'grey area' measures.

The way ahead must be regarded from the perspective of an interim solution. In the long run, competition and antitrust policy must supersede all these exceptional protection measures. After all, the objective is to lead to competition, regardless of the origin of the goods that are subject to protection. From the developing countries' vantage point, this is still far off in the future. They do not have a tradition of using competition policy; nor do they have any law in place or any institutions to implement competition policy.[15] The other solution is to make further improvements in existing exceptional protection measures. It is clear, however, that the extent to which antidumping provisions can be refined is limited. The Uruguay Round patently failed to do so, since the imposition of antidumping duties has increased and has been emulated by developing countries, which are now imposing such duties on one another, in particular among regional groups.

The more practical course of action in the medium term is to reform safeguards and restrain the use of antidumping and countervailing duties. The latter instrument poses less of a problem because it is triggered by a government's use of a specific subsidy and is consequently limited by the resources available to the government concerned. What is more, if one government decides to provide the 'gift' of a subsidy to the population of another country, that is actually not such a bad thing. There are several factors of political economy that will help to control such subsidization. Besides, export subsidies are now more closely monitored than before and can be redressed by the importing country through the Dispute Settlement Body.

The way ahead, then, is to reform the safeguard mechanism. This could be done in a number of ways. An important step was taken at the Uruguay Round, when safeguards were made more accessible by relaxing the conditions under which they can be used.[16] The relaxation of these provisions included an increase in the permitted duration of their use beyond the original three year limit, the introduction of a four year extension, a limitation of the possibility of retaliation by extending the period in which compensation is to be considered, and authorization of the use of quotas as a safeguard and thus permitting greater discrimination by source.

Three other features could also be incorporated into a new safeguard mechanism that would eliminate or reduce recourse to antidumping duties. (i) At the end of the second period of application of a safeguard, a country should be given only two choices: either to eliminate the measure altogether or to renegotiate the tariff on the good or service concerned. The country should also be explicitly prohibited from imposing antidumping duties on the import in question (ii) The extension period for safeguards could be reduced from four years to three so that they would be in cycle for renegotiation, thereby definitely making safeguards a transitional measure. (iii) Antidumping and safeguard measures should be reformed simultaneously so that there is no room for shifting over to antidumping duties as safeguard rules are tightened in the ways suggested by the three conditions for reform identified here.

Finally, all these measures are only as good as the institutions that enforce them. In order to improve these institutions, one effective formula is to create the greatest possible distance between them and any specific sector or interest group, to make the deliberations on safeguard measures transparent and open to the public so that all interested parties can have their say, and to ensure that the relevant legislation and the political leadership are committed to achieving the stated purpose of exceptional protection, namely, to be an exception, rather than a common practice.

Notes

1. See Guasch and Rajapatirana (1998) which makes the argument for competition law in some detail.
2. In a strict sense, safeguards are not exceptions to the most-favoured-nation principle since it is applied equally to all importers. However, there is provision grant compensation to principal sources who suffer losses due to the imposition of safeguard protection. These can differ, and hence in that sense safeguards are an exception from the most favoured nation principle.
3. Guasch and Rajapatirana (1998) show the increase for Latin American countries.
4. Viner (1923).
5. The use of average cost itself is flawed. It is based on the notion that long-term competitive equilibrium exists in the activity concerned where price,

average costs and marginal costs are equal. This is hardly the case at each moment in time.

6. David Palmeter points out that the US will have to amend its method of determining dumping margins since the actual percentages for administrative and profit rates are prescribed in the US while this is not the case with the revision of antidumping rules following the Uruguay Round (see Palmeter, 1996).

7. Witness the current controversy regarding the decline in real wages in manufacturing in the US which is ascribed to foreign competition mistakenly, as shown by Paul Krugman and Robert Lawrence (1993). The decline in real wages is associated with technical change rather than import of labour-intensive goods from low wage countries.

8. Victor (1983) indicates that there is inherent friction between antitrust and the administration of antidumping in the United States. He remarks that 'the dumping law has consistently been interpreted to protect competitors rather than competition'.

9. There was a strong disagreement between the US and Europe (led by France) on this issue. France argued for selective intervention but the US insisted that it would go against the most favoured nation principle, a cornerstone of the multilateral trading rules ensconced in GATT.

10. Michael J. Finger (1994).

11. Schott (1994).

12. Michael Finger *et al.* (2000) could refer to antidumping as safeguard policy.

13. Jackson (2000).

14. The literature on optimal trade intervention makes this very clear, as demonstrated in the theoretical contributions of Bhagwati, Corden and Johnson, to name the leading theorists who have analyzed this issue.

15. Peru is a rare exception as it has the National Institute for the Defense of Competition and Protection of Intellectual Property.

16. This section owes much to the thinking of Patrick Messerlin (2000).

Bibliography

ABBOT, KENNETH W. (1995) 'Trade Remedies and Legal Remedies: Antidumping, Safeguards, and Dispute Settlement After the Uruguay Round', Northwestern University School of Law, Chicago (mimeo).

DEARDORFF, A. V. (1989) 'Economic Perspectives on Anti-dumping Law', in John Jackson and Robert Stern (eds), *Anti-dumping-Law and Practice* (Ann Arbor: University of Michigan Press).

FINGER, MICHAEL J. (1993) '*Antidumping: How it Works and Who Gets Hurt*' (University of Michigan Press).

FINGER, MICHAEL J. (1998) 'Experience with Safeguards – Making Economic and Political Sense of the Possibilities that the GATT allows to Restrict Imports', World Bank Policy Research Paper No. 2000.

FINGER, MICHAEL J., FRANCIS NG and SONAM WANGCHUK (2000) 'Antidumping as Safeguard Policy', October (mimeo).

GUASCH, J. LUIS and SARATH RAJAPATIRANA (1994) 'The Interface of Trade, Investment and Competition Policies: Issues in Challenges for Latin America', Policy Research Working Paper No. 1393, World Bank, December.

GUASCH, J. LUIS and SARATH RAJAPATIRANA (1998) 'Soul Mates or Rival Siblings: Antidumping and Competition Polices in Latin America and the Caribbean', World Bank Policy Research Paper No. 1958.

HOEKMAN, BERNARD M. and PETROS C. MAVROIDIS (1994) 'Antitrust Based Remedies and Dumping in International Trade', Center for Economic Policy Research, Discussion Paper 1010, August.

JACKSON, JOHN (2000) *The World Trading System* (Cambridge, MA: MIT Press).

JACKSON, JOHN and EDWIN VERMULST (eds) (1989) *Anti-dumping Law and Practice* (Ann Arbor: University of Michigan Press).

KRUGMAN, PAUL R. and ROBERT LAWRENCE (1993) 'Trade, Jobs and Wages', NBER Working Paper No. 4478, September.

MESSERLIN, PATRICK A. (2000) 'Antidumping and Safeguards', in *The WTO After Seattle*, ed. Jeffrey J. Schott (Washington D.C.: Institute of International Economics).

MORKRE, MORRIS and K. H. KELLY (1994) *Effects of Unfair Imports on Domestic Industries: US Anti-dumping and Countervailing Duty Cases, 1980–88* (Washington D.C.: Bureau of Economics, Federal Trade Commission).

PALMETER, DAVID (1996) 'A Commentary on the WTO Antidumping Code', *Journal of World Trade*, August, Geneva.

RAJAPATIRANA, SARATH (1995) 'Post Trade Liberalization Policy and Institutional Challenges in Latin America and the Caribbean', Policy Research Working Paper No. 1465, World Bank, May.

RAJAPATIRANA, SARATH (1997) *Trade Policies in Latin America and the Caribbean: Priorities, Progress and Prospects* (San Francisco: International Center for Economic Growth).

SCHOTT, JEFFREY J. (1994) *The Uruguay Round: An Assessment* (Institute of International Economics).

SCHOTT, JEFFREY (ed). (2000) *The WTO After Seattle* (Washington D.C.: Institute for International Economics).

SPENCER, B. J. (1988) 'Countervailing Duty Laws and Subsidies to Imperfectly Competitive Industries', in Robert E. Baldwin, Carl Hamilton and Andre Sapir (eds), *Issues in US–EC Trade Relations* (Chicago: University of Chicago Press).

VICTOR, P. (1983) 'Antidumping and Antitrust: Can the Two be Resolved?', *Journal of International Law and Politics*, 15.

VINER, JACOB (1923) *Dumping: A Problem in International Trade* (University of Chicago Press).

5 Is the WTO Dispute Resolution System Serving the Developing World's Interests?

James R. Holbein and Dennis R. Nuxoll

INTRODUCTION

The World Trade Organization (WTO) was established on 1 January 1995, as a result of the Uruguay Round of multilateral trade negotiations under the General Agreement on Tariffs and Trade (GATT). As of 31 December 2000, the WTO had 140 members, with an additional 28 countries in the process of accession. The WTO, as an international organization, administers the GATT trade agreement; acts as a forum for ongoing multilateral trade negotiations; serves as a tribunal for resolving disputes; reviews the trade policies and practices of its members; and cooperates with other international organizations to standardize global economic policy-making.[1]

In November 1999 the WTO held a Ministerial meeting in Seattle, Washington, with a goal to initiate a new round of multilateral trade negotiations to amend the GATT. The meeting was disrupted by massive civil unrest. This meeting was widely perceived to be a failure for the WTO because the members were not able to agree to launch the new round of negotiations. Developing country members severely criticized the WTO as well as the process for decision-making.

The protests in Seattle concerning the WTO's global role have brought this organization into the collective consciousness of many around the world. Far from a toothless and drab international body, the WTO today wields influence over trade policies, environmental regulations, services, investment, agriculture and the settlement of disputes, among others, in member states. Indeed, high-profile WTO and GATT legal disputes over beef hormones, bananas, gasoline and tuna have been increasingly well-publicized over the past decade. The decisions of the dispute settlement mechanism have important effects on developed and developing countries.

This chapter will analyze whether the developing world is a net beneficiary or victim of the new, tougher dispute settlement system established in the WTO. It begins by presenting the background of how the dispute settlement process operates. The second part will analyze the dispute settlement mechanism effectiveness on developing countries. The last part will present case studies followed by a conclusion and policy recommendations for developing countries during the negotiation process in the WTO.

BACKGROUND ON THE DISPUTE SETTLEMENT PROCESS

The dispute settlement mechanism and the prompt settlement of disputes according to Adamantopoulus (1997) contribute more to trade stability and effective functioning of the WTO than any other aspect.[2] It is one of the main achievements of the Uruguay Round. The prompt settlement of disputes was deemed essential to the effective functioning of the WTO. In fact, the entire WTO dispute settlement system owes its creation to the United States' insistence for a new dispute resolution system at the end of the 1990s. This system was to be both more binding and quicker than the previous GATT system.

Article III of the Dispute Settlement Understanding (DSU) establishes the very prominent and critical role of the dispute settlement mechanism: It is 'a central element in providing security and predictability to the multilateral trading system. Members recognize that it serves to preserve the rights and obligations of Members under the covered agreements, and to clarify the existing provisions of those agreements ...'.[3]

Dispute Settlement Body

The WTO Agreement created a Dispute Settlement Body (DSB), comprised of all member states, which is charged with creating panels, adopting panel and appellate body reports, and monitoring compliance with rulings and recommendations. A dispute resolution begins when a WTO member requests a consultation with another member and notifies the DSB and other relevant committees. Any other involved member(s) must enter into consultation in good faith. These consultations are confidential. If a dispute is not resolved within sixty days after a request for consultation, the member bringing a complaint may submit a written request for a panel. The parties may also voluntarily undertake less formal processes, including good offices, conciliation, or mediation, which may continue even while a panel proceeds.[4]

The panel examines the matter before the DSB in light of the relevant provisions of the agreement in question, and produces findings to assist the DSB in making recommendations. The three member panels are comprised of experienced governmental and/or non-governmental individuals from diverse backgrounds, who are selected to ensure independence. If a dispute is between a developed country and a developing country, the developing country may request that the panel include at least one panelist from another developing country. If more than one member requests a panel on the same matter, a single panel will be established to address both requests in a manner that will not impair the rights of any of the disputing parties.

A panel may seek information and technical advice from appropriate bodies after informing the members involved. Panel deliberations are confidential. Panels issue interim reports to the parties. Parties may request that a panel review sections of its interim report and/or hold further meetings with the parties on identified issues. Unless a party wishes to appeal the panel's recommendation, a final report is submitted to the DSB for approval.[5] Typically, panel reports are submitted for approval within ten to thirteen months after the establishment of a panel.[6] The DSB will approve panel reports unless there is a consensus not to adopt the report or a party notifies the DSB that it is appealing the panel decision.[7] This is a major reform of the prior GATT system in which a consensus, such as unanimity, was required to form a panel and adopt a panel report. This gave effective veto power to members who were in violation of the GATT commitments. The new DSB system eliminates that problem.

Another important innovation was the creation of the Appellate Body to review panel reports. Only parties to disputes may appeal, and appeals are heard only on legal issues. The seven-member Appellate Body hears appeals from panel cases in three-person groups. As with panel proceedings, Appellate Body proceedings are confidential. The Appellate Body may 'uphold, modify, or reverse the legal findings and conclusions' of a panel. The DSB adopts or rejects the appellate body's decision. In turn, the WTO Agreement states that prompt compliance with recommendations or rulings of the DSB is 'essential to ensure effective resolution of disputes'. If an offending party fails to implement a ruling, the WTO may request voluntary compensation from, and/or temporarily suspend concessions that benefit that party.[8] Typically appellate body actions are completed within six months of the appeal. Several cases have established that the reasonable time to implement an adverse finding by a panel is fifteen months.[9]

DISPUTE SETTLEMENT EFFECTIVENESS ON
DEVELOPING COUNTRIES

Although many aspects of the WTO's interaction with developing countries are worthy of scholarly attention, the dispute resolution process under
the WTO is particularly innovative, as compared to the prior GATT
process. Of the WTO's 140 members, three-quarters are developing or
least-developed nations. Under the terms of the GATT 1994, the principle
of special and differential treatment grants developing countries extra
rights during the dispute settlement process such as extended time for
preparing and presenting arguments.[10]

Critics and proponents of this system now have five full years' worth of
data from the system's actual operation to analyze. Robert Hudec performed a detailed statistical analysis of the cases brought during the first
three years of the 'Understanding on Rules and Procedures Governing the
Settlement of Disputes' (DSU) operation. His work is insightful in many
ways in understanding the *impact* of the DSU. Hudec calculated that the
volume of cases during the first three years of the WTO disputes procedure was nearly double that under the previous GATT dispute settlement
procedure. He also found that the volume of complaints during the first
three years was 60 per cent higher than under the GATT. He concluded
that, 'measured either way, the increase in volume has certainly been large
enough to be considered a significant event'.[11]

Professor Hudec attributes this huge increase in cases to the new obligations that the WTO created. These new obligations take the form of new
substantive obligations such as the General Agreement on Trade in
Services (GATS), the Trade-Related Aspects of Intellectual Property
Rights (TRIPS), etc., which in turn have generated new disputes:

> There is one other kind of 'new obligation' that appears to have been a
> significant cause of the 46-case increase. Under the 'Single Undertaking'
> principle adopted in the Uruguay Round negotiations, developing
> countries were required to sign almost every agreement included in the
> WTO package of agreements. In addition, developing countries were
> asked to bind most of their tariff schedules, even if at relatively high
> 'ceiling bindings.' Both the volume of these new obligations and the
> interest in stronger discipline that lay behind them promised that the
> volume of WTO enforcement activity against developing countries
> would increase.[12]

Finally, Hudec establishes that there has been a dramatic increase in the
percentage of developing country defendants since the inception of the

WTO. Under the GATT only 13 per cent of defendants in cases were developing countries. Under the WTO dispute settlement process, however, Hudec reports that nearly 40 per cent of the defendants in cases are developing nations.[13]

Observations about WTO Dispute Settlement Related to Developing Countries

Given the proliferation of cases during the last two years, it is an appropriate time to again review the experience of developing countries in dispute settlement. Appendix 1 attached to this chapter provides a complete list of all WTO dispute settlement actions involving developing countries through December 2000.[14] Of the 163 matters in which complaints have been filed, 99 involved developing countries. From that group of matters, the following observations of interest to developing countries can be made.

1. Complainants Win Most Cases that are Brought to Panels

Almost all of the matters that have reached full panel and appellate body review resulted in findings that responding countries are imposing measures inconsistent with the GATT. This may well reflect the widely used practice of screening matters through consultations and the opportunities for settlement that abound in the system. It would appear that the only cases that make it to panel review are those where measures are clearly inconsistent with existing obligations and where domestic political pressures prevent settlement. This pragmatic assessment may well oversimplify the process, but in the overwhelming majority of cases involving developing countries (20 of 23), in which the panel and appellate process have been completed, complainants have won.

2. The Consultation Process is Effective

Consultations appear to be a useful screening device that can, when used properly, weed out weaker cases and permit countries to vent their concerns and trade problems without public scrutiny. Of the 99 matters analyzed, including multiple requests concerning the same measure, 41 have remained in the consultation stage. In an additional 22 matters, the parties have notified the DSB that a settlement has been reached or is apparent. In only 23 matters was the entire process completed, while 15 matters remain active. Far more cases are being dealt with in consultation and settlement than in the formal panel process. That is not to say that all of the matters have been resolved successfully from the complainants' point of view, but the purpose of the process is being served. Consultations are very useful to permit airing of grievances in a multilateral setting, under agreed rules, so that domestic political pressure can be blunted and the international rule of law can be applied.

3. Case-by-Case Cost–Benefit Analysis Required

Resolving trade issues requires pragmatic cost–benefit analysis on a case-by-case basis. Issues that must be considered by respondents are the efficacy of negotiating a solution given the political considerations that mitigate for and against settling or dragging out cases up to 30 months through the panel review, appellate body review and implementation. Further concerns include possible adverse impacts to existing political goodwill in the community of nations if a country is viewed as dragging its feet or intentionally delaying resolution.

Developing country complainants must weigh the substantial costs of enforcing rights through WTO litigation against the very real possibility that they will be left with no recourse except retaliation after months of litigation. A further criticism of the WTO dispute settlement procedure is that the time limits built into the system are very long – in certain circumstances a settlement process may legitimately take nearly two and half years. Given that offending parties often want the longest time to elapse before being forced to remove offending measures, these long delays can be effective trade barriers.[15]

4. Only the Largest Developing Countries are Effectively Participating

You have to 'pay-to-play'. As a result, it is primarily the large developing countries that can effectively participate. Twelve countries – Brazil; Korea; Mexico; Argentina; Chile; Thailand; India; Pakistan; Indonesia, the Philippines; Turkey and Hungary – were involved in 95 of the 99 disputes involving developing countries. Eighteen smaller economies were involved in 28 disputes (several matters involved multiple complainants from larger and smaller economies). The majority of WTO members are lower-income developing countries and least developed countries. Generally, they do not take advantage of the consultation system, with the exception of some of the smaller Latin American members, (Costa Rica, Trinidad & Tobago, Panama, Ecuador, Peru, Uruguay, Guatemala and Honduras).

As a means to give effect to the provisions for special and differential treatment for developing countries, they were given longer transition periods to implement their obligations. Transition periods expired on 31 December 2000 under many of the agreements. This is a big cause for concern.[16] Developing countries find that they cannot enforce these hard-won new rights against other countries, including the large developed economies, due to the high cost of investigating and prosecuting cases, and the lack of trained personnel. This diminishes the access most countries have to use the system effectively, and they therefore do not vent their problems effectively through the consultation process.

Developing countries are understandably concerned about the resulting pressure they feel. They have all accepted higher levels of obligations as a consequence of joining the WTO and now face the full effect of these measures due to the expiration of the transition periods. The opening of their markets results in extreme pressure on their vulnerable industrial and agricultural sectors. However, unlike the major players, they are unable to use the WTO system to help their vulnerable sectors to adjust or to ensure that they compete successfully in formerly closed markets. This combination of factors has led to frustration and a sense that they are yet again powerless to influence and use the trading system to grow and develop.

In addition, the process of dispute settlement is disproportionately costly to developing countries. The technical nature of the disputes and the legal complexity of the DSU process demands far-reaching legal preparation, and the skills of experienced, highly skilled lawyers and other trade experts. None of this comes cheaply, and many developing counties do not have the necessary legal capacity within the country. In some instances, they feel compelled to employ experts on the WTO process from developed countries in order to successfully prosecute or defend themselves in a WTO case. For developing countries, the decision to raise an issue in the dispute settlement process is often based on cost as much as the technical and legal merits of the case, while developed countries rarely need think in those terms.

An interesting phenomenon is the apparent lack of familiarity with WTO litigation displayed by some of the members attempting to use the process. In two of the three matters decided by panels that involved only developing countries, the decisions were based on procedural grounds, not merits.[17] This indicates that developing countries may have a learning curve to overcome before they pursue their rights more aggressively against each other. In both cases that were decided on procedural grounds, additional panels have been requested to review the same disputed measures.[18]

5. The Implementation Process Needs to be Addressed

The preferred solution when a measure is found to be inconsistent with WTO obligations, is removal of the measure. In many instances, replacement measures are legislated in an attempt to bring non-compliant provisions into compliance. In other instances, members who have been found in violation simply substitute another inconsistent measure. In circumstances where offending measures are not removed, the complaining party has the possibility of removal of concessions or imposition of retaliation in the form of higher tariffs on specific products. If small countries lose to large countries, this threat is important.

Retaliation in the form of removing trade concessions or increasing tariffs is ineffective against the powerful Quad counties (US, EU, Japan and Canada). Retaliation from the majority of other weaker WTO members would simply not be a credible threat. Furthermore, non-compliance would be no more of a political embarrassment than blocking the process was in the old GATT system.[19] Indeed, there is the danger that such action could work against the weaker countries since it could be used against them. The threat of retaliation serves as a far stronger tool for the developed countries than for the developing countries.

6. Many Developing Countries are Using the DSU Successfully against Both Developing and Developed Countries

What many developing country critics do not acknowledge is that the new WTO system has provided them with many benefits and substantial victories. While it is true that an increasing number of developing countries are defendants in WTO cases, it is not the case that developing countries always lose such cases. Furthermore, developing countries have also been involved in just over half of the cases involving developing countries as complaining parties. Victories over the United States in the Reformulated Gasoline,[20] Shrimp-Turtle[21] cases, and against the EU in the Bananas[22] case are well-known, well-documented highlights on the list of successful cases that developing countries have waged recently. There are numerous other less-known cases involving developing WTO Members. Several are of note for this chapter and have been highlighted herein.

7. The Developing Countries Need an Advocacy Office

Analysis of the cases to date leads to the conclusion that the lower-income developing countries and all developing countries truly need an advocacy office and access to 'legal aid' in order to function effectively. It is in the interest of all WTO members to ensure that every member fulfils their WTO obligations. Given the lack of funding and trained personnel as well as the relative lack of sophistication of many of the economies of member states, it makes sense for the larger community to assist them to comply.

8. The WTO must Broaden the Use of High Technology

A significant problem limiting developing country participation in dispute settlement is the high cost of maintaining a permanent delegation in Geneva. Given the high level of sophistication in telecommunications today, it would be cost-effective to ensure that all major meetings (General Council, Dispute Settlement Body, Committees on Trade, Services, Intellectual Property, etc.) are broadcast via teleconference to every Member. It would be logistically difficult to set up initially, but once the mechanisms are in place, it should become a standard practice. Enabling all Members to participate via teleconference in all meetings will ensure that information is exchanged more readily. It will also blunt the criticisms by many Members that they are locked out of the system because they do not have permanent representatives in Geneva.

Case Studies of Decisions Involving Developing Countries

A. Costa Rica – Restrictions on Imports of Cotton and Man-Made-Fibre Underwear

On 27 March 1995, the United States requested consultations with Costa Rica on trade in cotton and man-made underwear under the Agreement on Textiles and Clothing (the 'ATC'). At the same time, the United States provided Costa Rica with a 'Statement of Serious Damage', dated March 1995, on the basis of which the United States proposed the introduction of a restraint on imports of underwear from Costa Rica. The consultations were held but the United States and Costa Rica failed to negotiate a mutually acceptable settlement during these consultations. The United States then invoked Article 6.10 of the ATC, and introduced a transitional safeguard measure in respect of cotton and man-made-fibre underwear imports from Costa Rica on 23 June 1995. The measure was, by its terms, to be valid for a period of 12 months, effective as of 27 March 1995 (i.e., the date of the request for consultations). At the same time, the United States referred the matter to the Textiles Monitoring Body (the 'TMB').

The TMB found that the United States had failed to demonstrate serious damage to the United States domestic industry. Although further consultations took place between the United States and Costa Rica in November 1995, no agreement was reached as to the removal or compensation for the measure. In spring of 1996 Costa Rica sought a panel to resolve the dispute. On 8 November 1996, the panel found that the United States violated its obligations under Article 6.2 and 6.4 of the ATC by imposing a restriction on Costa Rican exports without having demonstrated that serious damage or actual threat thereof was caused by such imports to the United States' domestic industry.[23] Further, the United States was found to have violated its obligations under Article 6.6(d) of the ATC by not granting the more favourable treatment to Costa Rican re-imports contemplated by that sub-paragraph.[24] The panel also found that the United States violated its obligations under Article 2.4 of the ATC by imposing a restriction in a manner inconsistent with its obligations under Article 6 of the ATC.[25] Finally, the panel held that the United States violated its obligations under Article X:2 of the General Agreement on Tariffs and Trade 1994 (the 'General Agreement') and Article 6.10 of the ATC by setting the start of the restraint period on the date of the request for consultations, rather than the subsequent date of publication of information about the restraint.[26]

Costa Rica was able to successfully defeat the United States, although it took over two years to vindicate their rights. Costa Rica was able to obtain the full benefit of the concessions negotiated in the ATC. However, the US industry received the full benefit of the safeguard, because it remained in effect throughout the WTO litigation of the issue. An important consideration in an analysis of this dispute is whether the safeguard would have expired if Costa Rica had not asserted its WTO rights.

B. Brazil – Export Financing Programme for Aircraft

C. Canada – Measures Affecting the Export of Civilian Aircraft

Brazil and Canada have been involved in an interesting pair of cases involving export subsidies to their respective aircraft industries. In the case brought by Canada against Brazil, Canada alleged that the Brazilian aircraft maker, Embraer, received prohibited export subsidies in the form of interest rate equalization bonds issued under the Programme for the Financing of Exports (PROEX). A panel found that Brazil's PROEX programme indeed conferred prohibited export subsidies and ordered Brazil to withdraw the GATT-inconsistent subsidies.[27] Brazil appealed the panel decision to the Appellate Body, which upheld the panel's finding, although modifying other aspects of the report. Brazil then took steps to implement the recommendations of the DSB. However, Brazil continued to issue the bonds at issue after the Appellate Body Report, and Canada requested that the same panel review the implementation of the DSB's recommendations and rulings. The panel found that Brazil's PROEX programme was still inconsistent with the prohibition on export subsidies of the Agreement on Subsidies and Countervailing Measures (SCM Agreement).[28]

Brazil appealed the second panel ruling to the Appellate Body, arguing, *inter alia*, that although bond payments made after the ruling were GATT-inconsistent, since they were based on commitments made before the ruling, they could not be prohibited. The Appellate Body ruled that Brazil did not meet its burden of proof on the issue and therefore its continued bond payments under the PROEX programme was not consistent with its WTO commitments.[29] Canada requested from the Appellate Body authorization for retaliatory action against Brazil and Brazil requested that the matter be sent to arbitration. On 28 August 2000 the Arbitrators decided that the suspension by Canada applying tariff concessions to Brazil covering trade in a maximum amount of C$344.2 million per year would constitute appropriate countermeasures.[30] Canada now has the option of retaliating against Brazil or continuing to attempt to negotiate a mutually satisfactory resolution. In the companion case, Brazil successfully argued to a panel, as affirmed by the Appellate Body, that Canada was providing prohibited subsidies to its aircraft producer, Bombardier, through the Technology Partnerships Canada (TPC) programme and the Canada Account programme.[31] Canada made substantial changes in its programmes and the subsequent panel challenge and appeal to the Appellate Body by Brazil resulted in findings that Brazil had not demonstrated that Canada's revised programmes are inconsistent with the SCM Agreement.[32]

These cases illustrate several of the points made in the previous section. First, both complaining parties won their initial cases. Second, the larger developing countries are fully capable of participating effectively in all aspects of the dispute settlement process. This includes the ability to use the long time periods involved in litigating matters to conclusion through multiple Panel and Appellate Body reviews. Third, the implementation process needs to be improved. Both countries were found to have provided prohibited export subsidies, but only Canada modified its programme to become GATT-consistent. Brazil made some changes in the PROEX programme after it was found to be inconsistent with the SCM Agreement. It took several months longer for a panel and the Appellate Body to rule that the changes in the programme made by Brazil were still not in compliance with its WTO obligations.

It is each WTO member's sovereign right to decide whether to comply with its obligations under the agreements. However, the extensive time periods needed to authorize retaliation in instances where measures are found inconsistent with WTO rules is a weakness in the system that should be corrected. Such structural problems should be addressed in a new round of multilateral trade negotiations.

D. Turkey – Restrictions on Imports of Textile and Clothing Products

In this case, the government of India claimed that the unilateral imposition of quantitative restrictions by Turkey in 1995–96, on imports of a broad range of textile and clothing products, was inconsistent with Turkey's obligations under Articles XI and XIII of GATT 1994 and were not justified under Article XXIV of GATT 1994, which does not provide for the imposition of discriminatory quantitative restrictions. India also considered the restrictions, imposed in order to comply with the Turkey–EU partnership agreement, to be inconsistent with Turkey's obligations under Article 2 of the World Trade Organization Agreement on Textiles and Clothing (ATC). India alleged that the restrictions imposed by Turkey nullified and impaired the benefits accruing to India under the Agreement on Textiles and Clothing, GATT 1994, and the WTO Agreement.[33]

The panel and Appellate Body agreed that the restrictions imposed by Turkey were inconsistent with Articles XI and XIII of the GATT 1994 and Article 2.4 of the ATC and as such impaired benefits to India.[34] After conducting negotiations, India and Turkey concluded a mutual agreement with respect to the reasonable period of time for Turkey's implementation of the recommendations and rulings of the panel and Appellate Body.[35]

This case serves as a prime example of a developing country filing and winning a case. In this instance the dispute settlement system worked to secure the rights of its members. Unfortunately, however, this case also serves to highlight again the problem that resolution and remedy can take an extremely long time during which countries are being denied benefits and injured without recourse. This case began on 10 March 1996 (WT/DS34/1) with India's consultation request. The final Appellate Body decision came down in late 1999 and the mutual agreement cited above occurred in 2000, while full implementation and compliance will not take effect until 2001–2. The reality of waiting 5–6 years for relief from measures that are found to be GATT-inconsistent is unacceptable. This failure of the system to produce timely results must be addressed in the next round of multilateral trade negotiations.

CONCLUSIONS AND SUGGESTED ACTION

Developing countries consider that the WTO has failed to provide real substance or meaning, other than longer transition periods, for the 'special and deferential treatment' provisions of the GATT. Developing nations have in fact come to expect that the WTO system will not provide them with the 'special and deferential' treatment which they should be accorded.

Based upon our analysis of the matters concerning developing countries in the WTO dispute settlement process, we have drawn the conclusions summarized below:

1. Complainants win almost all of the matters that reach full panel and appellate body review;
2. The consultation process appears to be a useful device for countries to vent their concerns about trade problems without public scrutiny;
3. Case-by-case cost–benefit analysis is necessary to balance the competing political, economic and other considerations that impact trade matters;
4. With a few exceptions, only the largest developing countries are effectively participating, leaving over half the membership outside the system. Developing countries are unfamiliar with the system. Two of three panels involving only developing countries were decided on procedural grounds, not the merits;
5. The process often takes far too long, resulting in significant, proven trade barriers remaining in place for several years while the process grinds on;
6. Despite the problems with the system, many developing countries are using the DSU successfully against both developing and developed countries;
7. The WTO should enhance the newly created Advocacy Office; and
8. There should be broader use of technology to improve developing country participation in the WTO.

APPENDIX 1   WTO DISPUTE SETTLEMENT ACTIONS INVOLVING DEVELOPING COUNTRIES

Respondent and Case Number	Complainant	Result
Complaints by developed countries against developing country members		
A. Active panels		
Thailand, antidumping duties (metal products) (DS122)	Japan, EU, U.S. reserved rights	Thailand has requested the Appellate Body to review the Panel report
Argentina, bovine hides (DS155)	EU	Panel established
Argentina, import measures (footwear) (DS164)	U.S., EU	Panel established
India, motor vehicles (DS146, 175)	U.S., Japan, EU	Panel established

Respondent and Case Number	Complainant	Result
Argentina, antidumping (card-board and ceramic floor tiles) (DS189)	EU	Panel established
Chile, swordfish (DS193)	EU	Panel established
Philippines, motor vehicles (DS195)	U.S.	Panel established
B. The panel and appellate review process has been completed		
Brazil, aircraft (DS46)	Canada	Brazil revised laws, but panel found revisions did not comply with Subsidies Agreement; retaliation authorized
India, patent protection for pharmaceutical and agricultural products (DS50)	U.S.	India revised its legislation
Indonesia, automobiles (DS54, DS55, DS59, DS64)	U.S., EU, Japan	Indonesia reformed its automobile policy
Korea, alcoholic beverages (DS75, DS84)	U.S.	Korea amended its legislation
India, patent protection for pharmaceutical and agricultural products (DS79)	EU	India revised its legislation
Chile, alcoholic beverages (DS87)	EU	Chile amended its tax law
India – quantitative restrictions (DS90)	U.S.	India modified its QR regime in some instances and several measures expired without renewal
Korea, safeguard measure (dairy) (DS98)	EU	Korean safeguard not in compliance with WTO agreement
Mexico, antidumping (corn syrup) (DS101)	U.S.	Mexican antidumping process inconsistent with WTO agreement
Chile, alcoholic beverages (DS109, DS110 only – see DS87)	EU	Chile amended its tax law
Argentina, safeguard measures (footwear) (DS121)	EU; U.S.	Argentina safeguard not in compliance with WTO agreement
Mexico, antidumping (corn syrup) (DS132)	U.S.	Mexican antidumping process inconsistent with WTO agreement

Respondent and Case Number	Complainant	Result
Korea, Government Procurement (DS163)	U.S.	Korean procuring entity not covered by GPA
C. Settlement has been notified or is apparent		
Korea, shelf-life (DS5)	U.S.	Settlement reached bilaterally. Parties negotiated an agreement on shelf-life of imported products
Korea, bottled water (DS20)	Canada, U.S.	Settlement reached bilaterally. Korea agreed to take steps to remove law and regulation.
Hungary, export subsidies (agriculture) (DS35)	Canada, Australia, New Zealand, U.S.	Mutually agreed solution based on waive for Hungary
Pakistan, patent protection for pharmaceutical and agricultural chemical products (DS36)	U.S., EU	Settlement reached bilaterally. Pakistan agreed to implement intellectual property ordinances protecting complainant rights.
Korea, telecommunications (DS40)	EU	Settlement reached bilaterally
Turkey, taxation of foreign film revenues (DS43)	U.S.; Canada reserved rights	Settlement reached bilaterally. Turkey agreed to equalize tax on box office between foreign and domestic films.
Philippines, pork and poultry (DS74, DS102)	U.S., EU, Canada	Settlement reached. Philippines agreed to modify TRQ and other regulations.
Argentina, textiles and footwear (DS56, DS77)	U.S.	Argentina reduced taxes
India – quantitative restrictions (DS91, DS92, DS93, DS94, DS96)	Australia, Canada, Switzerland, EU, New Zealand	India modified its QR regime in some instances and several measures expired without renewal
D. Consultation requested		
Korea, inspection of agricultural products (DS3, DS41)	U.S.	Consultations – no panel requested
Brazil, automobiles (DS51, DS52, DS65, DS81)	Japan, U.S., EU	Consultations – no panel requested

Respondent and Case Number	Complainant	Result
Mexico, customs valuation (DS53)	EU	Consultations – no panel requested
Pakistan, hides, skins and leather (DS107)	EU	Consultations – no panel requested
Brazil, import payment terms (DS116)	EU	Consultations – no panel requested
India, export commodities (DS120)	EU	Consultations – no panel requested
India, import restrictions (DS149)	EU	Consultations – no panel requested
India, customs duties (DS150)	EU	Consultations – no panel requested
Argentina, antidumping (drill bits) (DS157)	EU	Consultations – no panel requested
Hungary, safeguard on steel products (DS159)	Czech Republic	Consultations – no panel requested
Korea, beef imports (DS161, DS169)	U.S.; Canada, Australia New Zealand reserved rights	Consultations – no panel requested
Argentina, patent protection for pharmaceuticals (DS171)	U.S.	Consultations – no panel requested
Brazil, import licensing (DS183)	EU	Consultations – no panel requested
Argentina, patent protection (DS196)	U.S.	Consultations – no panel requested
Brazil, minimum import prices (DS197)	U.S.	Consultations – no panel requested
Romania, minimum import prices (DS198)	U.S.	Consultations – no panel requested
Brazil, patent protection (DS199)	U.S.	Consultations – no panel requested
Mexico, live swine (DS203)	U.S.	Consultations – no panel requested
Mexico, telecommunications services (DS204)	U.S.	Consultations – no panel requested

Complaints by developing countries against developed country members

A. Active panels

EU, antidumping duties (bed-linen) (DS141)	India; Egypt	Panel found EU methodology was inconsistent with AD Agreement in some respects; EU appealed
US, textiles (cotton yarn) (DS192)	Pakistan; India reserved rights	Panel established
U.S., antidumping measures (steel plate) (DS206)	India	Panel established

Respondent and Case Number	Complainant	Result
B. The panel and appellate review process has been completed		
US, gasoline (DS2, DS4)	Venezuela, Brazil	U.S. revised its regulations concerning the baseline for imported gasoline
US, underwear (DS24)	Costa Rica	U.S. measure found inconsistent with agreement; measure expired
US, wool shirts (DS33)	India	U.S. withdrew measure before panel concluded its work
US, shrimp (DS58, DS61)	Malaysia, Thailand, Pakistan, India, Philippines	U.S. issued revised guidelines to implement law; complainants requested original panel to review implementation
EU, poultry (DS69)	Brazil; Thailand reserved rights	EU acted inconsistently with Art. 5.5 of Agreement on Agriculture concerning safeguard duty rate
Canada, aircraft (DS70, DS71)	Brazil	Canada revised program; Brazil appealed and lost in Appellate Body
C. Settlement has been notified or is apparent		
US, wool coats (DS32)	India	US restraint removed
US, antidumping investigation on fresh or chilled tomatoes (DS49)	Mexico	Investigation suspended
D. Consultation requested		
US, brooms (DS78)	Colombia	Consultations – no panel requested
US, countervailing measure (salmon) (DS97)	Chile	Consultations – no panel requested
EU, bananas (DS105)	Panama	Consultations – no panel requested; same measures challenged in DS27
US, tariff rate quota (groundnuts) (DS111)	Argentina	Consultations – no panel requested
EU, import duties (rice) (DS134)	India	Consultations – no panel requested
EU, anti-dumping investigation (cotton fabrics) (DS140)	India	Consultations – no panel requested

Respondent and Case Number	Complainant	Result
EU, special & differential treatment (coffee) (DS154)	Brazil	Consultations – no panel requested
South Africa, antidumping (pharmaceuticals) (DS168)	India	Consultations – no panel requested
EU, special & differential treatment (soluble coffee) (DS209)	Brazil	Consultations – no panel requested

Complaints by developing countries against developing country members

A. Active panels

Nicaragua, tax on imports from Honduras and Colombia (I) (DS188)	Colombia; Costa Rica, Honduras reserved rights	Panel established

B. The panel and appellate review process has been completed

Brazil, coconut (DS22)	Philippines	Provisions of agreements relied upon by Philippines inapplicable to the dispute
Turkey, textiles (DS29, DS34, DS47)	India, Thailand, Hong Kong	Turkey implementing panel report and agreed to increase India quotas
Guatemala, cement (DS60)	Mexico	Panel found Guatemala initiated antidumping investigation on insufficient evidence; Appellate Body reversed because Mexico did not identify the measure complained about

C. Settlement has been notified or is apparent

Malaysia, polyethylene and polypropylene (DS1)	Singapore	Malaysia modified laws
Venezuela, antidumping, OCTG (DS23)	Mexico	Venezuela terminated investigation
Guatemala, antidumping, cement (DS156)	Mexico	Mexico refiled case it lost (DS60); Guatemala then removed the measure
Colombia, safeguard (polyester) (DS181)	Thailand	Thailand withdrew request after Colombia terminated safeguard
Argentina, safeguards (cotton fabrics) (DS190)	Brazil; Pakistan, Paraguay reserved rights	Panel established to review Argentina's transitional safeguards

Respondent and Case Number	Complainant	Result
D. Consultation requested		
Brazil, coconut (DS30)	Sri Lanka	See DS22 above
Peru, countervailing duty investigation (buses) (DS112)	Brazil	Consultations – no panel requested
Argentina, subsidies (footwear) (DS123)	Indonesia	Consultations – no panel requested
Ecuador, antidumping (cement) (DS182)	Mexico	Consultations – no panel requested
Trinidad and Tobago, pasta (DS185)	Costa Rica	Consultations – no panel requested
Trinidad and Tobago, antidumping (pasta) (DS187)	Costa Rica	Consultations – no panel requested
Ecuador, antidumping (cement) (DS191)	Mexico	Consultations – no panel requested
Nicaragua, imports from Honduras and Colombia (II) (DS201)	Honduras	Consultations – no panel requested
Egypt, import prohibition on canned tuna (DS205)	Thailand	Consultations – no panel requested
Chile, price band system and safeguard measures on certain agricultural products (DS207)	Argentina	Consultations – no panel requested
Turkey, antidumping duties on steel and iron pipe fittings (DS208)	Brazil	Consultations – no panel requested
Egypt, antidumping duties on steel rebar (DS211)	Turkey	Consultations – no panel requested

Complaints by both developed and developing country members

A. Active panels

B. The panel and appellate review process has been completed

EU, bananas (DS16, DS27)	Ecuador, Guatemala, Honduras, Mexico, U.S.	EU banana regime found not fully consistent with WTO; U.S. and Ecuador authorized to suspend concessions to EU

C. Settlement has been notified or is apparent

EU, scallops (DS7, DS12, DS14)	Peru, Chile, Canada	Panel established, but EU adopted regulations modifying existing laws

| EU, grains (DS9, DS13, DS17, DS25) | Thailand, Uruguay, Canada, U.S. | Panel established, but EU implemented new regulations |
| Hungary, export subsidies (DS35) | Argentina, Canada, U.S., Australia, New Zealand, Thailand | Panel established. Settlement agreed, and complaint will be withdrawn after Hungary obtains waiver of WTO obligations |

D. Consultation requested

| EU Bananas II (DS158) | Guatemala, Panama, Honduras, Mexico, U.S. | Consultations – no panel requested |

Notes

1. See Marrakesh Agreement Establishing the World Trade Organization, Art. III, Legal Instruments – Results of the Uruguay Round, Vol. 31, 33 I.L.M. 81(1994) (hereinafter WTO Agreements).
2. See Adamantopoulus (1997).
3. WTO Agreement, Annex 2, Understanding on Rule and Procedures Governing the Settlement of Disputes (hereinafter, DSU), Art. 3, para. 2.
4. DSU Article 3–5. For a more detailed examination of operation of DSU panels, see Stewart and Karpel (2000).
5. DSU Article 6(16).
6. Stewart and Karpel (2000).
7. DSU Article 16(4).
8. DSU Article 17, 19.
9. *Japan – Taxes on Alcoholic Beverages*, WT/DS8/15, WT/DS10/15, WT/DS11/13 (14 Feb. 1997); *European Communities – Regime for the Importation, Sale and Distribution of Bananas*, WT/DS27/15 (7 Jan. 1998); *EU – Beef Hormones*, WT/DS26/14, WT/DS48/13 (29 May 1998). However, *Brazil – Export Financing Programme for Aircraft*, WT/DS46/R, adopted 20 August 1999, as modified by the Appellate Body Report, and the related cases establish ninety days for implementation under the SCM Agreement.
10. The authors gratefully acknowledge the assistance of Patrick Macrory, whose unpublished manuscript on developing country issues for a seminar for Egyptian trade officials provided thoughtful inspiration.
11. Robert Hudec (1990).
12. Ibid, p. 20.
13. Ibid, p. 24.
14. The Annex is drawn from *Overview of the State-of-Play of WTO Disputes*, 13 December 2000, WTO official document from http://www.wto.org/english/tratop_e/dispu_e/stplay_e.doc
15. B. Lal Das (1998).

16. See, Communication from Bangladesh, *Integrating Least-Developed Countries into the Global Economy: Proposals for a Comprehensive New Plan of Action in the Context of the Third WTO Ministerial Conference*, WT/GC/W/251, 13 July 1999.
17. Guatemala cement (Mexico), WT/DS60; Brazil desiccated coconuts (Philippines), WT/DS22.
18. Guatemala cement (Mexico), WT/DS156; Brazil desiccated coconut (Sri Lanka), WT/DS30.
19. Under the GATT system, the US took the EU to the dispute settlement process over their preferential treatment of bananas from African, Caribbean and Pacific (ACP) countries. When the panel ruled in favour of the US, the EU blocked the adoption of the report, resulting in its non-adoption. Similarly, under the new WTO system, in the case of Nicaragua against the US, the ruling was made against the US, who then refused to implement the recommendations on the grounds that they were against its vital interests.
20. *United States – Standards for Reformulated and Conventional Gasoline*, WT/DS2, 19 August 1997.
21. *United States – Import Prohibition of Certain Shrimp and Shrimp Products*, WT/DS58/AB/R, 12 October 1998.
22. *European Communities – Regime for the Importation, Sale and Distribution of Bananas*, WT/DS27/15, 7 Jan. 1998.
23. *United States – Restrictions on Imports of Cotton and Man-Made Fibre Underwear*, WT/DS24/R, 8 Nov. 1996 at paras. 7.52 and 7.55.
24. Panel Report, para. 7.59.
25. Panel Report, para. 7.71.
26. Panel Report, para. 7.69. On 11 November 1996, Costa Rica filed and later won an additional ruling which overturned the reasoning, but not the substance of the panel's fourth finding. *United States – Restrictions on Imports of Cotton and Man-Made Fibre Underwear*, WT/DS24/AB/R, 11 Feb. 1997.
27. *Brazil – Export Financing Programme for Aircraft*, WT/DS46/R, adopted 20 August 1999, as modified by the Appellate Body Report.
28. WT/DS46/RW, 9 May 2000.
29. WT/DS46/AB/RW, 21 July 2000.
30. WT/DS46/ARB, 28 August 2000.
31. *Canada – Measures Affecting the Export of Civilian Aircraft*, WTDS70/R, adopted 20 August 1999, as modified by the Appellate Body Report.
32. WTDS70/RW, 9 May 2000, as modified by the Appellate Body Report, WTDS70/AB/RW, 21 July 2000.
33. *Turkey – Restrictions on Imports of Textile and Clothing Products.*, WT/DS34/AB/R, 22 October 1999.
34. Ibid, p.18.
35. WT/DS34/10, 18 January 2000.

Bibliography

ADAMANTOPOULUS, KONSTANTINOS (ed.) (1997) *An Anatomy of the World Trade Organization* (Kluwer Law International).

BARSHEFSKY, CHARLENE (2000) 'U.S. Trade Policy and the Trading System', speech delivered to the School of Advanced International Studies, Washington, D.C., 2 March.

DAS, B. LAL (1998) *The WTO Agreements: Deficiencies, Imbalances and Required Changes* (Third World Network).

FINGER, J. MICHAEL and PHILLIP SCHULER (1999) *Implementation of Uruguay Round Commitments: The Development Challenge*, WTO/World Bank Conference on Developing Countries in a Millennium Round, 20–21 September 1999.

General Accounting Office (GAO) (2000) *World Trade Organization: US Experience to Date in Dispute Settlement System*, GAO/NSIAD/OGC-00-196BR, June 2000.

HOEKMAN, BERNARD M. and PETROS MAVROIDIS (1999) *Enforcing Multilateral Commitments: Dispute Settlement and Developing Countries*, WTO/World Bank Conference on Developing Countries in a Millennium Round, 20–21 September 1999.

HORN, HENRIK and PETROS MAVROIDIS (1999) *Remedies in the WTO Dispute Settlement System and Developing Country Interests*, paper for the World Bank, 11 April 1999.

HUDEC, ROBERT (1999) 'The New WTO Dispute Settlement Procedure: An Overview of the First Three Years', 8 *Minnesota Journal of Global Trade* 1, pp. 3–15 (Winter 1999).

McGRORY, MARY (1999) 'Labor's Battle in Seattle', *Washington Post*, 2 December 1999, p. A03.

STEWART, TERENCE P. and AMY A. KARPEL (2000) 'Review of the Dispute Settlement Understanding: Operation of Panels', *Law and Policy in International Business*, vol. 31, no. 3.

'UK Seeks Ministerial Meeting in New Year to Review WTO Process', *Inside US Trade*, vol. 17, no. 51, 24 December.

ZEKOS, GEORGIS I. (1999) 'An Examination of GATT/WTO Arbitration Procedures', *Dispute Resolution Journal*, November 1999.

Documents from the World Trade Organization

About the WTO, website at http://www.wto.org/wto/inbrief/

Communication from Bangladesh, *Integrating Least-Developed Countries into the Global Economy: Proposals for a Comprehensive New Plan of Action in the Context of the Third WTO Ministerial Conference*, WT/GC/W/251, 13 July 1999.

Final Act Embodying the Results of Uruguay Round of Multilateral Trade Negotiations, 15 April 1994, Legal Instruments – Results of the Uruguay Round vol. 1 (1994), 33 I.L.M. 1125 (1994).

Marrakesh Agreement Establishing the World Trade Organization, art. III, Legal Instruments – Results of the Uruguay Round vol. 31, 33 I.L.M. 81 (1994).

Overview of the State-of-Play of WTO Disputes, 22 June 2000, WTO official document from http://www.wto.org/english/tratop_e/dispu_e/stplay_e.doc

WTO Agreement, Annex 2, Understanding on Rule and Procedures Governing the Settlement of Disputes.

WTO Dispute Settlement Proceedings

Brazil – Countervailing Duties on Imports of Desiccated Coconut and Coconut Milk Powder from Sri Lanka, WT/DS30 (20 March 1997).

Brazil – Measures Affecting Desiccated Coconut, WT/DS22 (20 March 1997).

Brazil – Export Financing Programme for Aircraft, WT/DS46/R, adopted 20 August 1999, as modified by the Appellate Body Report.

Canada – Measures Affecting the Export of Civilian Aircraft, WT/DS70/R, adopted 20 August 1999, as modified by the Appellate Body Report, WTDS70/AB/R, adopted 20 August 1999.

European Communities – Regime for the Importation, Sale and Distribution of Bananas, WT/DS27/15 (7 January 1998).

European Communities – Beef Hormones, WT/DS26/14, WT/DS48/13 (29 May 1998).

Guatemala – Definitive Anti-Dumping Measure regarding Grey Portland Cement from Mexico, WT/DS156 (panel established).

Guatemala – Anti-Dumping Investigation Regarding Imports of Portland Cement from Mexico, WT/DS60 (25 November 1998).

Indonesia – Certain Measures Affecting the Automobile Industry, adopted 23 July 1998, WT/DS54/R, WT/DS55/R, WT/DS59/R, WT/DS64/R.

Japan – Taxes on Alcoholic Beverages, WT/DS8/15, WT/DS10/15, WT/DS11/13 (14 February 1997).

Turkey – Restrictions on Imports of Textile and Clothing Products, WT/DS34/AB/R (22 October 1999).

United States – Standards for Reformulated and Conventional Gasoline, WT/DS2 (19 August 1997).

United States – Import Prohibition of Certain Shrimp and Shrimp Products, WT/DS58/AB/R (12 October 1998).

United States – Restrictions on Imports of Cotton and Man-Made Fibre Underwear, WT/DS24/R (8 November 1996).

United States – Restrictions on Imports of Cotton and Man-Made Fibre Underwear, WT/DS24/AB/R (11 February 1997).

6 The Growing Participation in Multilateral Services Liberalization by Latin America and the Caribbean

*Sherry M. Stephenson**

INTRODUCTION

The General Agreement on Trade in Services (GATS) under the World Trade Organization (WTO) marked its fifth year of operation in January 2000. This important millennium date provides a nice benchmark from which to evaluate what has been accomplished by Latin America and the Caribbean with respect to the liberalization of trade in services at the multilateral level, both during and since the Uruguay Round of Multilateral Trade Negotiations (1986–94), and in particular to examine what role countries of the region have played in the services area.

After a controversial launch and difficult negotiations during the Uruguay Round, since the coming into effect of the GATS in January 1995, discussions and negotiations on trade in services have progressed in a relatively smooth manner. Witness to this are the successful conclusions of the Agreement on Basic Telecommunications in February 1997 and the Financial Services Agreement in December 1997. From an initial attitude of scepticism and mistrust, countries in Latin America and the Caribbean have on the whole been actively participating in these discussions and have undertaken additional commitments, some of them market-opening in nature, at the multilateral level.

As mandated in Article XIX.1 of the GATS, a new round of services negotiations was officially launched in February 2000, with the objective

---

* The author would like to acknowledge an enormous debt of gratitude to Soonhwa Yi for her valuable research assistance and input into this paper and Maryse Robert for helpful comments on the paper.

of furthering the progressive liberalization of trade in services. This launch met with almost complete concordance among WTO members, developed and developing alike, on the negotiating agenda. Latin America and the Caribbean were very much present in this general consensus on negotiating principles and objectives.

This chapter sheds light on the progress towards services liberalization achieved by Latin America and the Caribbean during the Uruguay Round negotiations and in the first five years of the operation of the GATS. It also examines their participation in the current multilateral services negotiations (GATS 2000), and reviews their submissions to these negotiations.

THE URUGUAY ROUND SERVICES NEGOTIATIONS

In the Western Hemisphere, trade in services comprises 25 per cent of total exports and over 60 per cent of total GDP on average. Trade in services is a major foreign exchange earner for smaller economies in the hemisphere. Many Caribbean and Central American countries rely heavily on trade in services, and services exports are larger than merchandise exports for two-thirds of these small nations where for some they can be double the value of goods exports.[1] In terms of economic activity, 54 per cent of the total labour force in the Western Hemisphere is engaged in some form of service activity: 39 per cent of male labour force and 69 per cent of female labour force, respectively.[2]

However, despite the significance of trade in services, negotiations during the Uruguay Round were quite contentious. Under the Punta del Este Declaration, services negotiations were separated from those of goods, and the two were launched separately in September 1986. Given the fact that the major exporters of services in the world economy have traditionally been developed countries; the European Union member countries and the United States, developing countries perceived that only developed countries would benefit from services liberalization. This perception led to their strong opposition to the launch of services negotiations, only brokered by the fact that both agriculture and textiles were also included as negotiating agenda items. Such resistance was transformed into reluctance and hesitation, once negotiations were initiated. Rather passive participation on the part of developing countries during the Uruguay Round resulted in a very low number of specific commitments and a small degree of openness for services trade.[3]

One of the main reasons that negotiations were so divisive was because of the lack of knowledge over what was being discussed. Services trade represented a large unknown and uncharted area in the realm of multilateral diplomacy. Thus most participants simply muddled through with little knowledge. Two factors contributed to undermine most countries' active involvement in the services negotiations. Those were notably: the paucity of statistics on trade in services, and the lack of economic studies estimating the economic impact of services liberalization. These two factors deserve further comment.

Deficiency of Statistical Data

It is widely acknowledged that services negotiators face a deficiency of available statistics on trade in services. The statistical paucity derives from the divergence between the GATS legal framework and the classification that has been adopted for services activities, and the traditional statistical framework within which tradable data are collected and reported. Importantly, the GATS legal framework does not match the concepts and categories used by statisticians. Currently, the only available source of data on services trade (cross-border transactions) on a global basis is the Balance of Payments (BOP) statistics collected by the International Monetary Fund (IMF) and found in the fifth edition of the IMF Balance of Payments Manual. These data, as all BOP data, are based on the concept of transactions between residents and non-residents. However, the concept of services trade under the GATS goes beyond this.

First the GATS defines services transactions as one of four possible modes: mode 1 being cross-border trade; mode 2, consumption abroad; mode 3, commercial presence; and mode 4, movement of natural persons. Thus the GATS covers not only transactions between service producers and consumers in two different countries (residents and non-residents) but also those transactions taking place between service producers and consumers of different nationalities located within the same territory or country. It also covers the movement of natural persons to provide a service abroad. The source of service transactions can thus be not only differences in location, but also in ownership, control and nationality. The few number of categories for which data are collected and reported within the fifth edition of the IMF/BOP Manual is therefore limited to cross-border transactions under modes 1 and 2.

Data on mode 3 are taken to be those sales by foreign affiliates or foreign affiliate trade (FAT) within a host country. However, the FAT definition of foreign ownership does not coincide with the GATS which is broader; similarly, the services classification used by FAT does not concord with the classification of the GATS. With a view to solving these problems, a set of guidelines for collecting data on foreign affiliates trade in services (FATS) has been developed.[4] However, at the present time only a few developed countries have begun to collect data on sales by foreign affiliates under these guidelines, and very little is as yet comparable. Data on mode 4 are partially available under the category of worker compensation in the balance of payments accounts. However these data do not include self-employed workers, and they group together workers in both the goods and service sectors, thus including transactions that are not related to service supply.[5]

Second, there is a divergence between the GATS framework and that of traditional statistics with respect to classification. The current classification scheme used by statisticians for the collection of data is far less disaggregated than that for services products set out in the classification list adopted by the WTO for the purpose of services negotiations (found in GSN/W/120). This difference is most flagrant with respect to telecommunications and financial services, where practically no detail in breakdown exists for the collection of trade statistics. Third, a divergence exists with respect to the actual service categories included in the various classification systems. There is a lack of concordance between some of the services categories used by the IMF and/or in the framework of the FAT, and those listed in the GSN/W/120.[6]

Due to the paucity of available statistics on services trade, services negotiators, especially those from developing countries, were not able to determine which of their service sectors was important for trade (export-oriented) or relatively less competitive (import-competing) for the purpose of requesting and offering GATS commitments. This contributed to their lack of preparation for the negotiations and ultimately undermined the ability of these countries to play an active role in the services negotiations during the Uruguay Round.[7]

Lack of Economic Studies

In terms of economic studies of the impact of services trade liberalization, these have been extremely difficult to carry out due to lack of data and the difficulties involved in trying to estimate price equivalents for the non-tariff type of barriers that restrict service providers. Barriers to services trade have been broadly placed into two categories for the purpose of the services negotiations: restrictions on market access (GATS Article XVI); and derogations on national treatment (GATS Article XVII).[8] These non-tariff barriers are hard to measure, which also means that the impact of liberalization is not easily captured. This difficulty in measuring economic impact of services liberalization deterred services negotiators for quite some time. Over the recent past, some pioneering studies have been undertaken to measure and quantify non-tariff barriers in selected service sectors.[9]

Commitments by Latin America and the Caribbean

The sceptical attitude towards the opening of services markets described above was initially manifested by Latin America and the Caribbean and resulted in very little participation in the Uruguay Round on specific commitments undertaken on trade in services.[10] Half of the countries made commitments on less than 40 of the 155 service sub-sectors defined for the purpose of the negotiations. The large majority of commitments were made in five of the eleven principal service sectors, namely: tourism (32 countries), financial services (30), communications (28), business services (26), and transport (25), while the other six sectors were practically ignored.[11] Table 6.1 sets out the number of service commitments undertaken by countries of the Western Hemisphere (Latin America and the Caribbean plus the United States and Canada) at the conclusion of the Uruguay Round. However, this numerical listing does not take into account the degree of actual liberalization or market opening contained in the GATS schedules. The number of commitments listed in the table is a reflection of the count of the total number of entries made in an individual schedule, and groups together measures with varying degrees of openness, from those with no restrictions to those with very restrictive limitations. The list even includes entries in national schedules that were listed as 'unbound'. The numerous ways in which the data can be presented makes deciphering the value of the commitments tricky.

A more in-depth analysis in this area relies upon a measurement tool that can provide a better evaluation of the actual significance of GATS commitments, particularly from the perspective of trade liberalization, or openness, achieved. The most objective measurement of openness that can be applied to the services area comes from examining the number of sub-sectors/ modes of supply in which a country has bound itself to apply no restrictions and has therefore listed 'none' for both market access and national treatment.[12] This measurement is the most significant one in evaluating GATS commitments because it takes into account in an objective manner the real degree of openness of the scheduled measures by capturing the number of bound commitments that a country has made that reflect fully liberalized access, with no limitations on either national treatment or market access attached. It is obtained by taking the number of commitments for a given sub-sector and mode of supply without any limitations

Table 6.1   Number of GATS commitments made by Western Hemisphere
countries, 1994

Countries	Number of commitments	Countries	Number of commitments
Antigua & Barbuda	68	Haiti	64
Argentina	208	Honduras	64
Barbados	24	Jamaica	128
Belize	8	Mexico	252
Bolivia	24	Nicaragua	196
Brazil	156	Paraguay	36
Canada	352	Panama	208
Chile	140	Peru	96
Colombia	164	St. Kitts & Nevis	24
Costa Rica	52	St. Lucia	32
Dominica	20	St. Vincent & the	32
Dominican Republic	264	Grenadines	
Ecuador	140	Suriname	16
El Salvador	92	Trinidad & Tobago	68
Grenada	20	United States	384
Guatemala	40	Uruguay	96
Guyana	72	Venezuela	156

Source: WTO, National schedules of GATS commitments.

attached as a share of total possible GATS commitments. Such a measurement allows a more significant interpretation to be made of the liberalizing
extent of the commitments since it is devoid of weighing as well as of sub-
jective judgments. The method takes into account only those bound measures in both categories of market access and national treatment that
represent full liberalization of market access and non-discriminatory treatment for all service providers for a given service sub-sector/mode of
supply. Results from this method are shown in Table 6.2.

One Latin American country (Argentina) falls in the category of
'moderately open' with respect to the liberalizing content of its GATS
commitments. Significantly, more than two-thirds of Latin American and
Caribbean countries have committed to full market openness for less than
10 per cent of total possible service sub-sectors/modes of supply, and one-
half of these for less than 5 per cent. Thus, according to this measure, it
can be concluded that the extent of liberalization in the services area
achieved at the conclusion of the Uruguay Round in April 1994 by Latin
America and the Caribbean was quite limited. Part of this modest result

Table 6.2   Degree of services liberalization achieved in the GATS 1994: schedules of countries in the Western Hemisphere

Very high (100–60%)	Moderately high (<60–40%)	Moderate (<40–20%)	Moderately low (<20–10%)	Low (<10–5%)	Very low (<5%)	
		Argentina	Colombia	Antigua	Barbados	Belize
		Canada	Dominican	& Barbada	Bolivia	Brazil
		United	Republic	Chile	Costa Rica	Dominica
		States	Ecuador	Guyana	El Salvador	Honduras
			Jamaica	Haiti	Guatemala	Peru
			Mexico	Trinidad &	Paraguay	Suriname
			Nicaragua	Tobago	St. Kitts &	St. Vincent &
			Panama	Venezuela	Nevis	the
			Uruguay		St. Lucia	Grenadines

Notes: The degree of liberalization is calculated as a per centage of the number of commitments where no restrictions have been attached to both market access and national treatment for a specific services sub-sector and mode of supply out of total possible commitments. Countries are grouped into categories in the table without being ranked within those categories. Calculations have been done by the OAS Trade Unit based on the methodology developed by Hoekman (1995).

with respect to both a low number of specific commitments and a low degree of effective liberalization derives from the way the GATS itself was structured. GATS does not oblige WTO members to schedule a specified number of commitments, either in numerical terms or in terms of sectors covered. A country needs to make only one commitment in one sector to legitimize its acceptance of the Uruguay Round Final Act, a fact that explains the great deal of variance in the GATS schedules both in terms of number and coverage of commitments. Moreover, the GATS was structured as an agreement that emphasizes progressive liberalization; few countries (and no developing countries) during the Uruguay Round were asked to make commitments of any significant degree of actual market opening.

POST-URUGUAY ROUND PARTICIPATION IN WTO SERVICES NEGOTIATIONS

Following the opening of markets for goods through significant reductions of tariffs and non-tariff barriers over the period 1985–95, developing countries of the region began to turn their priority to the reform and liberalization of the service sector. This new emphasis has likewise been reflected in their heightened participation in the GATS, post-Uruguay Round. The section below highlights the commitments that Latin America and the Caribbean have undertaken in the WTO extended negotiations on basic telecommunications and financial services concluded in 1997. The significant success of both of these negotiations is largely a reflection of the fact that most of the governments involved, including Latin America and the Caribbean, saw the need to pursue reforms in these sectors, including liberalization, elimination of entry barriers, and the development of regulatory principles.

Basic Telecommunications

The vast bulk of the world's telecommunications market has been made subject to some form of competition with the entry into force of the Fourth Protocol of the GATS or the Agreement on Basic Telecommunication (ABT) in February 1998.[13] In these negotiations, twenty (20) Latin American and Caribbean countries made specific commitments, and all of these but Brazil also committed to adopt in whole or in part the Reference Paper on Pro-Competitive Regulatory Principles.[14]

According to Low and Mattoo (1999), 'specific commitments' made by a government may be categorized into four types: (i) less than 'status quo'; (ii) the 'status quo' level; (iii) further actual liberalization in the context of negotiations; and (iv) undertakings for future liberalization.[15] These categories are not mutually exclusive, but this distinction is useful in thinking about the relationship between WTO negotiations and the domestic liberalization process. In the Western Hemisphere most of the twenty-two participating governments scheduled commitments at the level of the 'status quo'. More commitments were undertaken for value-added services than for basic telecommunications; many undertook some form of commitment to allow competition in long-distance services.[16]

Several developing countries in the hemisphere participated in a new form of scheduling in these negotiations in the form of pre-commitments for future liberalization. For example, Argentina, Jamaica, and Venezuela scheduled to liberalize international services in the years 2000, 2001, and 2013 respectively. By means of such pre-commitments, countries can take advantage of the GATS to strike a balance between their reluctance to unleash competition immediately on protected national suppliers and their desire not to be held hostage in perpetuity either to the weakness of domestic industry or to pressure from vested interests.

Commonly listed limitations in the schedules are those on the number of suppliers, restrictions on the type of legal entity and limitations on the participation of foreign capital. For example, Argentina, Bolivia, Grenada and Jamaica, either do not allow foreign entry or have postponed it, as these countries are allowing newly privatized telecom companies to exploit fixed monopoly or duopoly concession terms for between six to ten years. The benefit of this type of conditional liberalization has been questioned by policy analysts.[17]

The GATS Telecom Reference Paper, negotiated as a voluntary accompaniment to the GATS Agreement on Basic Telecommunication, fosters competition in the telecom sector by providing pro-regulatory principles to curb the anti-competitive behaviour of telecom providers with monopolistic characteristics. These pro-competitive regulatory principles apply to a major supplier who has the ability to materially affect the terms in which others may participate in the market for basic telecommunications services (with respect to price or supply or both), or to abuse a dominant position as a result of control over essential facilities (that is, the public telecommunications transport network).[18]

In terms of actual regulatory practice, however, several countries in the hemisphere have established independent regulatory bodies for telecom services during the recent period. This is the case of Brazil (with Anatel being established in 1998 to supervise anti-competitive practices), as well as Argentina, Chile and Mexico who have established independent regulatory bodies in the form of CNC, Subtel and Cofetel, respectively.[19]

Financial Services

During the extended post-Uruguay Round negotiations on financial services, 102 WTO members concluded the Financial Services Agreements (FSA) in December 1997. Seventy (70) among them, accounting for 97 per cent of the world's financial services trade, submitted their improved schedules, bringing financial services under the GATS most-favoured-nation (MFN) principle.[20] These commitments entered into force through the acceptance of the Fifth Protocol in January 1999. Fifteen Latin American and Caribbean countries submitted newly improved schedules on financial services.[21] However, none of them accepted the Memorandum of Understanding on Financial Services that also resulted from the negotiations. The United States and Canada did.

Nonetheless, numerous improvements were made in the expanded commitments on financial services. Many Latin American countries moved to a more open stance with respect to the entry through foreign direct investment of foreign-owned banks and insurance companies.[22] Improved commitments highlight expanded coverage of commitments and the allowance of new entry in the form of subsidiaries for insurance and banking.

With respect to mode of supply, it is notable that most Latin American countries did not make commitments on modes 1, 2, or 4 in either the insurance or the banking sector (except for Uruguay). This posture, similar to that of other WTO developing members, was most likely promoted by a desire for retention of control over cross-border flows of capital, combined with regulatory caution. Several Latin American countries with respect to their 1994 GATS commitments have liberalized commercial presence, or mode 3, but investment is still made subject to ceiling levels. Brazil, Chile, Peru and Uruguay allow new entry of foreign subsidiaries in both insurance and banking (Brazil allowing up to 100 per cent ownership, upon approval) but this is made subject to decrees or authorizations.[23] Mexico increased the possibility of foreign participation or investment in the financial sector up to an overall 40 per cent, with a 10 per cent ceiling per individual foreign company in insurance and securities, and a 5 per cent ceiling for individual foreign companies in banking.

These patterns of varying degrees of commitments by mode may be interpreted as indications of considerable continued regulatory caution with respect to the financial sector and a marked reluctance to bind liberalization of cross-border trade in financial services. As a result, liberalization in the financial sector is concentrated primarily on mode 3, or commercial presence, while modes 1 and 2 are kept unbound. Also, while Canada and the US scheduled commitments at a 'status quo' level, many Latin American and Caribbean countries scheduled commitments at 'less than the status quo'. Others followed what is known as 'grandfathering', or the adoption of more stringent or restrictive conditions on market access or national treatment for new service suppliers than those that are applied to foreign companies already established in the market. This is the case of Brazil, which adopted a grandfathering measure for the banking sector.[24]

Regulatory reform is an important issue in the area of financial services, in order to allow for the implementation of liberalizing commitments. With respect to the acceptance of the Fifth Protocol, Brazil and the Dominican Republic reported that their financial systems were in need of regulatory reform, and that this would be a prerequisite for the ratification and acceptance of the Fifth Protocol. However, regulatory issues in the form of prudential and solvency requirements and financial safeguards continue to remain outside of the scope of the GATS, making it problematic to discuss either the content or the appropriateness of such measures in the WTO context.

The Understanding on Financial Services that accompanied the specific commitments under the Fifth Protocol is a scheduling convention to promote market access in financial services markets. It states that each member 'shall list in its schedule pertaining to financial services existing monopoly rights and shall endeavour to eliminate or reduce them'. WTO members that adopted the understanding (only Canada and the US in the Western Hemisphere) agreed that the Understanding should be placed on record as part of their commitments. However, the coverage of relevant obligations they adopted with respect to banking and insurance activities and auxiliary/advisory services (is limited to mostly modes 2 and 3).[25]

Post-Uruguay Round Work on Services and Latin America

Three articles of the GATS remained unfinished at the conclusion of the Uruguay Round, namely those related to safeguards (Article X), subsidies (Article XV) and government procurement (Article XIII). Since 1995, the Working Party on GATS Rules has been continuing discussions on these issues and attempting to develop rules in these areas, all of which are mandated by the GATS. On each issue, developed and developing WTO members tend to display at times considerable differences in their positions. Latin American countries have been active in the discussions, and in certain cases have submitted proposals.[26]

In the case of *safeguard disciplines*, the deadline for conclusion of the negotiations ongoing within the Working Party on GATS Rules has been extended from 15 December 2000 to 15 March 2002. While developed countries are reluctant to formalize disciplines on safeguards and tend to support a limited scope of action with respect to mode 1 only (cross-border trade), developing countries on the other hand continue to push strongly for the inclusion of language that is as broad as possible in this area, and have tended to make their willingness to further open their services markets contingent upon a functioning safeguard clause. Discussion has centred on whether safeguards should be general or only for specific commitments, if they should benefit all providers of services or only those companies controlled by nationals, on the type of emergency situations that would justify a safeguard, on the viability to define the criteria for injury and causality, and on what type of measure should be taken to carry out a safeguard action.[27]

Most Latin American and all Caribbean countries share the position that a functioning safeguard clause would be useful in the services area at the multilateral level, similar to what exists for goods in the GATT 1994. However, the questions of how to define these disciplines and over what modes they would apply and how, are still outstanding. Interestingly, the position held by Latin America on safeguards at the multilateral level is quite the opposite to that which the majority of these countries have manifested at the sub-regional level in the Western Hemisphere, where none of the integration agreements at present (with the exception of one) contain either a general safeguard provision or an operational safeguard clause for services trade.[28]

In the case of *subsidies*, GATS Article XV recognizes that subsidies may distort trade, but also that they may play an important role in development. It calls for negotiations to establish subsidy disciplines and to examine the case for countervailing remedies.[29] Current discussion on subsidies in the Working Party on GATS Rules is addressing nine basic themes: definition of domestic industry, the issue of acquired rights, the concept of 'like services', compensation, indicators and criteria for defining a subsidy, applicable measures, modal application, and the issue of 'unforeseen circumstances'.

Latin American countries have shown a certain enthusiasm and activism in developing multilateral disciplines on subsidies. Argentina jointly presented with Hong Kong China a communication on subsidy issues with a view to try and clarify some of the difficulties around the definition of a 'subsidy' in the services area, and what type of criteria are necessary in order to determine the harm resulting from the use of one.[30] Other Latin American countries, namely Chile, Colombia and Uruguay, have spoken in favour of developing multilateral subsidies disciplines. Chile also provided a submission with a view to analyzing the effect of subsidies on international services trade. However, in the context of the exchange of information process mandated by Article XV in order to deepen the knowledge of actual practices, Latin American and Caribbean countries have not yet provided a reply to the questionnaire agreed by the Working Party.

Again, there is a wide gap between the positions taken by countries in the region at the multilateral level and the sub-regional agreements. While there seems to be a general consensus by Latin America and the Caribbean that subsidy disciplines would be useful to develop under the GATS, only one agreement on services in the Western Hemisphere foresees the possibility of applying general subsidy disciplines to the service sector, while none of the other agreements contain provisions in this area.[31]

Much less interest and enthusiasm have been displayed in the ongoing discussions on *government procurement* than on safeguards and subsidy disciplines. Little progress has as yet been made to develop multilateral disciplines to fortify GATS Article XIII. For developing countries, government procurement activities comprise well over half of their GDP. Disciplines on market access, along with important obligations for transparency and non-discrimination, would subject the bulk of procurement in the services area to scheduling commitments with a view to liberalization. Thus most countries in Latin America and the Caribbean are not very enthusiastic at this prospect, while developed WTO members (including the US and Canada) would prefer to bring procurement seriously to the negotiating table and develop multilateral disciplines along the lines of those used by the World Bank in its lending programmes. Discussions on government procurement have been limited to conceptual issues, in particular the relevance for services of the terms and definitions contained in the GATT and the distinction between government purchases and concessions. The positions and practices of a few Latin American countries on government procurement can be found in their responses to the questionnaire on the subject prepared and circulated by the WTO Secretariat in 1996.[32] Once again, the position of countries in the hemisphere at the multilateral level is in some cases quite at odds with what has been achieved at the sub-regional level where a few of the sub-regional agreements have indeed already incorporated procurement disciplines on both goods and services.

In this area NAFTA broke new ground by including government procurement for services within the scope of the procurement chapter, and many sub-regional agreements have followed this example. Similar provisions have already been included or are under development in all but one of the integration agreements in the Western Hemisphere.[33] Thus in these three areas, safeguards disciplines, subsidies and government procurement, several Latin American and Caribbean countries have been both willing and able to go beyond the incomplete multilateral GATS framework. Given this reality, it is interesting to note that the positions of these countries in the GATS discussions at the multilateral level do not reflect the deeper commitments and the more far-reaching approach that they have adopted in a regional context which has led to deeper integration.

Contributing to Preparations for the Seattle Ministerial Meeting

During the months preceding the WTO Ministerial Meeting held in Seattle in December 1999, many proposals were submitted by Latin American and Caribbean countries. A submission by Brazil focused on the issue of how to sequence the outstanding work of the GATS subsidiary bodies prior to beginning the market access component of the negotiations. Submissions by Bolivia, the Dominican Republic, El Salvador, and Honduras, Caricom (Caribbean Community and Common Market) members, Colombia, Uruguay, and Venezuela supported the inclusion of the concept of greater flexibility and special treatment in drawing up the guidelines and procedures for the services negotiations. Another submission by the Dominican

Republic, El Salvador, and Honduras, along with nine other developing countries, centered on the full implementation of commitments undertaken by developed countries in mode 4.

A submission by Caricom members emphasized the importance of giving practical orientation to Article IV of the GATS and requested that special attention be given to market access needs of small developing economies. A submission by Argentina also discussed possible negotiating modalities, preferring to leave the choice open for whichever modality might best suit the needs of participants.[34] Finally a submission by Chile, jointly with Australia and New Zealand, focused on the objectives of the GATS 2000 negotiations.

NEW MULTILATERAL SERVICES NEGOTIATION GATS 2000 AND LATIN AMERICA

The Special Session of the GATS Services Council officially launched the new negotiations on services in February 2000, as part of the built-in agenda for progressive liberalization mandated in Article XIX of the GATS. The negotiations and work on services is carried out in three subsidiary bodies: the Committee on Specific Commitments, the Working Party on Domestic Regulation, and the Working Party on GATS Rules, as well as in the meetings of the Special Session of the GATS Council on Services.

WTO Members agreed to a road-map for the services negotiations in May 2000. They were seen as comprising two phases: (a) the 'rule-making' part during which WTO members are to complete the negotiation of disciplines in the areas discussed; (b) the 'market access negotiations' phase, where WTO members are to negotiate further specific commitments and further sectoral disciplines. However, the road-map does not provide for any direction with regards to sequencing and timing of the different issues that are being considered by the Special Session. It only states that current work in the Working Party on GATS Rules should be completed prior to the conclusion of the negotiations.[35] Since the launch of the GATS 2000 negotiations, the Special Session has been discussing four major issues: (i) assessment of trade in services; (ii) elements of a proposed first phase of negotiations; (iii) negotiating guidelines and procedures; and (iv) treatment of autonomous liberalization.

Assessment of Trade in Services

GATS Article XIX: 3 mandates an assessment of trade in services in overall terms and on a sectoral basis, with reference to the objectives of the GATS, including those set out in Article IV: 1 (facilitation of the increasing participation of developing countries), in order to provide the necessary elements for the elaboration of the guidelines and procedures for each round of services negotiations. This requirement could be viewed in two ways: (a) either that the assessment is a prerequisite to establishment of the guidelines, or (b) that the assessment is the ongoing parallel process to the negotiations, by which a government can identify its negotiating position and priorities. Most developing WTO members adhere to the first position, while developed members prefer the latter.

Since 1999, the Council for Trade in Services has carried out an information exchange programme endorsed by the Ministers at the Singapore Ministerial Conference. The programme aims to facilitate access to all WTO members, in particular developing country members, to information regarding laws, regulations and administrative guidelines and policies affecting trade in services. During this exercise, ten key issues were identified: (i) the need to improve classification and definition of particular sectors and activities; (ii) the need to ensure that domestic regulation type measures and disciplines would not raise unnecessary barriers to trade; (iii) the presence of important obstacles to movement of natural persons, including restrictions on obtaining work permits and visas, recognition of qualifications, compulsory membership in professional associations; (iv) the role of mutual recognition agreements; (v) non-transparent and discriminatory taxation regimes; (vi) a need for transfer of technology; (vii) issues relating to electronic commerce; (viii) subsidies granted by developed countries and their impact on developing countries services sectors; (ix) the relationship between services and goods sectors and the need to remove barriers in the complementary sectors; and (x) the need to further clarify the boundary between mode 1 and 2.

The Council has also discussed the serious lack of statistical information on services trade that could allow for a quantitative assessment. In light of the very slow progress on the improvement of services trade statistics mentioned above, this means that effectively WTO members must again enter into market access negotiations without having information on services trade flows available, including for determining the potential economic impact of services liberalization.

While some developed WTO members have made a great deal of effort in assessing their own situation with respect to services trade, most developing countries including Latin American countries are still in need of serious statistical and analytical analysis in this area, as well as in need of developing a comprehensive inventory of the legal measures affecting services trade. In fact, some analysts feel that amassing a comprehensive set of information at the national level on the barriers that affect services trade or restrict international competition in services is the most important predication from an economic policy and negotiating perspective.[36] It is of note that for Latin America, only Argentina submitted the assessment of trade in services for its economy.[37]

Negotiating Guidelines and Procedures

GATS Article XIX: 3 mandates that negotiating guidelines and procedures should be established for each round. Due to the failure of the WTO Seattle Ministerial Conference, agreement was not reached in 1999 on guidelines and procedures, and thus the Council for Trade in Services launched the GATS 2000 round of negotiations without guidelines. The Special Session took over the agenda from the Council for Trade in Services. Following agreement on the road-map in May 2000, the Special Session has been focusing its attention on the elaboration of guidelines and procedures to carry out market access negotiations after the stock-taking exercise of March 2001, with the help of proposals from WTO members.[38] Upon request by the members, the WTO Secretariat prepared a document in January 2001 containing draft guidelines and procedures for the services negotiations on the basis of these submissions as well as the draft Seattle Ministerial Text and already-existing provisions of the GATS. Following criticism by developed countries that this first draft was focused too heavily on the needs of developing countries for flexibility, including the possibility of opening fewer service sectors and the grant of special treatment of least-developed countries, the guidelines were revised by the Secretariat and reissued in February 2001.

Significantly, the revised text retains the main ideas from the first draft with respect to negotiating modality in that: (a) the reference point for the negotiations shall be the current service schedules of members (which set out their market access and national treatment commitments) and that the deadline for concluding the negotiations should be determined at a later date;[39] (b) no service sector or mode of supply should be excluded 'a priori' from the negotiations; and (c) countries should be given credit in the negotiations for 'autonomous liberalization', or market access measures that go beyond those agreed to by participants in the first services negotiations.

New criticism was directed to the revised document by several developing countries (the Group of 24 and the African Group) who felt that the text had gone backwards in omitting several key development-oriented proposals that were contained in the first version. Agreement on negotiating guidelines was finally reached in late March 2001.

Negotiating Modalities

Negotiating modalities are also to be specified as part of the negotiating guidelines and procedures before the market access phase of the negotiations is undertaken. According to Article XIX: 4, progressive liberalization under a negotiating modality (ies) to be adopted by the Special Session will be 'facilitated through bilateral, plurilateral or multilateral negotiations directed towards increasing the general level of specific commitments undertaken by member countries'. A number of countries in the region have contributed to the discussion on negotiating modalities and made proposals in this regard. Such proposals centre around the request-offer approach, the sectoral approach, the cluster approach, and the formula approach.

The request-offer approach is a bilateral exchange of requests and offers, followed by bilateral negotiations of market access and national treatment commitments on a mode-by-mode basis across all services sectors. The modality increases WTO member countries' participation in the negotiations by allowing all participants to promote their specific interests directly on with respect to a specific service sector or sub-sector in a given market. It was on the basis of this modality that negotiations during the Uruguay Round took place. Abugattas (2000) points out another merit of the approach is it expedites the evaluation of the possible impact of the specific commitments that mirror the level of market openness as a result of the negotiations.[40] The 'request-offer' approach has been supported by developing countries because it calls for less information on barriers to market access than other approaches. Brazil has specifically come out in favour of following this negotiating modality in the current GATS 2000 negotiations. The US supports this approach, in combination, however, with several other approaches.

The sectoral approach focuses on the undertaking of an agreed set of commitments in an individual service sector, such as air transport or maritime transport. It may be carried out plurilaterally or multilaterally. The approach was adopted during the extended Uruguay Round negotiations for the basic telecommunications and financial services sectors. In the current round of GATS services negotiations the EU strongly supports this approach and has proposed the creation of subsidiary bodies dealing with negotiations on specific services sectors. However, among countries in the hemisphere, this proposal has not received explicit written support to date.

The cluster approach carries out the negotiations on the basis of an identification of sectors or sub-sectors related to a given service sector and the adoption of a coherent, pre-established and harmonized set of commitments for all of these services activities which are felt to be essential components of being able to effectively provide the service in question.

Chile and Australia, in a joint paper, advocate the cluster approach in order to organize service industries into groups of interconnected services so as to allow for more coherent and effective negotiating procedures. In a separate paper setting out some of their suggestions for the GATS 2000 negotiations, they define a 'cluster' as a service mode around which several interconnected services are articulated and which allow the main service to operate efficiently. The choice of clusters would be decided on a voluntary basis, where it was felt relevant for the appropriate service sectors. In this regard, Chile and Australia set out several service sectors that might be examples of clusters. These include multi-modal transport, electronic commerce, environmental services, and some professional services such as legal services.[41] In this regard, the question of classification is critical since the identification of all relevant sub-sectors related to a given service activity is the wheel of the cluster approach.

The Dominican Republic, El Salvador, and Honduras have jointly proposed the negotiation of a Tourism Annex to the GATS, based on the concept of a 'cluster' of tourism services.[42] Their proposal underlines how trade liberalization in the very heterogeneous tourism sector would be more effective if the many highly related activities currently classified under other services sectors were to be included in a 'cluster' of tourism-related activities, thus focusing on the tourism sector as a whole for the purpose of negotiations. The need to deal effectively as well with the trade implications of anti-competitive conduct in tourism-related activities is also underlined. The proposal puts forward a draft text for an Annex on Tourism including sections on definitions, competitive safeguards, consumer safeguard, access and use to information, cooperation for sustainable development of tourism, and relationship of the WTO/GATS draft Annex to other international organizations. Several tourism-related activities drawn from various service sectors across all services sectors are set out in an attachment to the draft Annex.[43] A second proposal submitted by the Dominican Republic, El Salvador and Honduras plus Nicaragua and Panama in late 2000 reinforced the concept of a 'cluster' of tourism industries and includes a set of tourism characteristic products based on the definition given by the WTO to the Tourism Satellite Account at its conference in June 1999.

The formula approach (model schedule) sets out agreed objectives for the liberalization of a specific service sector and can be achieved in various ways. For example, agreement might be reached on the removal of certain types of limitations found in national schedules (for instance the exclusion of cabotage in maritime transport negotiations), or compliance may be required with certain negotiated specified obligations (like the Memorandum of Understanding in Financial Services that specifies the content of market access commitments and includes other provisions dealing with specific issues), or commitments additional to the individual requests-offers, like the Reference Paper on the Basic Telecommunications. A more far-reaching version of the formula approach would be to provide for an overall standstill with respect to unbound or unscheduled measures, as the United States has proposed. The incorporation of a discipline on ratcheting in an agreed model schedule would go much further towards facilitating progressive liberalization of services trade. This discipline requires the binding of any new level of liberalization with respect to services trade, without the possibility of retrenching.[44]

The various types of 'formula' approaches described above require an acceptable degree of reciprocity as well since all members signing onto them must abide by the same disciplines and implement the same level of liberalization. Although no interest has been expressed to date by Latin America and the Caribbean in this modality, these countries may at some point be interested in the formula approach for certain service sectors as a way to facilitate the liberalization of modes 3 and 4 through negotiated agreement on the elimination of requirements to the movement of capital and natural persons that might be more difficult to reach in isolated request-offer negotiations (for instance equity, nationality, residency, qualification, and so on).

Treatment of Autonomous Liberalization

In compliance with Article XIX: 3, the negotiating guidelines for the market access component of the GATS 2000 negotiations are also to establish modalities for the treatment of liberalization undertaken autonomously by WTO members since the previous negotiations. How can autonomous liberalization be defined? One way is through examining if such liberalization is based on reciprocity. Only if a country has reduced barriers to trade in services autonomously and not in return for a reciprocal reduction by its trading partner, can this be defined as autonomous liberalization. Mattoo (2000) identifies this as a type of 'ex ante' behaviour: autonomous liberalization is a type of 'ex ante' assurance of credit, whereas other forms of liberalization involve reciprocity as they are based on the reciprocal exchange of concessions.

The big question surrounding this issue arises when the liberalizing country seeks 'credit'. How would such credit be granted?[45] This is an important issue, especially for Latin American countries that undertook enhanced liberalization in telecommunications under the basic telecommunications negotiations. Hoekman (1998) suggests thinking of credit in terms of 'the *quid pro quo* to be put on the table by high-income countries and major middle-income emerging markets in return for a significant increase in bindings by developing countries'.

In this regard, the US has proposed the following: 'Any member that has liberalized autonomously in a particular sector, mode, or type of measure since the end of the Uruguay Round and through the end of the current round should make the nature of the liberalization known to interested trading partners. Then the member and interested trading partners should discuss and seek agreement on their respective bindings relative to the autonomous liberalization'. Chile supports this type of request-offer approach for the treatment of autonomous liberalization.[46] Brazil, however, maintains a much stronger stance with respect to this question, advocating the elaboration of a multilaterally agreed modality to quantify the autonomous liberalization that has been carried out by WTO members.[47] The granting of credit would thus take place under agreed principles.

FURTHER LIBERALIZATION AT THE REGIONAL LEVEL

In conclusion, Latin America and the Caribbean have come a long way towards developing a substantial interest and activism in the area of trade in services since the mid-1990s. From a limited participation in the first multilateral trade negotiations (Uruguay Round) encompassing services and a very modest level of overall service commitments with little liberalizing content, Latin American and Caribbean governments have come to recognize the importance of services trade to the growth and efficiency of their economies and have moved to adopt a much more proactive stance towards liberalization. This change in attitude, bolstered in large part by a widespread domestic consensus on the desirability of regulatory reform, has been manifested at the multilateral level in growing participation in the GATS and in the current multilateral services negotiations (GATS 2000). After many Latin American and Caribbean countries undertook new or expanded commitments in the extended negotiations on basic telecommunications and financial services under the WTO in 1997, they have continued to contribute substantively to the current GATS 2000 negotiations. From submissions to the preparations for the Seattle Ministerial Conference in

December 1999, to input in the discussions of the work of the GATS sub-sidiary bodies, and lastly to the submission of proposals to the GATS Council in Special Session on the issues of services classification, of nego-tiating guidelines and procedures, the choice of a negotiating modality, and the sequencing of negotiations, Latin American countries in particular have been making their positions known and their voices heard.

Despite increased participation in the services work of the GATS and in the negotiating discussions, many of the submissions by Latin American countries to the multilateral services negotiations under the GATS reflect an undercurrent of caution towards what some countries appear to fear as too rapid a liberalization of the service sector. Thus many submissions insist upon retaining the appropriate *flexibility* for developing WTO mem-bers to undertake 'fewer commitments' and 'proceed progressively' with liberalization. Elaborating a common approach to the issue of providing credit for autonomous liberalization is also of concern to many Latin American countries.

This cautious activism at the multilateral level contrasts with a strong proactivism at the regional level in the area of services liberalization, where all of the Latin America and Caribbean countries without exception have negotiated one or more (and sometimes several) sub-regional integra-tion agreements encompassing trade in services. All of these agreements go beyond the GATS in either developing deeper disciplines, or providing for greater liberalization and market access opportunities for service providers, or enhancing transparency – or a combination of all three.[48] Two sub-regional agreements even posit the complete removal of all restrictions affecting services and service providers falling within their arrangement, while other agreements posit an effective standstill or prohi-bition on the adoption of any new restrictive measures.[49] A few agree-ments even set out the unconditional application of both MFN and national treatment.

The willingness of Latin American and Caribbean countries to go beyond the GATS and undertake substantial liberalizing commitments and to either harmonize certain essential regulations affecting service providers or to promote the conclusion of recognition agreements as an alternative means to facilitate services trade in a reduced-country setting, deserves comment.[50]

Not being willing to offer similar liberalization at the multilateral level most likely reflects the greater ease and ability to arrive at consensus on these often-sensitive issues in a context with smaller numbers of more like-minded governments. It certainly also mirrors the differing goals of members to sub-regional agreements who are striving to reach a level of 'deep' economic integration in line with their political and strategic objectives. Members to sub-regional agreements perceive that not only is the negotiating process easier in a setting of fewer participants, but the implementation of such commitments may be as well since this involves extending such obligations or commitments only to the other members of the agreement. The reality of the situation may, however, often differ from this perception since implementing services commitments of a liberalizing nature necessarily involves the modification of domestic laws, regulations, decrees, and procedures, as these are the means through which services trade is actually controlled. Reforming domestic regulation in a small country setting will generally involve the same amount of work as carrying this out on a multilateral basis. Nonetheless, the perception remains that services liberalization is easier to achieve among a limited number of participants with clearly defined, similar objectives. Perception aside, in the region, those countries that have been willing to initiate and sustain domestic reforms for services on a wide scale have been able to bind these reforms at the sub-regional level and to push the liberalization process forward on this scale at a much faster pace in the case of most arrangements than it has proceeded under the GATS. The will to go beyond multilateral liberalization at the sub-regional level may also be a reflection of the awareness of countries in the hemisphere of the need to comply with the obligations of GATS Article V, which requires all economic integration agreements to be more liberalizing and far-reaching in their effects than the GATS. This is in order to ensure that these agreements (representing a violation of the MFN principle in trade) result in trade creation rather than trade diversion for the wider trading community.

Lastly, Latin America and the Caribbean have also been participating in negotiations at the hemispheric-wide level under the Free Trade Area of the Americas (FTAA) negotiations. While undertaken by a much larger number of countries (34 participants), the FTAA negotiations are also serving to stimulate reflection on what has worked at the multilateral level under the GATS and what has worked at the sub-regional level, and what may be improved upon with respect to both in a hemispheric-wide agreement. This should make the hemispheric-wide services agreement a much stronger and more coherent instrument than the GATS is in its present form. Thus Latin America and the Caribbean have progressed substantially in the services area over the past decade, and the growing importance of services trade will ensure that it will continue to occupy the attention of countries in the hemisphere for a long time in the future.

Notes

1.   See Prieto and Stephenson (1999).
2.   WTO Background Data: Employment by Economic Activity, Press Release 167.6.2000.
3.   Only one-third of WTO members committed on between 81 and 145 sectors out of 155 sectors. See WTO S/C/W/94 for further information.
4.   See Chang *et al.* (1999).
5.   See Karsenty (2000).
6.   See UN (2000).
7.   In order to improve availability on services statistics, an Inter-Agency Task Force of Statistics on International Trade in Services was created and drafted the Manual on Statistics of International Trade in Services (MSITS) in early 2000. The task force consists of EUROSTAT, OECD, UN, UNCTAD, IMF, and WTO. It explicitly takes into account the needs of services trade negotiators for the first time in designing an expanded framework for the collection of statistics on services trade. With a view to addressing the needs of the users, the task force held a meeting in July 2000 of senior statisticians (providers) and senior trade negotiators (users) to discuss the draft Manual that is now in the process of revision.
8.   See Warren and Findlay (2000).
9.   Ibid.
10. As of 15 April 1994, twenty-eight countries of the thirty-four WTO members in the Western Hemisphere submitted schedules of GATS commitments. Ecuador, Haiti, St. Kitts and Nevis, and Panama submitted their schedules in 1996 and 1997. The Bahamas is not yet a WTO member. The number of commitments refers to a count of the entries a country has placed in its GATS schedule for a given service sub-sector in the areas of market access and national treatment. The total universe of possible commitments is a count of 620 with respect to each, or 1,240 in total.
11. Those sectors are construction and engineering, distribution, education, entertainment, health, and recreation, cultural and sports services.
12. This method, pioneered by Hoekman, gives a value of '1' for an entry of 'none' for the same sub-sector and mode of supply scheduled for both market access and national treatment. These matched 1's provide a measure of the openness of the service sectors in a country because this measure takes into account only those commitments of full liberalization that indicate the binding of liberalized market access (or the absence of any restrictions) for *both* market access *and* national treatment. Its measure therefore involves no value judgment about the degree of openness in a particular subsector and/or mode of supply. The percentage of matched 1's out of the total GATS count (1,240) has been calculated for each country in the Western Hemisphere and the result set out in Table 6.2.
13. See WTO S/C/W/74. Governments representing about 82 per cent of world revenue committed to ensure some form of telecom competition as of February 1998 and another 6 per cent have committed to introduce competition on or before 2005. As of November 1998, 89 WTO members have included telecommunications services in their schedules of commitments.

Out of 19 members, one-quarter committed 14 or more telecom sub-sectors (the total number of telecom sub-sectors is 15 of them); another 40 per cent between 10 and 13; over one-quarter between 6 and 9; and the rest, 9 per cent, five or less. Eighty-three members committed on basic telecommunications and 70 on value-added telecoms.

14. Sixty-eight (68) members committed on some or all aspects of the Reference Paper. From the region these countries are Antigua & Barbuda, Argentina, Barbados, Belize, Bolivia, Chile, Colombia, Dominica, Dominican Republic, Ecuador, El Salvador, Grenada, Guatemala, Jamaica, Mexico, Peru, Suriname, Trinidad & Tobago, and Venezuela. Canada and the United States also scheduled commitments. St. Vincent & the Grenadines submitted only a draft offer for the specific commitments. As of October 2000, fourteen of these countries had accepted the Fourth Protocol, namely Antigua & Barbuda, Belize, Canada, Colombia, Dominica, Ecuador, El Salvador, Grenada, Jamaica, Mexico, Peru, Trinidad & Tobago, USA, and Venezuela. The Agreement is subject to ratification in both Brazil and the Dominican Republic.

15. See Low and Mattoo (1999) and Warner (2000).

16. Fourteen countries undertook commitments for long distance services. These include: Argentina (as of November 2000), Bolivia (as of November 2001), Canada, Chile, Dominican Republic, El Salvador, Grenada (as of 2006), Guatemala, Jamaica (as of 2013), Mexico, Peru, Trinidad and Tobago, the United States, and Venezuela (as of November 2000). Antigua and Barbuda will allow competition for international long-distance services as of 2012. Mexico only allows for international long-distance providers to use the national infrastructure and satellites to make the calls until 2002.

17. See Mattoo (2000) who asserts that granting time-protected monopoly rights does not improve market conditions and entry restrictions are thus less justified in the face of growing evidence of the benefits of competition. In Latin America, countries that granted monopoly privileges to newly privatized telecom operators (formerly state enterprises) saw connections grow at 1.5 times the rate achieved under purely state monopolies but at only half the rate of telecom connections. Another area of lesser benefit is that of employment: an increase in telecom employment of over 20 per cent has occurred in markets allowing for varying degrees of competition as compared to some 3 per cent in monopoly markets in Latin America. See WTO No. 2748/Rev.1.

18. The principles are notably: (i) competitive safeguards with the objective of preventing anti-competitive practices, including cross-subsidization and misuse of information as a means of impeding competition; (ii) ensure the right to interconnection – provision of interconnection by a major supply on a non-discriminatory basis and a timely manner; (iii) the right to define and carry out a universal service obligation; (iv) transparency of licensing criteria; (v) the creation of an independent regulatory body, separate from the supplier of basic telecom services; and (vi) fair and non-discriminatory allocation and use of scarce resources, such as frequencies and rights of way, on a timely, objective, and transparent manner.

19. See Bastos Tigre (2000).

20. See WTO (1998) 'The Results of the Financial Services Negotiations under the GATS', http://www.wto.org/english/tradtop_e/servfi_e/fiback_e.htm.

21. Those are Bolivia, Brazil, Chile, Colombia, Costa Rica, Dominica Republic, Ecuador, El Salvador, Honduras, Jamaica, Mexico, Nicaragua, Peru, Uruguay, and Venezuela. Canada and the United States also scheduled commitments. Twelve of these countries have already accepted the Fifth Protocol, namely: Canada, Chile, Colombia, Costa, Rica, Ecuador, El Salvador, Honduras, Mexico, Nicaragua, Peru, USA, and Venezuela. Bolivia and Costa Rica made commitments on financial services for the first time in February 1997. Both Brazil and Uruguay are in the process of ratifying the Fifth Protocol.

22. However, Peru and Venezuela continue to maintain broad MFN exemptions corresponding to reciprocity requirements in banking and insurance sub-sectors.

23. See Holz (2000).

24. The measure specifies that banks established before 5 October 1988 are allowed to maintain the aggregate number of branches that existed at that date. For foreign banks authorized to operate in the country after that date, however, the number of branches is subject to the conditions set out at the time the authorization is granted.

25. See Warner (2000).

26. The possibility of disciplines in these three areas is also being discussed in the context of the services chapter within the Free Trade Area of the Americas (FTAA) negotiations.

27. These issues were summarized in the Secretariat document S/WPGR/27/Rev.1 of May 1999.

28. Only the Caricom Protocol II agreement in the Western Hemisphere for countries of the Caribbean includes an operational safeguard article at the time of this writing. Most of the sub-regional agreements do not contain a general safeguard article for services trade. This is the case of NAFTA, the Andean Community's service agreement contained in Decision 439, the Mercosur Protocol of Montevideo, the Group of Three and four of the NAFTA-type agreements.

29. The main service sectors receiving subsidies are those of air and maritime transport (in developed countries) and telecommunications (in developing countries).

30. See GATS S/WPGR/W/31.

31. This is the case of the NAFTA, the NAFTA-type agreements, the Andean Community Decision on services and the Caricom Protocol II where none of the agreements contain provisions on subsidies with respect to services. These are, in fact, excluded from the coverage of these agreements. The Mercosur Protocol on Services is an exception to this, specifying that general subsidy disciplines, once elaborated, will apply to services.

32. See S/WPGR/W/11. Those countries in the Western Hemisphere that have submitted replies to the questionnaire on government procurement practices are: Argentina, Brazil, Canada, Chile, Colombia, Costa Rica, Mexico, Peru, and the United States.

33. Similar provisions on procurement to those of NAFTA are included in the Group of Three agreement and in certain of the bilateral free trade agreements (those between Bolivia and Mexico, Costa Rica and Mexico, Mexico and Nicaragua, Central America and the Dominican Republic, and Central

America and Chile). The Andean Community and Mercosur members are in the process of developing separate instruments on government procurement that will apply to both goods and services. Caricom Protocol II is the only agreement that does not include procurement within its scope, in either actual or potential form.

34. The submission by Brazil prior to the Seattle Ministerial Meeting addresses the sequencing for the different issues in the negotiating agenda and recommends two distinct phases for this process: the phase of negotiations for additional specific commitments should only begin once the rule-making phase has been completed. See WT/GC/W/333. As mentioned above, the deadline for completing the development of disciplines on safeguards was extended to 15 March 2002.

35. See WTO S/CSS/3. The WTO Secretariat prepared a text for the 'other matters relating to negotiations under Article XIX', drawing upon proposals by Australia and Singapore, and Mercosur members (Argentina, Brazil, Paraguay and Uruguay). The text is contained in WTO document S/CSS/M/3, which is not publicly available at the time of this writing.

36. See Hoekman (1999).

37. See S/CSS/W/44 of 29 January 2001, for further information.

38. To date five submissions have been presented to the Special Session regarding negotiating guidelines and procedures. These are by the US (S/CSS/W/4), the EU (Informal Paper dated 12 July 2000 entitled 'Negotiating guidelines: drafting elements'), Hong Kong China (S/CSS/W/6), the African Group (S7CSS/W/7), and the Group of 24 developing countries (G-24), including most Latin American countries: Argentina, Bolivia, Brazil, Colombia, Dominican Republic, Ecuador, El Salvador, Honduras, Mexico, Nicaragua, Panama, Paraguay, Peru, Uruguay, and Venezuela. See S/CSS/W/13.

39. The United States had proposed that the starting point of the negotiations should be the actual sector-by-sector limitations that governments currently impose on foreign service providers rather than those written into their WTO services schedule, and that the services negotiations should be completed by December 2002. Countries of Latin America and the Caribbean hold to the view set out in the Secretariat draft document.

40. See Abugattas (2000).

41. See paper prepared by Chile and Australia on 'GATS 2000: Towards Effective Liberalization of Trade in Services – Proposals for Action', presented to the APEC Committee on Trade and Investment, May 2000.

42. See submission on Tourism Services; Job No. 5658, Job No. 4406, S/CSS/W/7, and S/CSS/W/4, respectively.

43. The proposal draft Annex on Tourism and the listed sub-sectors in the attachment can be found in WT/GC/W/372.

44. See Piñera (2000) and Prieto and Burrows (1999). A 'ratcheting clause' has been included at the sub-regional level in both NAFTA and all of the NAFTA-type agreements that have subsequently been negotiated by Mexico or Chile.

45. This is an important issue, especially for Latin American countries that undertook enhanced liberalization in telecommunications under the basic telecommunications negotiations. Abugattas (2000).

46. See Prieto and Burrows (1999) and S/CSS/W/4.

47. See Brazil's proposal for the 1999 Ministerial Conference (WT/GC/W/333) and subsequent proposal on the possibility of granting credit for autonomous liberalization. The US has also proposed a formula approach for setting agreed targets for multilateral liberalization against which the value of autonomous liberalization measures might be gauged (S/CSS/W/4).
48. For an analysis of how far and in what way the sub-regional agreements in the Western Hemisphere go beyond the WTO/GATS, see Stephenson (2001).
49. The two sub-regional agreements that set out as their objective the elimination of restrictive measures affecting service suppliers are the members of the Andean Community and of Mercosur. The NAFTA and NAFTA-type agreements impose a prohibition on the introduction of any new restriction that is not specified in the annexes of non-conforming measures to the agreements. Caricom members are trying to identify measures affecting services trade in order to avoid the adoption of any new restrictions and thus implement an effective standstill.
50. See Stephenson (2000).

Bibliography

ABUGATTAS MAJLUF, LUIS (2000) 'Liberalization of Trade in Services: Options and Implications for Latin American and Caribbean Countries of the WTO and FTAA Negotiations', paper presented at meeting of Latin American Trade Network (LATN), Washington D.C., November 2000.

BASTOS TIGRE, PAULO (2000) 'The Political Economy of Latin American Telecommunications: Multilateral Agreements and National Regulatory Systems', paper presented at meeting of Latin American Trade Network (LATN), Washington D.C., November 2000.

CHANG, PHILLIP, GUY KARSENTY, AADITYA MATTOO and JURGEN RICHTERING (1999) 'GATS, the Modes of Supply and Statistics on Trade in Services', *Journal of World Trade*, vol. 33, June.

EVENETT, SIMON J. and BERNARD M. HOEKMAN (2000) 'Government Procurement of Services and Multilateral Disciplines', in *GATS 2000: New Directions in Services Trade Liberalization*, edited by Pierre Sauvé and Robert Stern (Washington D.C.: Brookings Institute Press).

FEKETEKUTY, GEZA (2000) 'Improving the Architecture of the General Agreement on Trade in Services', in *Services Trade in the Western Hemisphere: Liberalization, Integration, and Reform*, edited by Sherry Stephenson (Washington D.C.: Brookings Institute Press).

GAUTHIER, GILLES with ERIN O'BRIEN and SUSAN SPENCER (2000) 'Déjà vu, or Beginning for Safeguards and Subsidies Rules in Services Trade', in *GATS 2000: New Directions in Services Trade Liberalization*, edited by Pierre Sauvé and Robert Stern (Washington D.C.: Brookings Institute Press).

HOEKMAN, BERNARD M (1995) 'Tentative First Steps: An Assessment of the Uruguay Round Agreement on Services', paper presented at a World Bank Conference on The Uruguay Round and the Developing Economies, Washington D.C., January 1995.

HOEKMAN, BERNARD M (1998) 'Making Services an Engine of Growth', World Bank mimeograph.

HOEKMAN, BERNARD M (1999) 'Towards a More Balanced and Comprehensive Services Agreement', paper presented at the Conference on Preparing for the Seattle Ministerial organized by the Institute for International Economics, Washington D.C., October 1999.

HOLZ, EVA (2000) 'International Agreements in Latin American Financial Services: Effects on National Regulation Perspectives', paper presented at a meeting of the Latin American Trade Network (LATN), Washington D.C., November 2000.

KARSENTY, GUY (2000) 'Assessing Trade in Services by Mode of Supply', in *GATS 2000: New Directions in Services Trade Liberalization*, edited by Pierre Sauvé and Robert Stern (Washington D.C.: Brookings Institute Press).

KONO, MASAMICHI, PATRICK LOW, MUKELA LUANGA, AADITYA MATTOO, MAIKA OSHIKAWA and LUDGER SCHUKNECHT (1997) *Opening Markets in Financial Services and the Role of the GATS*, WTO Special Studies (Geneva: WTO).

LOW, PATRICK and AADITYA MATTOO (1999) 'Reform in Basic Telecommunications and the WTO Negotiations: The Asian Experience', Working Paper WTO Services Division.

LOW, PATRICK and AADITYA MATTOO (2000) 'Is There a Better Way? Alternative Approaches to Liberalization under GATS', in *GATS 2000: New Directions in Services Trade Liberalization*, edited by Pierre Sauvé and Robert Stern (Washington D.C.: Brookings Institute Press).

MASHAYEKHI, MINA (2000) *GATS 2000 Negotiations: Options for Developing Countries*, UNCTAD Working Paper.

MATTOO, AADITYA (2000) 'Shaping Future Rules for Trade in Services: Lessons From the GATS', paper prepared for an NBER Conference on Trade in Services, Seoul, June 2000.

NICOLAIDIS, KALYPSO and JOEL P. TRACHTMAN (2000) 'Liberalization, Regulation, and Recognition for Services Trade', in *Services Trade in the Western Hemisphere: Liberalization, Integration, and Reform*, edited by Sherry Stephenson (Washington D.C.: Brookings Institute Press).

PIÑERA, CARLOS (2000) 'Mexico's Free Trade Agreements: Extending NAFTA's Approach', in *Services Trade in the Western Hemisphere: Liberalization, Integration, and Reform*, edited by Sherry M. Stephenson (Washington D.C.: Brookings Institute Press).

PRIETO, FRANCISCO JAVIER and ALISON BURROWS (1999) 'Chile and Australia GATS 2000: Towards Effective Liberalization of Trade in Services Proposals for Action', paper presented at World Services Congress, Atlanta, Georgia, November 1999.

PRIETO, FRANCISCO JAVIER and SHERRY M. STEPHENSON (1999) 'Liberalization of Trade in Services', in *Trade Rules in the Making: Challenges in Regional and Multilateral Negotiations*, edited by Miguel Rodriguez Mendoza, Patrick Low and Barbara Kotschwar (Washington D.C.: Brookings Institute Press).

STEPHENSON, SHERRY M. (2000) 'Deeper Integration in Services Trade in the Western Hemisphere: Domestic Regulation and Mutual Recognition', paper prepared for the OECD Workshop on Regulatory Reform and the Multilateral Trading System: Insights from Country Experience, Paris, December 2000.

STEPHENSON, SHERRY M. (2001) 'Services', chapter 7 in *Toward Free Trade in the Americas*, edited by José Manuel Salazar Zirinachs and Maryse Robert (Washington D.C.: Brookings Institute Press.)

THOMPSON, RACHEL (2000) 'Formula Approaches to Improving GATS Commitments', in *GATS 2000: New Directions in Services Trade Liberalization*, edited by Pierre Sauvé and Robert Stern (Washington D.C.: Brookings Institute Press).

UNITED NATIONS (2000) The Draft Manual on Statistics of International Trade in Services (MSITS), New York.

WARNER, MARK A. (2000) 'Competition Policy and GATS', in *GATS 2000: New Directions in Services Trade Liberalization*, edited by Pierre Sauvé and Robert Stern (Washington D.C.: Brookings Institute Press).

WARREN, TONY and CHRISTOPHER FINDLAY (2000) 'Measuring Impediments to Trade in Services', in *GATS 2000: New Directions in Services Trade Liberalization*, edited by Pierre Sauvé and Robert Stern (Washington D.C.: Brookings Institute Press).

WTO Secretariat, Multiple services reports and negotiating proposals, see www.wto.org.

7 E-Commerce, Latin America and the WTO

Patricia Gray Rich[*]

INTRODUCTION

The 1997 Agreement on Basic Telecommunications (ABT) reached under the General Agreement on Trade in Services (GATS) was a milestone in the history of the multilateral trade system. This agreement affected more than 90 per cent of the world market for telecommunications. In the developing world, liberalization and privatization reforms have been substantial. Telecommunications and networking possibilities are no longer limited to narrowband, land-line analogue wireless telephony. The choice of available technologies is expanding at a tremendous rate.

Participation by developing countries in the World Trade Organization (WTO) process has been important for improving their competitiveness in their own sector and establishing a foundation for reaping the benefits of the information age. The WTO is a member-driven organization where the burden of the analytical work, development of proposals and negotiation of agreements and disputes falls on member countries and their representatives and thus requires continuous active involvement.[1] This chapter is specifically aimed at helping developing – and, in particular, Latin American – countries to assert their self-interest effectively during the negotiations on electronic commerce, or e-commerce.

Following this Introduction, the first part of the chapter will present a snapshot of the nature of e-commerce – what is meant by it, and what it can and cannot do – with a view towards clarifying certain misconceptions about e-commerce. The second part addresses barriers to and opportunities for e-commerce in Latin America. This section discusses the issue of the 'digital divide' between and within countries and how the gap can be narrowed. The third part follows up with an applied analysis and suggestions

* The author is especially grateful to Eduardo da Costa of NEST-Boston for providing valuable insights into this paper, to Felix Zimmerman of the London School of Economics, and to Professor Anthony Oettinger and John LeGates at Harvard University for their valuable comments and suggestions.

for small businesses going on-line in Latin America. These sections lead up to the last part, in which an exploration of the most pressing e-commerce issues being discussed at the WTO is followed by conclusions and recommendations for more effective participation in the WTO negotiation process.

THE NATURE OF E-COMMERCE

Broadly speaking, the term 'e-commerce' can refer to any system capable of completing electronic transactions. The term can include payments made over any electronic or money-transfer system, Electronic Data Interchange (EDI) networks or the Internet. However, much of the current excitement and confusion have to do with the growing presence of e-commerce on the Internet. From a business perspective, the potential of e-commerce is based on the new opportunities opened up by the Internet for handling traditional business transactions faster and more efficiently.

The Internet is a vast, swiftly expanding worldwide network of computers that are interconnected over existing telecommunications networks (over 200 million to date). Establishing a network involves large up-front fixed costs, but incorporating an additional user into an existing network costs very little. This may offer a great deal of potential to firms. Success is driven by the dynamics of increasing returns. The more competing buyers and sellers are brought together in one place, the more liquid a market becomes and the more efficient the price-setting mechanism is: (a) prices are lower because e-commerce breaks down entry barriers, and greater competition leads to lower prices; (b) goods and services are presented in a more homogeneous form than previously in order to sell them in an electronic marketplace (where no one can see them or inspect them), thereby paving the way for commodity-style pricing for homogenous goods; and (c) e-commerce lowers the real cost of selling and marketing products, thus allowing an overall price reduction. (However, this cost reduction is not necessarily passed on to the consumer. Online buying is often not different from off-line buying price-wise.)

Electronic marketplaces between buyers and sellers are being created in which establishing a critical mass of users is far more important to the ultimate success of an exchange than having the most advanced technology.[2] Competition is intense, and new opportunities are being explored in many directions. The New Economy, as it is so confidently called by many, is being shaped by the development and diffusion of computer hardware and software and by access to cheaper and rapidly increasing electronic connectivity. According to Nua Internet Surveys,[3] the number of people with Internet access reached an estimated 378 million worldwide in September 2000, up almost 80 per cent from the same period in 1999, and it is estimated that as of November 2000 the number reached 407 million worldwide. Internet access in Latin America is estimated to have doubled from 5.3 million in 1999 to 10.7 million in 2000, an increase of 102 per cent and by the end of 2000, access increased to 16.4 million. For the first time the United States and Canada will account for less than 50 per cent of the global online population.[4]

The Web has spillover effects that permeate the rest of the economy. Not only are individuals and businesses going online throughout the world in increasing numbers, but the products and services used in everyday life are becoming increasingly integrated into the networked economy. Businesses and governments have discovered the potential of the Internet as a place to sell surplus goods, dispose of used equipment and make requests for purchases. Nonetheless, the evolution of digital business is still in an early stage. A recent survey by the National Association of Manufacturers found that more than two-thirds of American manufacturers still do not conduct business electronically.[5]

There has not been enough time to gain much insight into the impact of the Internet because it is such a new phenomenon. Those who have tried, including research institutions and government agencies, lack adequate data to clearly evaluate its impact.[6] This is important to bear in mind as Latin America begins to participate in this process more fully and when addressing the issue of e-commerce in the WTO. Investment decisions concerning the creation and expansion of the modern technical infrastructure required for active participation in the information society are increasingly complex.[7] It is particularly difficult to decide how and where to invest in the necessary technical infrastructure. Firms do not know how heavy their overall site traffic will ultimately be, and so determining how much capacity to buy is difficult. Many software solutions are so new and untested that choosing one over another not only requires a great deal of research but also a leap of faith. Information technology (IT) in general is often viewed as a technological panacea, and it is often thought that all that is needed to solve social organizational inefficiencies is better technology. While there is no shortage of attention being devoted to the Internet in the media, little background information or other data is provided to help the public understand how business processes translate Internet technologies into *economic value*.

Each new wave of technology brings theories and expectations about the value and function of these changes. Each wave is associated with considerable rhetoric about the anticipated impacts, both positive and negative, of new technologies. Lessons from prior encounters with new technologies and economic breakthroughs tell us that we cannot predict the possibly profound social, technological and economic changes awaiting us. What is the size, scope and speed of the growth of e-commerce on the Internet? What is the actual number of users online worldwide or in a particular country? What is their impact on developed or developing economies? Nobody really knows. Is the Web an opportunity or a risk? The answer is both.

What It Can Do: It is Not About Technology

Electronic commerce is not about technology alone but about business opportunities and new business models. Over the period 1998–2001, the reliability, speed and to some extent security of the Internet have improved substantially. More businesses are connecting to the Internet and traditional businesses are using the Internet to conduct e-business and exchange information with customers, suppliers and distributors. XML (Extensible Markup Language) is being accepted as the standard language for the exchange of information online between firms. This makes it possible for firms to move into systems that allow for more open, data-rich and flexible links with supply partners, built around an Internet core.[8] This Web standard for data exchange is rapidly becoming the preferred language for automating online business. Its ability to deliver information of almost any sort in digital form at low cost offers more flexible customer–supplier relations that also entail greater competition.

As more and more countries use the Internet for trade, and as the number of industries affected by it rapidly expands, the Internet's influence on international trade may grow very quickly. Were this to be the case, e-commerce negotiations in the WTO would become of great interest for developing countries. A recent study at the London School of Economics (2000) using a gravity model for 56 developed and developing countries to assess the impact of the Internet on trade flows from 1996 to 1999 suggests that the effect of the Internet on trade is positive, that its effects on exports are stronger for poor countries than rich countries and that the results are statistically significant.[9]

Meantime, at least in the United States, a large gap is forming at the corporate level between those who are actively and aggressively integrating the Internet into their business and those who are slow to embrace it. Not surprisingly, this gap is driven by relative size and infrastructure maturity.

Bigger firms have larger budgets for IT and have been able to maintain their existing infrastructure. They enter the Internet world much faster than small firms in the same sector. This is also happening in Latin America, in particular in multinational corporations. However, the first phase of electronic commerce diffusion is also being driven by small firms created by entrepreneurs seeking the same degree of success as their peers elsewhere in the developed world.

The Internet has prompted a large number of mergers for the purpose of undertaking new activities, as in the automotive industry, where GM, Ford and DaimlerChrysler are working to build the world's largest online marketplace. While these new electronic marketplaces hope to achieve significant savings, it is difficult to gauge the impact these new arrangements may have on their supply communities. Concerns have been raised about the potential for these large players to use online trading exchanges to reduce competition. The overall impact will depend on the extent to which actual efficiencies can be achieved as opposed to simply squeezing supplier margins. It can also open up opportunities for Latin American suppliers of car parts. Overall, electronic commerce will undergo considerable changes in the next decade as firms respond to new technical capabilities and come to understand them more fully.

In sum, the Web-effect can be summarized as follows:[10]

- It begins with *access*. Intensive marketing efforts result in improved access to millions of consumers who, in their turn, have easy access to the Web.
- This access is creating a *preference* to do business and conduct relationships on the Web in every market in the world. This involves vertical markets, marketing practices, real estate, automobiles, books, and nearly every retail segment.
- It has created *empowered* customers by providing a tool with infinite options they never had before, making customers more demanding than in the past. The control has shifted to a large extent from the seller to the buyer.
- It creates new *opportunities* to improve customer service, streamline account and financial practices, and make better use of information and the purchasing needs of customers.
- It also involves *risks* because of the uncertainty and rapid pace of the Internet environment.
- Strategy *conflict* is by far the most critical barrier to doing business on the Internet. The Web presents an opportunity for companies to re-examine how they buy and sell goods. Many companies have tried

to deliver on their brand promise on the Web. Some have succeeded and others have failed. The challenge is not a trivial one.

- Customer loyalty is about delivering what has been promised, and the sum of a user's experience on a Web site is what builds *trust*.

Local and Country-Specific

There are other important issues that need to be carefully examined as well. For instance, a great deal has been said about how the Internet is free of country borders. However, in practice, many private and public decisions about marketing, sales, production, control or R&D are country–specific and, like all politics, *local*. Both global and local aspects shape the decision-making process, in which suppliers, consumers and local government all play an important role. In this context, states remain central players. According to Oettinger (1998), although there is growing interdependence among national economies, local differences limit trade liberalization along local, national and regional lines. The formation and breakup of new acquisitions and alliances happen in response to local factors, and many times for political reasons. For business to succeed in this environment Web-related issues need to be addressed quickly, efficiently and at the highest levels within a firm or organization. Unfounded claims of borderless economies, competition and convergence can mislead suppliers and consumers when it comes to deciding what and how much to allocate to IT investments. Decision-makers need to base their choices on how important the Web is going to be to *their businesses* in the next two to three years, and then act accordingly.

Strong emphasis has been given to the need to acquire technology, if countries are to compete in a digital world. However, technology is not valuable, meaningful, or consequential in and of itself; it only becomes so when people actually understand it and use it, and this varies from country to country. It is a mistake to expect returns on technology rather than returns on the business *use* of technology. Information technology by itself cannot increase or decrease productivity, only its effective use can. It is at the point of use that investments in technology and new business models are realized, or not. These are principles that are being recognized more and more clearly by CEOs and company executives in assessing e-commerce performance for their firms in the US. Furthermore, technologies are social, and dynamic. They are continuously being modified and/or abandoned in unpredictable ways. As technology changes, so does its social meaning, its use and its implications for our work and lives.[11] (This is actually happening in the US today.) This is a key issue to bear in mind when seeking to analyze the building of a networked economy, be it in the United States, Europe, Latin America or other developing areas.

Buying technology is not a complete transaction in itself, but rather a down payment on the establishment of a relationship. The use of the technology requires deep knowledge of the customer's needs, whether in automobiles, airlines, banking, engineering, or retail stores, of their overall situation, and of the vendor's capabilities, none of which are fungible or easily comparable. This will take time, and the level of support that the manufacturer will provide is often not immediately known.[12] (In Latin America there are especially serious user-support deficiencies that need improvement.) Since operating systems change frequently, all that can be done is to make intelligent guesses as to the future path of the technology being acquired. We are dealing with imperfect information from the start. It is a major challenge for traditional businesses to figure out how to migrate from traditional processes to Internet-enabled business models; they face both dangers and opportunities. Some companies are succeeding, while others are in turmoil. A recent global study by A.T. Kearney,[13] based on interviews with 251 executives (CEOs) across industry segments, claims that increasing complexity and a rapidly changing business environment are causing re-engineering activities to take more time than originally anticipated. These are important lessons for Latin America to take into account in determining what pace, shape and business models to use during its own networking and associated decision-making processes.

BARRIERS AND OPPORTUNITES FOR LATIN AMERICA

Electronic commerce conducted on the Internet has been spreading rapidly throughout the world and will continue to do so in the decades to come. However, what is special about electronic commerce in Latin America? Does the technology-driven intensification of international trade in goods and services pose an opportunity or a threat to these countries? Furthermore, does it set a task for policy-makers in the region? The answers to these questions are obviously highly relevant to how Latin American countries will deal with the WTO negotiation process or other forms of integration.

Whereas in Scandinavia and the US, the countries that are at the vanguard of the Internet revolution, almost 50 per cent of the population has access to this new form of communication, Latin America lags considerably behind the developed world, with current access rates of around

5 per cent in the main countries. It is likely that Latin America will continue to be a technological *adopter* rather than becoming an *innovator* itself.

Natural Resource Dependency

It is important to have an unembellished picture of the starting point from which most Latin American economies are entering the digital age. The results of two decades of structural adjustment and subsequent liberalization and opening of Latin American markets have produced a stronger dependency on exports of natural resources and agricultural products. The structural movement of many economies away from the manufacturing of final and intermediate products and towards the increased exploitation of natural resources such as timber, minerals, agriculture or fisheries means that the emphasis of many economies has shifted from later to earlier stages in international supply chains.[14] Electronic marketplaces enhance the transparency of international markets for all the goods that are traded on them. Developed-country firms in many industries, such as chemicals or heavy industries, are currently setting up electronic marketplaces to realize cost savings on their procurement side. Greater market transparency is likely to squeeze the profits of developing-country firms that are supplying highly homogenous goods to multinationals operating in increasingly concentrated industries.

Exporters of natural resources also have to adopt electronic commerce practices and participate in newly established marketplaces simply to stay in business. Falling transaction costs for these exports translate into falling end prices. Due to low price elasticities of demand, Latin America cannot expect lower transaction costs to result in large increases in the international demand for natural resources. It is likely that gains from the introduction of electronic commerce into international trade in natural resources will mainly be reaped by large multinational corporations operating in the US, Japan and Europe rather than by their input suppliers from the developing world. Since Latin American firms are competing with each other in many natural resource markets, some of them will surely have the opportunity to gain first-mover advantages by setting up an electronic commerce-based order system before their competitors do so and thus gain market shares which may then lead to longer-term procurement relations. This is an issue that needs to be addressed within sub-regional integration groupings.

It would be wrong to conclude that Latin American countries necessarily have to rapidly reduce their dependency on primary goods while entering the Internet age. However, successful long-term economic development will depend more than ever on the successful diversification of Latin American production portfolios and, in particular, on the achievement of human-capital-intensive manufacturing capabilities and a growing service sector. In Latin America the main bottleneck seems to be the lack of human capital in the form of IT skills (and knowledge of English as a foreign language), aside from its traditional production problems in terms of quality standards.

New Opportunities for the Manufacturing Sector

The manufacturing sector in Latin America is likely to profit much more from the diffusion of electronic commerce practices than from the natural resource sector. This is where the largest potential for expanding Latin American exports certainly lies in terms of business-to-business activities. The closer a manufacturing firm is to the final customer within a supply chain, the more likely it is to profit from electronic commerce. Latin American manufacturing firms will be able to buy their inputs more cheaply on an electronic marketplace, which puts pressure on their suppliers. It is likely that Latin American manufacturing firms will buy fewer inputs from nearby firms than they used to before the digital age. Moreover, manufacturing firms can assume closer relationships with their customers on the distribution side and thus reduce the role of the middlemen which used to sell their products to other firms (business to business) or to final consumers (business to consumer) without adding any material value to the product. New electronic marketplaces will be open to every firm. Latin American firms may therefore have the chance to replace some developed-country firms as suppliers of intermediate products for industries in the developed world. In the past, supply relations were relatively stable and closed to outside competition, since they were often based on expensive Electronic Data Interchange systems.

Many smaller Latin American firms were not able to adopt these systems due to their high acquisition cost. As a consequence, they were excluded from some potential markets. Yet it is evident that the mere introduction of electronic commerce systems into the marketing and procurement functions of Latin American manufacturing firms does not guarantee their successful participation in the world market. Increased competition at the international level generates rising expectations of product quality, making it necessary to constantly innovate and improve existing products.

Given internationally acceptable product quality standards, Latin American firms may have a great potential, however, to utilize their relative wage-cost advantages and take the place of developed-country firms in the production of intermediate and possibly final goods in international supply chains for the textile or machinery industry. Moreover, intensifying contact with international customers also speeds up the dissemination of knowledge about customer preferences and new production technologies towards Latin American firms, which may adopt new technologies more quickly than in the past.

The Digital Divide

The great divide between rich and poor countries that has long been observed in relation to economic wealth and social conditions is now under discussion in the realm of information and communications technologies. While 15 per cent of the world population provides nearly all of the world's technology innovations, 50 per cent is able to adopt these technologies and the other 35 per cent is disconnected from the whole process. In Latin America these technologically-excluded regions include southern Mexico, pockets of tropical Central America, some Andean countries and most of tropical Brazil.[15]

Is there really a digital divide as such? Do developing countries need higher IT diffusion rates to have higher economic growth rates and be able to catch up? Or are investments in public infrastructure, health and education more important in order to catch up? How different is this divide from the traditional ones previously talked about? In many ways, we are looking at the same issues that slow-down development and that have widened the gap between North and South. What is different is that it is now cloaked under the name of the 'technological divide' to some extent. Nonetheless, the attention that IT and the digital divide have received from government officials may serve to heighten awareness of existing inequities and help create a sense of urgency in addressing these issues within and between countries and in taking steps to overcome them.

Many reports have been focusing not just on the *connectivity* gap between the North and South but on the *content* gap, which is just as important. There are reasons to believe that countries that do not have sufficient access to infrastructure and education will be increasingly excluded from the international trading system. Without appropriate content directly relating to local people's lives, and in their native language, the relevance of the networking revolution for developing countries will remain in doubt.

The growth of IT in developing countries, and to some extent in developed countries, masks the striking disparities existing between rich and poor countries. According to the Pyramid Research Group, in 1999 Latin America had 139 telephone mainlines per 1,000 persons while OECD countries had 561. There were mobile phones for 66 out of every 1,000 persons while OECD countries had 332, and Internet access for 1.5 out of every 1,000 persons while for OECD countries the figure was 64.1. Industrialized countries, with only 15 per cent of the world's population, are home to 88 per cent of all Internet users.[16] Spending on IT is similarly concentrated in developed countries. While OECD countries spend 1.8 per cent of their GDP on IT and technological inputs, Latin America spends 0.5 per cent. Three-quarters of all Websites are in English, a language understood by only one in ten people on the planet. Spanish and Portuguese appear in only 4 per cent of all Web pages.[17] An Index of Technological Progress (ITP), which measures how many citizens use personal computers, Internet hosts, fax machines, mobile phones and televisions in 110 economies for the period 1992–97, showed that the top ten economies are all OECD countries.[18]

The same occurs in the control of traffic on Internet routes. The Internet began as a product of the US public sector (academia and defence); it was built around a single standard (Internet protocol) and has been predominantly American. This is so not only in terms of sites, servers and e-commerce business transacted on it, but also in the sense of content, culture and language. US taxpayers paid for the Internet in its initial stages and the US business sector and users after it reached a commercial stage. This can be appreciated from Figure 7.1 and the predominance of the US Internet routes and bandwidths. Although formally there is no ownership of or responsibility for the traffic that runs on mainly leased telecommunications lines, the few central decisions concerning protocol and the allocation of Internet addresses are US-based. However, due to international pressure, efforts are now being made to have such powers be shared at an international level.

Bridging the Digital Divide

Although the digital divide is real, there are ways to cushion the impact of these problems. There is a need to define how trading partners, service providers and networks should divide risks and costs among themselves. An equitable distribution would encourage investment and increase the likelihood of governments promoting these policies without coming under pressure from interest groups. This would increase the likelihood of having reform policies rapidly adopted and maintained. Developing countries, including those of Latin America, have a poor environment for entrepreneurship. Aside from legal, regulatory and financial constraints, early-stage

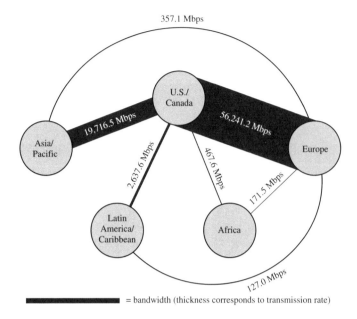

= bandwidth (thickness corresponds to transmission rate)

Figure 7.1 The largest international Internet routes and their corresponding bandwidths
Source: www.Telegeography.com (2000)

firms lack a network of experienced advisers as well as specialized legal and accounting services. Culture plays an important role in this as well. The United States has a tradition of rewarding risk-takers, in contrast to Europe and, to an even greater degree, Latin America. This factor has been decisive in enabling the US to take its current lead in IT over other countries.[19] It is also noteworthy that economies that fare well with new technologies have certain traits in common, basically: (a) an economic environment conducive to domestic investment, and (b) a consistent respect for civil liberties conducive to research and expansion of communications.

The Internet presents numerous opportunities for increasing the efficiency and equity of government services and improving the lives of the poorest. Like all innovations, it has the potential to transform societies internally and open up enormous possibilities for development. IT can be highly beneficial to individual communities and countries, and under the right circumstances IT can improve education, health, job creation, governance and other services. It can overcome many of the disadvantages of distance. For many countries in Latin America, especially in the Andean region, wireless telecommunications hold great promise for overcoming many deficits in infrastructure and access, especially in the rural sector.[20] However, the task is not an easy one. It calls for a solid commitment and involvement on the part of government, business and citizens alike. The market, acting alone, will not be enough to bridge the digital divide. Market failure presents a significant barrier to growth, especially for poor and rural populations who lack public access to IT infrastructure. If the rural poor have no access to infrastructure, they will fall further behind. When a new technology is introduced in a social environment marked by scarce resources and opportunities, there is a greater likelihood that those with more resources will employ them to gain additional ones. Groups of disadvantaged individuals who have not had access to even basic levels of education are more likely to be sidelined from the start. Governments must fill the gaps that open up in areas where the market alone will not assure equitable solutions.

In this regard, special attention should focus on providing basic access to the Internet and on promoting community-centred projects in rural and poor urban areas. Governments may want to promote regional connectivity as a way of minimizing costs in developing adequate telecommunications access, especially in the mountainous regions of the countries belonging to the Andean Community.

Latin America should take note of what is happening in South-East Asia as well. There, government officials are actively supporting the diffusion of these technologies for developmental purposes. There is a solid commitment to support the poor in both the urban and rural sectors by encouraging Internet use in the areas of education and health, promoting interconnectivity and helping small farmers in remote areas.[21] In Latin America, the Internet is mostly limited to urban areas and to the middle and upper classes, which is a mistake, as these countries are missing an opportunity to improve on income distribution and, in the long term, achieve more equitable development. Latin America has an added advantage over multilingual regions like South-East Asia; with two closely related, dominant languages – Spanish and Portuguese – its people are in a good position to do business throughout a large region crisscrossed by overlapping regional groupings, including Mercosur, NAFTA and the Andean Community. As mentioned before, the larger a network, the more valuable it becomes to its business and household users, since it provides them with access to more firms, people and places.

Policy-makers, local governments and the private sector need to act now to determine the appropriate priorities for their countries. Active participation is required, since networking an economy is not an overnight process; it requires education, widespread legal reforms and significant investments in infrastructure. Competition is an important condition for attaining the maximum benefits from the Internet revolution, and education is the main enabler.

Readiness for the Networked World

A study conducted by the Center for International Development (CID-2000) at Harvard University to serve as a starting point for an IT planning process designed for developing countries has become very popular among governments and institutions. It is a particularly useful tool for towns and regions.[22] This guide uses specific indicators to measure a country's readiness for the networked economy. Although care should be taken not to generalize the concept of readiness for all countries, it is nonetheless an important starting point, inasmuch as it represents a first attempt to assist developing economies to understand what needs to be done to join the networked world. It also creates awareness of the consequences of not joining and being left behind. Besides investment in infrastructure and content, these are other factors necessary for network readiness as well (CID 2000):

- The availability and efficiency of traditional physical transport infrastructures such as roads, railways, ports and airports are extremely important for the movement of IT equipment and of IT-facilitated trade in goods.
- The nature and quality of postal services, private shipping services, warehousing, licensing and permits are decisive for local distribution. Each of these factors can place limitations on the movement of goods that affects the growth of business activity in relation to information and communications technologies. Inefficient customs services can also be an impediment.
- The reliability and cost of electrical power is an important factor.
- Rates for local telephone calls can discourage extensive Internet use.
- Proper functioning of IT equipment is also dependent upon local conditions that in turn affect how the technology performs.

Furthermore, investment in human capital cannot be overemphasized. Students should be taught from the earliest age possible to use information technologies to enhance and improve their learning experience. This could be accompanied by including courses on information technology in the school curricula. At the same time, teachers need to be trained to use the Internet and computers as tools for the students' benefit. Training government officials and civil servants as well as employees in the private sector will also pay off by increasing IT awareness in society.

E-commerce provides a major opportunity to developing countries. However, in the end, it is important to bear the following in mind. (a) The most expensive technology is not the essential issue: entrepreneurship is. (b) Infrastructure, although important, is not the determinant of success: how to use the available technology is. (c) While embarking upon 'e' activities, countries should bend a well-known maxim and act *locally* but exert their influence *globally* via the Internet. Both national and international concerns must be dealt with. (d) The Internet, while important, is nonetheless only a complementary input to a country's development process.

GLOBAL E-COMMERCE STRATEGIES FOR SMALL BUSINESSES

At some point in their development cycle, small and medium-sized enterprises (SMEs) in Latin America, as elsewhere, have to decide what to do in foreign markets. Are they ready to go international? Do they meet some or most of the conditions for success in the global marketplace? Is the company willing to reposition itself as a global company and make the international arena its mainstream place of business?[23]

Companies, big and small, are sampling the waters, trying out, checking possibilities, and studying alternatives. It is in any small country's best interest to see change as a market opportunity and to investigate the techniques and tools that are now available. The Internet can be a powerful tool for small companies because it tends to level the playing field for firms of any size. On the Net it is very difficult to figure out who or where you are and how big your company is (at least at the beginning). In fact, for various kinds of businesses, this is not important. The following items summarize the process of going online for the international market:

- Researching the business opportunity
- Researching the customer
- Reaching out to the customer
- Showing the company's 'face' online
- Closing the deal
- Providing customer support

Researching the Business Opportunity

The first phase of the process is to research the business opportunity. There are various ways of doing this. The Internet has opened up a broad search area for the identification of opportunities, for the establishment of partnerships across national borders, and for direct links between small companies. 'Virtual companies' are now possible: in fact they are already economically relevant today and will become even more so in future.

It is a traditional maxim that, in order to be able to sell in any particular market, a physical presence in that market is necessary in order to keep abreast of relevant events. With the advent of the Internet, a small company now has the opportunity of being there *virtually*. This means that a firm has ready access to a vast pool of information about the region or country, can read their newspapers, participate in their chat-rooms, and can even listen to their local radio or watch their TV stations. Facts, figures, and statistics on a whole range of issues are available on the Net. This does not mean that all this information is easy to find, or that it is all accurate, but at least it is available, and it is to be hoped that search engines will become more sophisticated in future.

A traditional international trading company links the producer of goods and services in one country with consumers in another country. They operate on a large scale and either focus on one particular market segment or on specific big companies and are not, in general, a big help for small companies trying to go international. With the Internet, it is now possible to establish a partnership between a 'small company' that produces a given item and another small company, or several other small companies, that know the relevant target markets very well. How do you research the potential market for a given product? If you input a keyword into a search engine, you will find sites that specialize in a specific good, and it is then merely a question of contacting the administrator of each site and negotiating a link to your site.

Another opportunity for partnerships across countries is for two or more companies to join complementary skills or product lines to sell on each other's or even third markets. Some of these partnerships are obvious: language translation or 'localization' of products for specific markets, product on one side and package on the other, and so forth. Others are more subtle. In the software business, for instance, companies can purchase 'components' (pieces of software that are reusable) from anywhere in the world, work out the necessary licences, and package them into another product that they can then put up for sale in the global market.[24] In the retail fashion market, a partnership can quickly be between a company that produces gymnastics sports clothes in Mexico and a 'batik' design shop in Bali for sales to Buenos Aires. The opportunities are countless.

Researching the Customer

It is impossible to overestimate the overwhelming amount of information available on the Net about potential customers. Although finding the exact information may be time-consuming, it is well worth it once the right sources are found. In the developed world, and the US in particular, there are statistics about so many things (most of which are now being made available online) that it is very likely that the owners of a small company in Latin America can find useful information or products that are in his/her direct interest (for example handicrafts, lamps, machinery, and so forth).

Another opportunity is the possibility of establishing permanent links with 'virtual communities' as described by Hagel and Armstrong.[25] A virtual community, unlike a 'virtual company', is a group of people from different parts of the world that share a specific set of interests and whose main form of communication is the Net. If a Latin American product fits in with the interests of any of these communities (and chances are that when a Latin American company wants to go abroad, many related communities will exist), the company can try to approach them and gauge, their reaction. There are specific rules for approach, however, and traditional direct marketing might not be one of them.[26]

In cases where governments are the customers of a Latin American company, it will be important to keep looking for new opportunities coming out of WTO agreements. Governments will find it increasingly necessary to offer their tenders for purchases online and to treat international bidders fairly. The European Union has gone a step further and set the date of 2003 for 25 per cent of its own purchases to be conducted online.

Reaching Out to the Customer

Unlike other forms of marketing and sales effort, when a company in Latin America launches a Website, nobody knows they are there. The first step in webbing a business is planning. The first decision is how electronic the commercial transaction is going to be. Is it just to help customers with the search process? Will they be able to order online? How is payment going to be processed? Is the product or service deliverable online? The next step is to define the site's architecture. If the company does not feel comfortable in this area, it is better to hire someone who is. This step is crucial for the success of the endeavour. Considering all the progress made on the Internet, ordering online is still not comfortable from the users' point of view. They must be reassured of the quality of the product, the delivery time, what to do in case of returns (a 'no questions asked' return scheme within a few weeks), and the contact source in case anything goes wrong.

Many of the services offered on the Net today are free (although this is changing). This is reminiscent of the times when academia mainly used the network, and information was posted on the Net as a public service. Information-content companies today have to find a way of generating earnings, though. Non-store-front commerce, in its many forms (direct mail, catalogues, order-by-phone in response to TV ads, and so on), has been around for many years and makes hundreds of billions of dollars annually. It is of course advisable to use traditional tools to reach the customer. Brochures, leaflets, magazine and newspaper ads, and direct mailings should be used as a complement to electronic marketing in order to bring the user to the company's site. At the stage at which business is today, a firm can seldom rely on the Internet alone. A good mixture of *old* and *new* techniques, which varies from case to case, should be developed for any particular business.

Showing the Company's Face Online

Net users expect a site to be lively, ever-changing and up-to-date. When planning the Web-site, its dynamic nature must be taken into consideration: What features are going to change? how often? What can a firm post on the web that its potential visitors will find interesting and attractive? Local culture is a very important aspect of international trade, and companies must be aware of it. It is important to tailor sites to the particular culture of their main customers and not to think, even for a minute, that one's cultural behaviour is somehow standard.

Closing the Deal

It is probably better to start thinking about credit cards or COD (charge on delivery), as practised in China. International credit-card companies have branches in many countries and in major cities throughout Latin America. If this is not the case in a particular country (or if there is mistrust about using such procedures), the next best arrangement would be to have an intermediary in a developed country to facilitate the payment system. Electronic payment will also develop in some form, but the ease of access, tax regulations, and rules on international monetary flows will certainly vary from country to country, and it is important to study each case separately. For very small companies in remote locations that do not have access to a major credit-card company, the use of intermediaries will probably be the norm.

There are international companies that deliver packages efficiently in short periods of time, such as DHL Worldwide Express, Federal Express and United Parcel Service, but direct delivery to each customer, depending upon the kind of product on sale, is not always appropriate. The exporter might have to consider having some kind of storage facility in the target country. In this case, companies should avoid building up too large on inventory of products.

Providing Customer Support

The Internet is a very suitable tool for customer service, support and maintenance (in the manufacturing industry, after- or post-sales support). This activity may be crucial for a company's success and a very rewarding generator of additional revenues. Customer support involves services associated with a product that was sold, or additional services associated with a service that was sold.[27] Provided that a company's customers or perhaps distributors are on the Net, there is a possibility of organizing the entire range of after-sales services on the Internet. This tool is ideal for overcoming language barriers and geographical distances.

After considering all these relevant aspects of the business of going online, SMEs will be in a better position to decide what to do. If they decide to go forward, a directly related book and site can be consulted for useful hints and current versions of texts.[28] An interesting project concerning the facilitation of physical import–export transactions is the 'tradepoint' initiative. Although the architecture of the network was devised before the Internet, UNCTAD's Trade Point Programme has incorporated this new tool and it is now receiving and posting a large number of business opportunities on the Net. Trade points exist physically in many cities in Latin America and are worth a visit.

E-COMMERCE AND THE WTO

One of the roles of international organizations such as the International Telecommunications Union (ITU), the World Intellectual Property Organization (WIPO) and the WTO is to deal with information and communications issues such as those associated with the Internet. The General Council of the WTO agreed to reinvigorate its work programme on electronic commerce after last year's Seattle meeting. The council invited four subsidiary bodies – the Goods, Services and TRIPS (Trade-Related Aspects of Intellectual Property Rights) Councils and the Committee on Trade and Development – to pick up where they had left off and to report back to the General Council by December 2000. The work programme is also to include issues relating to the development of the infrastructure for e-commerce.

Countries need to participate in the proceedings conducted by all these institutions because the agreements and commitments that will be signed during the negotiation process will have a direct impact on their economies. The determination of the degree to which countries can regulate Internet-based trade, what taxes they can impose and what trade barriers they can erect to help out domestic suppliers will depend on the WTO disciplines that member countries decide to apply. In e-commerce transactions, the distinction between goods and services can be blurred. The lack of distinction matters because WTO rules treat goods and services quite differently. Goods tend to be subject to tariffs while services can be limited by restrictions on national treatment. For services, equal treatment is required for domestic and internationally based services providers or quantitative controls may be placed on access to foreign markets. The general view of member governments of the WTO is that a whole range of transactions carried out over the Internet is already covered under the structure and trade liberalization commitments of GATS. There is more disagreement regarding the classification of a limited number of products available on the Internet as services or goods (mostly items such as books and software). The GATS classifies services according to the mode of delivery. Improved commitments to open trade in cross-border services (mode 1) and consumption abroad (mode 2) are also important if electronic commerce is to achieve its full potential. However, it is difficult to establish a distinction between supply under modes 1 and 2 in the case of e-commerce. Countries will need to decide on this classification. The liberalizing impact may be greater under mode 2. Classification also determines the country of jurisdiction for purposes of regulation and dispute settlement. Under mode 1, the transaction would be considered to be taking place where the *buyer* resides. Under mode 2, the regulatory regime is that of the country where the *supplier* resides. Mode 1 would protect the consumer, and mode 2 the supplier.

In choosing which mode to apply under GATS, it may be best to decide which electronic transmissions are treated as services subject to GATS rulings, with the understanding that a review would take place further on, as countries come to better understand the shape and direction of e-commerce. The advantage to this approach is that adopting one definition across the board would solve the issue in case of a dispute, whether the object of a dispute is a good or a service. It avoids uncertainty.[29] However, if quantitative restrictions were to become enforceable, the outcome could be inferior to the results achieved under GATT. For the time being, e-commerce could be subjected to GATS rulings while future contested issues could be addressed and settled through the Dispute Settlement mechanism. At the same time, it is essential that individual service sectors look at the implications of cross-border trade in e-commerce and develop their own sector-specific scheduling strategy to ensure that their own objectives are met.

The application of GATS provisions to e-commerce, under Article VIII on monopolies, exclusive service providers and business practices, could benefit from further elaboration. Article VIII is limited in its application when a monopolist is supplying the service in question. In many countries telecommunications services are supplied by a public monopoly, which often also becomes the monopoly provider of Internet access. In the absence of suitable rules, national regulations and laws may be used as government-made barriers to e-commerce. This would be a key area to liberalize by allowing private Internet service providers (ISPs) into the market. Conversely, a monopoly may be a logical means of taking the risks and making the commitments involved in embarking on a new and expensive venture such as the networking of an economy.

At present, there is no mechanism for arriving at a common approach or mutual recognition with respect to domestic regulatory regimes. Regulatory bodies for ISP issues should include not just members of government agencies but also, if possible, network specialists and private-sector participants in order to achieve a rapid expansion of e-commerce. Countries should try to attract as many firms as possible to bring down prices and increase competition in service provision.

Intellectual Property on the Internet

The Trade Related Intellectual Property Rights (TRIPS) Agreement dealt with in the WTO applies to transmissions on the Internet, while the World Intellectual Property Organization (WIPO) is handling the bulk of the work relevant to this topic. In December 1996, two new treaties came into existence under the auspices of WIPO: the WIPO Copyright Treaty and the WIPO Performances and Phonograms Treaty. These treaties further strengthen the rights of authors, performers and music producers over their own intellectual property (IP). Although these treaties have not yet come into force, they will eventually be brought into the WTO and incorporated into TRIPs.

The growth of the Internet has generated pressure to increase the granting of intellectual property rights and enforcement of protections such as copyrights and patents. The underlying argument is that some forms of information, when made accessible on the Internet, are easily copied. Policy-makers must carefully address intellectual property issues within a policy framework. However, the traditional view that tighter intellectual property protection improves innovation incentives does not appear to hold in such a highly interactive and dynamic environment as the Internet. In this environment, much of the creative activity is interactive and involves the contributions of many different parties. The community nature of the Internet constitutes a good environment for sequential, incremental improvement, where each creator improves on the work of the other. The standard IP model equates imitation to copying, but when innovation is sequential, imitation goes beyond copying as it adds value. Imitation can actually increase the overall incentives to create new content in a dynamic environment, especially since most creative activity tends to be partly imitative, as, for example, in the LINUX case. LINUX is a free version of the UNIX operating system that has become very popular on the Internet as the power operating system of choice. UNIX has been used at the heart of the Internet since its inception. Internet communication software protocols were originally developed on UNIX, but, unlike Microsoft Windows, UNIX has never had a single version, but is instead a family of closely related implementations. LINUX is the latest one to appear. There has to be a delicate balance between patents as guaranteed monopoly rights (that also facilitate investment) and incentives for innovation, on the one hand, and, on the other, rapid imitation that leads to more competition and would be welfare-enhancing.[30]

Granting patents indiscriminately, as has been happening recently in the US, can actually hurt future performance, especially for developing countries as latecomers to the IT process. Since Latin American countries tend to be imitators in the IT industries, excessive IP protection may hurt their chances of catching up.

Customs Tariffs

The current moratorium on electronic commerce tariffs at the WTO is extremely popular with business and some governments. However, there is an argument that taxing electronic commerce will be an important source of future revenue that can be directed towards solving social problems. Governments of developing countries do not seem entirely happy with the prospect of permanently granting e-commerce duty-free status, and not without reason. On the one hand, it is important to bear in mind that trade and exchange across borders is certainly affected more by non-tariff barriers than by taxation of trade. Although customs duties are an important source of revenue for developing countries, it is also important not to put up barriers to a new and growing industry by restricting market access. It would even be advisable to lift import restrictions on all PCs, software and IT-related activities if developing countries are going to be successful during the catching-up period as they move towards a more networked economy. Some countries already have chosen to sign the Information Technology

Agreement (ITA), which requires the signatories to free up trade in a large number of information-technology products.[31]

The full implications of levying duties should be studied carefully and more time taken before any permanent decisions are made on this matter. Developing countries must be wary of entering into a commitment to accept a zero-duty regime before considering the full implications. The moratorium on tariffs could be applied to quantitative restrictions as well. This issue has not emerged at the WTO, but signing an agreement precluding them may not be a prudent step until the full implications are better understood.[32]

Trade Facilitation Issues

E-commerce also raises questions about trademarks and 'domain names' (addresses on the Internet). WIPO, along with the Internet Corporation for Assigned Names and Numbers (ICANN), is now working on these issues.[33] Domain names are a concern for developing countries as they may be monopolized by a few certification or standard-setting private agencies that are situated in technologically advanced countries. A more immediately troublesome development has been the systematic attempt made by various individuals to register desirable Internet domain names with the sole aim of later selling them at a profit, a practice aptly known as 'cyber-squatting'. The ICANN recently selected five members for its Board of Directors, one from each of five geographic regions: Africa, Asia/Australia/Pacific, Europe, Latin America/Caribbean and North America. This may improve developing countries' representation in this institution.

The Economic Commission for Europe (ECE) has also taken an active role in promoting trade facilitation. As a contribution to the reduction of technical barriers to trade, the ECE is developing and agreeing on standards and procedures worldwide, in particular those related to trade in goods and services between computerized information systems. Two standards are now being used for the electronic transmission of commercial data for industry: UN/Electronic Data Interchange for Administration, Commerce and Transport (EDIFACT), the international standard elaborated under the aegis of the ECE and applied worldwide, to support the development and implementation of global standards and the American National Standard Institute (ANSI), American Standard Code for Information Interchange (ASCII), used mainly in the US. UN/EDIFACT and ANSI recently joined forces and prepared a common language for the Internet for the twenty-first century called ebXML (Electronic Business with XML).[34] The UN/Center for Facilitation of Procedures and Practices for Administration, Commerce and Transport (CEFACT) Legal Working Group prepared a draft Electronic Commerce Agreement that is intended to serve the commercial requirements of business-to-business (B-to-B) electronic partners. The objective is to conduct commercial activities on the Internet within a sound legal framework.[35]

Lastly, the United Nations Commission on International Trade Law (UNCITRAL) developed a model law on e-commerce that constitutes the equivalent of a written document, signature and original in electronic form. Many countries have adopted this model law while others have introduced their own legislation related to trade facilitation. At its one hundred sixth session in January 2000, the United States Congress signed a bill authorizing the use of digital signatures into law.

Participation and Negotiations

The negotiating method for Latin America in the WTO should be directly linked to the e-commerce readiness of their economies. The quickest benefits from e-commerce for developing countries can be realized by applying e-commerce to gain competitiveness in their traditional export markets and by using it to reduce the cost of imports.

Trade negotiations will demand a re-examination of important domestic policies, particularly on telecommunications and financial services, as well as on the distribution, delivery, availability and marginal cost of hardware and software. Developing countries need to be given adequate time to study thoroughly the implications and optimal ways of placing the Internet and e-commerce fully in the service of development. Locking in on commitments is not a good idea for developing countries or, to some extent, for developed countries at this early stage, when there is little empirical information available about the social and economic impact of these powerful new tools. This should not, however, translate into barriers to progress in this area, given the incipient nature of e-commerce. A better alternative would be to provide for a review of these issues five years after their adoption, as e-commerce takes on a more definite form and direction.

CONCLUSIONS AND RECOMMENDATIONS

The Internet is a new tool for handling traditional business transactions faster and more efficiently. It offers many opportunities, and it also presents many challenges. However, even firstcomer countries such as the United States do not easily understand it. Many of the software solutions are new and untested, and choosing one over another requires a leap of faith. Over the past four years the reliability, speed and security of the Internet has improved substantially. For business to succeed in this environment, Web-related issues need to be addressed quickly and efficiently at the highest levels within a firm or organization. The public and private sectors also need to play an active role in determining the pace and shape of the networking process.

Electronic commerce has been spreading rapidly and gives every indication of continuing to do so throughout the world, and Latin America should give serious consideration to the steps it will need to take to ensure that it is not left behind. As more and more countries use the Internet for commercial transactions, its influence in international trade may grow very quickly. This offers new opportunities for exporters in Latin America, especially in the manufacturing sector and through business-to-business transactions. The digital divide is real, and if left unaddressed, it may deepen further. There is a lot of catching-up to do, and there is no time to waste. This could also be said of the long-standing economic and social divide between developed and developing countries. There are ways to bridge the digital divide. Information technology, if managed properly and made a priority for governments, can improve education, health, and employment. It can open up concrete possibilities for development, especially for poor and rural populations. Investment in human capital so that more can be learned about how to use the technology, is more important than the level of sophistication of the technology itself.

As in other parts of the world, large enterprises are incorporating the Internet into their business environment much faster than small and medium-sized firms in Latin America. At some point in their development cycle, small and medium-sized firms need to decide how and when to become part of this process. Each country and firm is different. There are no general rules. However, the Internet can be a powerful tool in facilitating market and global access that has not been immediately available in the past.

To what degree countries can decide on the form and pace of e-commerce will also depend on the WTO discipline that member countries decide to apply. That is why it is of paramount importance for them to understand the implications for their economies and their own goals and desires for a networked economy before signing on to agreements concerning issues addressed at the WTO.

If and when there is a next Round, Latin America needs to participate actively and positively in the implementation of e-commerce rule-making. The need for regional consensus on important issues cannot be over-emphasized – not only within a WTO setting but in other organizations as well. Enough time should be given for Latin America to examine the implications of intellectual property rights, customs tariffs, and Internet-based regulations in their own economies. The negotiating method should certainly go in tandem with the e-commerce readiness of their economies. However, trade negotiations will demand a re-examination of the Latin American Countries' own domestic policies as well.

Many questions still remain that need to be answered. In particular, what does it mean to work in an 'Internet-worked' organization? What are the social, cultural and personal implications of working this way? What are the changes in quality of life for people who work in 'Internet-worked' organizations? What are the demands on information technology departments as organizations develop, implement and use Internet-working technologies? An examination of these issues would be extremely useful in guiding and shaping a digital world and a networked environment that is compatible with local customs and needs. Latin America will want to move forward on an informed basis and with realism while taking care to maintain the momentum of this ongoing process, given the nascent nature and the opportunities and challenges offered by e-commerce.

Notes

1. For an in-depth analysis on how the WTO operates, see Michalopoulous, Chapter 2 in this volume.
2. For an interesting account on the rise and growing importance of B-to-B exchanges, see Sculley and Woods (1999).
3. See *Nua Internet Surveys* 'How Many Online'? (2001) (www.nua.ie).
4. See *Digital Economy 2000*, US Department of Commerce, June 2000.
5. See www.nam.org/ecommerce.
6. For instance, in a presentation by the Office for the Controller of the Currency, Department of Treasury, in September 2000 at Harvard University, the speaker recognized the lack of data in determining the weight allocated to use of the Internet in relation to banks' performance.
7. On the topic of how government policy affects investment decisions in IT, see Taschdjian (2000).
8. XML is like Latin was in medieval Europe: it is no one's native language but everyone can use it to exchange information. It is a simple, structured text that describes a business document such as purchase order, and because it is merely text it can be exchanged freely across the Internet and read by any computer. It provides a vehicle for creating site-to-site interfaces for Internet-based communication.
9. According to this study, sunk costs have historically been very important for a large share of trade in goods. The Internet can reduce these costs, as suppliers can advertise to numerous buyers at the same time, thus increasing the exports of countries that have not historically had strong trade ties. See Freund and Weinhold (2000).

10. Derived from Windham (1999).
11. See Carley (2000).
12. For an interesting and insightful account of where the Net may be going which is still highly relevant today, see LeGates (1995).
13. See Gibbon (2000).
14. Felix Zimmerman of the London School of Economics was responsible for the section related to natural resource dependency and opportunities for the manufacturing sector.
15. See Sachs (2000b). www.cid.harvard.edu.
16. See *Human Development Report 1999* (UN, 2000).
17. See Primo Braga (2000).
18. See Rodriguez and Wilson (2000).
19. Anthony Oettinger, in a lecture at Harvard University, on 20 September 2000. Of course there may be exceptions, such as Singapore, for instance.
20. For a summary of WAP potentials see www.wapforum.org; also *Scientific American Special Report* 'The Future of Wireless WEB', October 2000.
21. For a thorough analysis of what is happening in South Asia in the rural sector, see 'Internet in South Asia', *Economic and Political Weekly*, November 1999.
22. See Sachs (2000a). Studies on market readiness are presently being done for the Andean Community. This guide is inspired by Michael Porter's model of competitiveness and firms.
23. The content of this section drew heavily from ideas by Eduardo da Costa of Nest Boston.
24. See, for instance, www.software.net/dist.htm
25. Hagel and Armstrong (1997).
26. Direct marketing is, for most 'surfers', against the netiquette. It seldom works.
27. Pearlson and Whinston (1993).
28. For instance, see da Costa (2001). www.globalecommerce.com or Windham (1999).
29. For an analysis on this issue, see Panagariya (1999).
30. A study by Bessen and Maskin (1997) concludes that the strengthening of intellectual property rights throughout the 1990s has not translated into higher levels of innovative activity.
31. See www.wto.org/tratop-e/inftec
32. Singh (1999).
33. ICANN is a non-profit corporation formed in 1998 to assume responsibility for the IP address space allocation, protocol parameter assignment, and domain name system management now performed under US government contract. For more information, see www.icann.org
34. See www.unece.org/press00/13
35. For a description of these programs, see www.unece.org

Bibliography

BESSEN, JIM and ERIC MASKIN (1997) 'Intellectual Property on the Internet: What's Wrong with Conventional Wisdom'? www.harvard.edu/iip/econ/bessen.html, Cambridge, Massachusetts.

CAHNERS In-Stat Group (2000) www.instat.com/pr/2000. 'US Companies Invested $89 Billion on Internet Strategies in 1999, Spending to Increase to $120 billion in 2000'.

CARLEY, CATHLEEN (2000) 'Organizational Change and the Digital Economy: A Computational Organization Science Perspective', H.J. Heinz III School of Policy and Management, Carnegie Mellon University, Pittsburgh, Pennsylvania.

DA COSTA, EDUARDO (2001) *Global E-commerce Strategies for Small Businesses*, (Cambridge, Massachusetts: MIT Press).

Economic and Political Weekly (1999) 'Internet in South Asia', vol. XXXIV nos 46 and 47, Sameeksha Trust Publication, November 20–26.

FREUND, CAROLINE L. and DIANA WEINHOLD (2000) 'On Estimating the Effect of the Internet on International Trade', Federal Reserve Board, Division of International Finance, Washington, D.C., and Development Studies Institute, London School of Economics, London, October.

GIBBON, EDWARD (2000) 'The Winds and Waves Are Always on the Side of the Ablest Navigator', Strategic Information Technology and the CEO Agenda, AT Kearney Inc. www.atkearny.com, Chicago, Illinois.

HAGEL, J.III and A. G. ARMSTRONG (1997) *Net Gain: Expanding Markets through Virtual Communities* (Boston: HBS Press).

Human Development Report 1999 (2000) (New York: United Nations).

LEGATES, JOHN C. B. (1995) 'The Internet: Is it a Bird? Is It a Plane? Will it Fly'?, Center for Information Policy Research at Harvard University, Cambridge, Massachusetts.

MICHALOPOULOS, CONSTANTINE (2001) 'Latin America in the WTO', chapter 2, *Latin America: Its Future in the Global Economy* (Macmillan Press, UK).

OETTINGER, ANTHONY G. (1998) 'Context for Decisions: Global and Local Information Technology Issues', Center for Information Policy Research, at Harvard University, Cambridge, Massachusetts.

One Hundred Sixth Congress of the United States of America, second session, S.761 (2000), 4 January, Washington, D.C.

PANAGARIYA, ARVIND (1999) 'E-Commerce, WTO and Developing Countries', UNCTAD Paper, Geneva.

PEARLSON, K. and A. WHINSTON (1993) 'Customer Support Issues for the 21st Century', in www.cism.bus.utexas.edu/ravi/keri.html

PRIMO BRAGA, CARLOS A. (2000) 'The Networking Revolution: Opportunities and Challenges for Developing Countries', InfoDev Working Paper, The World Bank Group, Washington, D.C.

RODRIGUEZ, FRANCISCO and ERNEST J. WILSON III (2000) 'Are Poor Countries Losing the Information Revolution?', University of Maryland at College Park, an InfoDev Working Paper, The World Bank Group, Washington, D.C.

SACHS, JEFFREY D. (2000a) 'Readiness for the Networked World: A Guide for Developing Countries', Center for International Development at Harvard University, www.readinessguide.org, Cambridge, Massachusetts.

SACHS, JEFFREY D. (2000b) 'A New Map of the World', *The Economist*, by invitation, www.cid.harvard.edu.cidinthenews/Sachs, Cambridge, Massachusetts.

Scientific American (2000) 'Special Report: The Future of Wireless Web', October, vol. 283, www.sciam.com

SCULLEY ARTHUR and WILLIAM WOODS (1999) *B2B Exchanges: The Killer Application in the Business-to-Business Internet Revolution* (ISI Publications).

SINGH, A. DIDAR (1999) 'Electronic Commerce: Issues for the South', South Centre, Working Paper no. 4, Geneva.

TASCHDJIAN, MARTIN (2000) 'From Open Networks to Open Markets: How the Infrastructure Investment Decision is Affected by Public Policy', Programme on Information Resources Policy at Harvard University, Cambridge, Massachusetts.

US DEPARTMENT OF COMMERCE (2000) 'Digital Economy 2000', Economics and Statistics Administration, Office of Policy Development, www.ecommerce.gov Washington, D.C.

WINDHAM, LAURIE (1999) *Dead Ahead: The Web Dilemma and the New Rules of Business* New York: Allworth Press.

8 Moving toward a Common Set of Multilateral Investment Rules: Lessons from Latin America

Maryse Robert

INTRODUCTION

While investment rules are mostly absent from the multilateral system, the past decade saw a phenomenal increase in the number of bilateral and regional investment agreements concluded worldwide. The last ten years also witnessed an acceleration in the liberalization of foreign direct investment (FDI) regimes and strong growth in FDI inflows. This is particularly true in Latin America and the Caribbean. The 1990s marked the return of private capital to the region. FDI inflows increased by almost 1,000 per cent between 1990 and 1999, from $8.9 billion in 1990 to $90.5 billion in 1999. The region has become as attractive as developing Asia, which received $106 billion in FDI inflows in 1999. Brazil, the Latin American leader, competes advantageously with the People's Republic of China (PRC), having obtained $31 billion in FDI inflows in 1999 whereas the PRC received $40 billion.[1] After years of imposing controls excluding or restricting the entry of foreign firms, Latin American and Caribbean countries embarked on a series of ambitious economic reforms in the mid-1980s and early 1990s. They abandoned the import-substitution model and at the beginning of the twenty-first century most countries in the region are now seeking to attract investment from abroad as a way to foster economic growth and development and to stimulate transfer of technology and competition.

The 1960s and the early 1970s were characterized by a shortage of private flows to Latin America and the Caribbean. Countries had to rely essentially on multilateral lending by international financial institutions. The oil crises of the 1970s fundamentally changed this. As prices soared, earnings from oil exporters were deposited in commercial banks and recycled by these banks in developing countries. In Latin America, several countries, including Mexico and Brazil, saw an opportunity to finance their ever-growing fiscal deficit. Higher commodity prices and relatively low real interest rates encouraged this trend. But as the real exchange rate appreciated, exports became less competitive and the balance of payments worsened. When Mexico had a debt crisis in August 1982, the whole region experienced a severe flight of capital. Even Colombia and Chile, two countries that played by the rules, suffered from the 'neighbourhood effect'.[2] It would take almost an entire decade for private capital to return to the region.

The 1980s were a rather difficult period for Latin America and the Caribbean. Low commodity prices, high interest rates, and a strong dollar compounded the difficulties relating to the outflow of capital due to negative resource transfers to pay interests on the commercial debt. Schemes devised to solve the debt problem included debt swaps, buybacks, and initiatives such as the Baker and Brady Plans. Market-focused and outward-oriented reforms implemented as early as the mid-1980s paved the way for attracting private capital to the region in the 1990s. Foreign direct investment and portfolio investment increased significantly, whereas official flows dropped in relative terms, with the exception of 1995 and the Mexican 'tequila' crisis.

Type of FDI Flows

The type of FDI flows varies a lot throughout the region. Mexico, Central America and the Caribbean are mostly home to efficiency-seeking investors for whom these countries served as an export platform in sectors such as automobiles, electronics, and textiles. Some Caribbean countries (Trinidad and Tobago and Jamaica, for example) also receive resource-seeking investments. It is worth noting that several smaller countries (Costa Rica being a prime example) have been very successful in attracting high-tech companies, therefore taking advantage of the positive externalities associated with such investment.[3]

In the 1990s, economic reforms, in particular the liberalization of trade and investment regimes and new privatization policies played a key role in encouraging long-term capital flows and in improving the region's economic fundamentals. Moreover, low interest rates in developed countries triggered a substantial increase in portfolio investment, a new phenomenon in Latin America and the Caribbean, as international investors, including institutional investors, sought better returns in the region and bought stocks and bonds. Sebastian Edwards notes that the 1990s most probably signalled the end of the 'neighbourhood effect'. The 'cross-market contagion' declined during the decade although at the turn of the century this trend is presently changing. Strong fundamentals matter and 'international investors were quick to realize that there are significant differences among Latin American countries'.[4] In addition to laws and regulations that are more investment-friendly, Latin American and Caribbean governments also entered, bilaterally and regionally, into binding obligations to improve their investment climate. The multilateral system has not provided such opportunity yet. In fact, there is no comprehensive agreement on investment at the World Trade Organization (WTO). Its investment framework is rather limited in scope since it is primarily confined to performance requirements in the Agreement on Trade-Related Investment Measures (TRIMs), which covers goods only, and to the provisions of the General Agreement on Trade in Services (GATS) through commercial presence and movement of natural persons as the third and fourth modes of supply of a service.[5] The current system lacks 'modal neutrality', that is, in the words of Patrick Low and Arvind Subramanian (1996), 'equality of policy treatment regardless of the means by which producers choose to supply a given market – whether through imports, foreign direct investment, temporary presence of natural persons, or the licensing of domestic producers'.

The WTO framework suffers from a clear imbalance. It includes disciplines on trade in goods and services. Investment in services is included but investment in goods has yet to be fully covered.[6] Moreover, the traditional components of an investment agreement, such as investment protection, are not addressed by WTO rules.

At a time when 34 countries in the Americas are negotiating a hemispheric investment agreement within the Free Trade of the Area (FTAA) process, the issue of 'how and when' the WTO system will tackle the whole set of multilateral investment rules remains to be resolved. After reviewing the numerous endeavours to negotiate investment rules in the GATT/ WTO framework, from the early attempts (and the failed Multilateral Agreement on Investment (MAI) negotiated by members of the Organization for Economic Co-operation and Development (OECD) to the disciplines of the WTO Agreements). This chapter discusses the challenges of negotiating multilateral investment rules at the WTO in the current policy context, building on the experience of Latin America in their bilateral and regional investment agreements and the FTAA negotiations.

INVESTMENT RULES AND DISCIPLINES IN THE WTO

As mentioned earlier, there is no comprehensive WTO agreement on investment but a number of agreements resulting from the Uruguay Round that include investment-related provisions. These agreements are: the Agreement on Trade-Related Investment Measures (TRIMs), the General Agreement on Trade in Services (GATS), the Agreement on Subsidies and Countervailing Measures (SCM), the Agreement on Trade-Related Aspects of Intellectual Property Rights (TRIPS), and the Plurilateral Agreement on Government Procurement (GPA).

Agreement on Trade-Related Investment Measures (TRIMs)

The TRIMs Agreement does not go beyond the GATT since it establishes an illustrative list of prohibited performance requirements, those contrary to the principle of national treatment (Article III of GATT 1994) such as local content and trade-balancing requirements and those inconsistent with the general obligation of eliminating quantitative restrictions (Article XI of GATT 1994). These include trade and foreign exchange-balancing restrictions and domestic sales requirements. Member countries had 90 days from the date of entry into force of the WTO Agreement to notify all inconsistent TRIMs to the Council for Trade in Goods. Developed countries had to eliminate these TRIMs within two years of the date of entry into force of the WTO Agreement, whereas developing countries had until 1 January 2000. Least-developed countries are required to undertake the same commitments within seven years, that is by 1 January 2002. The Council may extend the transition period for developing and least-developed countries. On 31 July 2001, the Goods Council adopted decisions granting extension of the transition period for the elimination of TRIMs to the following countries: Argentina, Columbia, Malaysia, Mexico, Pakistan, the Phillippines and Romania. The WTO General Council approved a waiver for Thailand. The new decisions extend the deadline for these countries for eliminating the TRIMs notified under Article 5.1 of the TRIMs Agreement by two years (from 1 January 2000 to 31 December 2000) with a possible further two years.

General Agreement on Trade in Services (GATS)

The GATS is not an investment agreement, but it includes several investment-related provisions. First, the definition of services incorporates four modes of supply, one of which, the third mode, 'commercial presence in the territory of any other member', is essentially an investment activity and a right of establishment. Commercial presence means, under GATS Article XXVIII, 'any type of business or professional establishment, including through the constitution, acquisition or maintenance of a juridical person, or the creation or maintenance of a branch or a representative office, within the territory of a Member for the purpose of supplying a service'. It is worth noting that such definition is not as comprehensive as the definition of investment found in most bilateral investment treaties and free trade agreements signed in the Americas.[7] The fourth mode, which is the supply of service 'through presence of natural persons of a Member in the territory of any other Member', is also linked, albeit indirectly, to investment issues because it implies the temporary entry of managerial and other key personnel.

The GATS is the WTO Agreement with the most far-reaching implications for a multilateral investment agreement because of its all-encompassing most-favoured-nation (MFN) provision (GATS Article II), applies across the board to all members and services sectors. Although MFN exemptions are allowed, if listed in an Annex at the time of the entry into force of the Agreement, they are temporary in nature and subject to multilateral review. The GATS also provides that preferential treatment may be granted to a foreign service supplier who is a member of an economic integration agreement if such agreement has substantial sectoral coverage and provides for the absence or elimination of substantially all discrimination through the elimination of existing discriminatory measures, and/or prohibition of new or more discriminatory measures (GATS Article V). Other GATS provisions of a general nature that are investment-related include transparency obligations, general exceptions, and security exceptions. Unlike the North American Free Trade Agreement (NAFTA), the GATS do not contain a right of non-establishment promoting services trade along lines of comparative advantage. Such right ensures that no Party may require a service provider of another Party to establish or maintain a representative office or any form of enterprise, or to be resident, in its territory as a condition for the cross-border provision of a service. A right of non-establishment prohibits regulators to require establishment as a precondition for delivery of a service.

The GATS provisions regarding national treatment (Article XVII) and market access (Article XVI) are conditional, a clear departure from common practice in investment agreements with respect to the national treatment provision.[8] They are granted according to specific commitments listed in members' schedules indicating to which sectors and modes of supply these provisions apply. The GATS thus makes use of what is known as a 'positive list' by identifying which sectors are covered by the agreement. More specifically, this means that 'new discriminatory measures' are allowed in sectors not included in a member's schedule. Moreover, in sectors where commitments have been made, existing measures inconsistent with the agreement do not have to be eliminated as long as they are listed in a member's schedule.[9]

Schedules include a number of 'unbound' entries for each mode of supply, which means that a WTO member is not bound by any commitment in the GATS for a particular mode in a particular sector with respect to either national treatment or market access. Commercial presence is the mode with the lowest percentage of unbound commitments. When commitments are unbound, countries are not obliged to maintain the same level of openness or to further liberalize. Commercial presence has been scheduled for full liberalization by about 20 per cent of WTO members. Liberalization movement of natural persons (mode 4) was much less prevalent with full liberalization by less than one per cent of WTO members. The GATS includes commitments to further liberalize trade in services. WTO members are currently engaged in a second round of negotiations, which began in January 2000.

Agreement on Subsidies and Countervailing Measures (SCM)

The Agreement on Subsidies and Countervailing Measures (SCM) contains disciplines covering investment-related issues. In fact, some examples of investment incentives (fiscal, financial or indirect) fall under the meaning of subsidy, as defined in the SCM. Except as provided in the Agreement on Agriculture, such investment incentives are prohibited if they are given upon export performance or use of domestic over imported goods (Article 3). Others, which may not be prohibited but are found to cause adverse effects, are subject to compensation. However, as noted by the WTO, 'the underlying concepts of the SCM are oriented toward trade in goods, and as such may not in all cases be easily applied to investment incentives'. For example, an investment incentive is usually granted *before* any production begins, which means that 'neither a recommendation to withdraw or modify a subsidy, nor a countervailing duty applied to the exported goods, will be able to "undo" or to change an investment that already has been made'.[10]

Agreement on Trade-Related Aspects of Intellectual Property Rights (TRIPS)

The Agreement on Trade-Related Aspects of Intellectual Property Rights (TRIPS) is the first ever comprehensive multilateral agreement to set minimum standards protecting all areas of intellectual property rights, to include domestic enforcement measures, and to be covered by a dispute settlement mechanism. Its impact on investment issues, although indirect, is nonetheless significant. The TRIPS Agreement contributes to strengthening the protection afforded to foreign investment by reinforcing the protection of intellectual property rights, one of the key elements often listed in the definition of investment found in most recent bilateral investment treaties (BITs) and free trade agreements currently in force worldwide.

Plurilateral Agreement on Government Procurement (GPA)

The Plurilateral Agreement on Government Procurement (GPA) also includes investment-related provisions. The GPA is one of the plurilateral agreements set out in Annex 4 of the WTO Agreement, which means that not all WTO members are bound by its obligations. The cornerstone of the GPA is non-discrimination, either with respect to domestic products, services and suppliers (national treatment), or with respect to goods, services and suppliers of other Parties (most-favoured-nation or MFN treatment). With regard to all laws, regulations, procedures and practices regarding government procurement covered by this Agreement, each Party shall ensure that its entities shall not treat a locally-established supplier less favourably than another locally-established supplier on the basis of degree of foreign affiliation or ownership; and that its entities shall not discriminate against locally-established suppliers on the basis of the country of production of the good or service being supplied, provided that the country of production is a Party to the Agreement. The GPA applies to government procurement of entities selected by each Party and covers central government entities, sub-central government and other entities, services and construction services.

POST-URUGUAY ROUND: WTO AND OECD INITIATIVES

Shortly after the end of the Uruguay Round, two initiatives were undertaken by the WTO and the OECD to address the issue of investment in a multilateral context. At the Singapore Ministerial Meeting in December 1996, WTO members agreed to create a Working Group on the Relationship between Trade and Investment (WGTI). The mandate of the Group was not to negotiate an investment agreement but rather to begin analytical and exploratory work on the linkages between trade and investment. Earlier, in May 1995, the OECD Ministers had launched negotiations on a Multilateral Agreement on Investment (MAI).

OECD-Multilateral Agreement on Investment (MAI)

The United States successfully convinced its OECD partners to start negotiating in 1995, a multilateral agreement on investment. It would be a free-standing international treaty open to non-member countries, with high standards of liberalization, investment protection and effective dispute settlement procedures. The 1997 deadline to complete the negotiations was extended to the 1998 Ministerial Meeting held in Paris on 27 April. However, the MAI negotiations ended in failure in the Fall of 1998, after the French government had announced that it was pulling out. For some analysts, the reasons for this failure were attributed to the numerous issues which remained to be resolved (exceptions, culture, the coverage of sub-national levels of government, extra-territorial measures, labour and environment, among others). Others highlighted that a coalition of non-governmental organizations (NGOs) had campaigned against the agreement and successfully used the Internet trying to convince everyone that the MAI was a bad deal only benefiting multinational corporations. Finally, others closer to the negotiations, have suggested that the MAI failed because the agreement did not generate the benefits necessary to motivate the body politics and the business sector 'to bite the bullet' and push for the conclusion of the negotiations. In the United States, the Administration had no political appetite to fight for the MAI in early 1998, after having been unable to convince Congress to renew the fast-track negotiating authority in November 1997.[11]

The business sector in most OECD countries was also not very enthusiastic because the MAI would not have eliminated the very few investment barriers currently in place in these countries. Members were prepared at best to bind existing liberalization. Another element played against the agreement. The MAI was a single-issue negotiation, which meant that the trade-offs needed to be made within the context of the investment provisions.[12] In the Americas, the United States, Canada and Mexico participated from 1995 to 1998 in the MAI negotiations, whereas Argentina, Brazil, and Chile took part in these negotiations starting in 1997.

Investment Rules: Do We Need Them?

The fact that investment liberalization has taken place at the national level without a multilateral framework, and the failure of the OECD-based MAI negotiations, may suggest to some analysts and countries that such framework is unnecessary or too difficult to achieve. However, the objective of 'modal neutrality' mentioned earlier would call for multilateral rules and disciplines to liberalize investment. In the past, investment was essentially seen as a substitute to trade. High tariffs would encourage firms to invest in a country and serve the national market. But this relationship is not as significant today, as trade liberalization is now a worldwide phenomenon.

The globalization of the world economy and the internationalization of production have shown that investment has also become a complement to trade.[13] Firms have more choices. They can choose which 'modality' (trade, FDI, licensing, land, and so forth) to use to maximize access to resources and markets, and, in the process, increase their competitiveness. Firms often combine investment and trade to exploit, in the most optimal manner, opportunities offered by their 'portfolio of locational assets'.[14]

Before discussing the arguments in favour of a multilateral investment framework, this section addresses the potential impact of bilateral and regional investment rules, and describes succinctly the agreements that Latin American countries have entered into at both the bilateral and regional levels, as well as the objectives of the investment negotiations within the FTAA process. The region have adopted a three-pronged approach with respect to investment issues they have:

- Unilaterally liberalized their domestic investment regimes;
- Concluded numerous bilateral investment treaties;
- Negotiated bilateral and regional trade agreements, which include an investment framework.

They are currently involved in the FTAA negotiations and are participating, with other WTO members, in the reflection on whether to negotiate comprehensive investment rules at the multinational level or deepen the WTO investment regime.

BILATERAL AND REGIONAL TRADE AGREEMENTS

Bilateral Investment Treaties (BITs)

Traditionally, investment agreements have set standards for the treatment and protection of the investment and investor, in addition to including an admission clause and providing an effective dispute settlement mechanism between the investor and the Host State. These agreements, most of them bilateral in nature, do not include a market access component and do not *per se* attract investment flows. Rather, they act as a complement to the economic determinants of these flows. BITs are therefore 'enabling in character', which means that, 'by themselves, they have little or no effect'.[15] This is not to say that BITs are irrelevant. In fact, they contribute to improving the investment climate of the Host State and reducing the risk of investing in that country.

During the last decade, a growing number of Latin American and Caribbean countries concluded bilateral investment treaties that go beyond the traditional BIT approach. These new agreements include a right of establishment with no admission provision, and therefore add a 'market access' component to the 'protection element' of a typical BIT. More than 70 bilateral investment treaties have been signed between countries of the Americas since the early 1990s. Of these treaties, all those signed by the United States, and by Canada after negotiating the North American Free Trade Agreement (NAFTA), include a right of establishment and a list of reservations, for instance sectors that are not covered by some investment provisions such as national treatment and MFN treatment. These treaties exert a positive influence on the investment regime of a country by locking in the liberalization achieved at the national level.

Regional Trade Agreements: The Signalling Effects of Investment Liberalization

Regional trade agreements contribute in a similar fashion to improving the investment climate. They represent a commitment to a transparent, stable and predictable policy environment. The signalling effect of unilateral trade and investment liberalization, particularly for small countries, is much more powerful when bound in international agreements. Countries gain in credibility when narrowing the gap between bound and applied levels of market openness. In addition, it is also worth emphasizing that small countries stand to benefit from a liberalized regional trade and investment framework because market-seeking foreign firms interested in a region will no longer exclude countries with a small domestic market when analyzing locational advantages.

Regional trade agreements are likely to have a significant impact on FDI flows when they result in a more liberal investment policy and the opening up of sectors which had in the past been closed to foreign investors. They may also have a positive influence on FDI inflows by speeding up investment liberalization either before the conclusion of the agreement or during the implementing phase. Economic growth generated by regional trade agreements may also encourage higher levels of FDI inflows. Trade barriers, such as stringent and restrictive rules of origin in a free trade area (FTA), which discriminate against non-member countries are another important – albeit undesirable outcome from an allocation of resources' standpoint – factor that may lead to an increase in FDI flows into a region, more specifically tariff-jumping FDI in this case. Firms may wish to switch from exports to FDI in order to reap the benefits of the regional market.

It is fair to say that all countries do not benefit equally from a regional investment framework. States that choose to restrict access to some of their sectors or industries may not see much increase in FDI inflows. Similarly, countries which had a fairly open investment regime prior to the entry into force of the agreement, may not experience a surge in FDI flows. In fact, it is difficult to determine *a priori* which countries will benefit the most from a liberalized investment framework because other policy determinants and economic variables play a significant role in explaining an increase in FDI inflows. Each country must be able to exploit its own country-specific advantages, and, in that regard, policy choices still matter.

Regional or bilateral trade agreements concluded by Latin American countries generally include an investment chapter or protocol. The Free Trade Agreement (FTA) among members of the Group of Three (Colombia, Mexico, and Venezuela), and the bilateral FTAs signed respectively by Mexico with Bolivia, Chile, Costa Rica, Nicaragua, and the Northern Triangle (Guatemala, El Salvador, and Honduras), and between Chile and Canada, have all embraced the NAFTA model and incorporated a protection element and a market access component in their investment chapter. Meanwhile the free trade agreement between the Central American countries and the Dominican Republic includes an additional element, an admission clause that somewhat offsets the right of establishment of the national treatment provision. The Colonia Protocol for the Mercosur (the Common Market of the South) member countries also includes an admission clause, whereas the Buenos Aires Protocol for non-Mercosur members follows the traditional approach adopted in bilateral investment treaties as does the free trade agreement between Chile with each of the Central American countries.[16] The investment agreement between Caricom (the Caribbean Community and Common Market) and the Dominican Republic also follow the traditional approach in bilateral investment treaties. The Andean Community's Decision 291 contains a few investment provisions, and so does Caricom's Protocol II, which establishes that members shall not introduce in their territories any new restrictions relating to the right of establishment of nationals of other Member States save as otherwise provided in the agreement.

Except for Mexico and the NAFTA, it is difficult to determine the impact of most of these agreements on FDI inflows because statistics are unavailable. Mexico greatly benefited from an increase in FDI inflows shortly before and after the entry into force of NAFTA. Flows doubled to over $4 billion annually before NAFTA was brought into effect and rose to over $10 billion in 1994. The liberalization of Mexico's investment regime enshrined into the NAFTA the preferential access to the US market (as long as rules of origin are met), and low-cost labour led to a major increase of FDI flows into Mexico. Mercosur members, in particular Brazil and Argentina, also experienced a significant increase in FDI flows. Privatization policy, macroeconomic reforms, and investment liberalization at the domestic level, as well as the elimination of most tariffs between members, have also contributed to attracting more investment to the region.[17]

Hemispheric Investment Negotiations: The Free Trade Area of the Americas

Latin American countries are taking part, along with the United States, Canada and the Caribbean, in a regional negotiation to create the Free Trade Area of the Americas (FTAA). In addition to investment, there are eight negotiating groups in the FTAA: market access; agriculture; services; government procurement; intellectual property rights; subsidies, antidumping and countervailing duties; competition policy; and dispute settlement.[18]

The objective of the FTAA Negotiating Group on Investment (NGIN) is to establish a fair and transparent legal framework to promote investment through the creation of a stable and predictable environment that protects the investor and the investment, without creating obstacles to investments from outside the hemisphere. Essentially, the mandate of the NGIN is to develop a framework incorporating comprehensive rights and obligations on investment and a methodology to consider potential reservations and exceptions to the obligations.

Work prepared for the FTAA Working Group on Investment (WGIN), which met nine times between September 1995 and September 1998 and set the stage for the current negotiations, has shown that investment instruments in the Americas share important commonalities:[19]

- Most agreements have adopted a broad, open-ended, asset-based definition of the term investment, which is more encompassing that the traditional enterprise-based definition of foreign direct investment. They also provide for fair and equitable treatment, some form of protection, national treatment, and MFN treatment.
- They guarantee the free transfer of funds related to investment and include a non-exhaustive list of types of payments for which the transfer of funds is to be guaranteed. Investment agreements in the Americas prohibit expropriation unless it is done for a public purpose, on a non-discriminatory basis, in accordance with due process of law, and on payment of compensation.

- Dispute settlement provisions are also included. State-to-state investment disputes are covered by the general dispute settlement mechanism in free trade agreements, while there are specific provisions to that effect in bilateral investment treaties. There are also provisions on investor–state disputes allowing Parties to submit their claim either to an *adhoc* tribunal or a more institutionalized mechanism such as the International Convention on the Settlement of Investment Disputes between States and Nationals of other States (ICSID).

Two different approaches have been adopted with respect to the entry of investments and investors of a Party into the territory of another Party. Newer instruments such as those included in the NAFTA, the Group of Three, and the bilateral free trade agreements concluded by Mexico with Bolivia, Chile, Costa Rica, Nicaragua, and the Northern Triangle, and by Chile with Canada, create a right of establishment for investors and investments of the other Party. In fact, these instruments have been designed with the purpose of assuring the free entry of such investments – albeit with country-specific reservations – into the territory of the host country.

MULTILATERAL INVESTMENT RULES

In analyzing whether to negotiate comprehensive multilateral investment rules, Latin American countries and other WTO members have to consider the arguments in favour of such undertaking and the results and signals that WTO rules on investment would send to foreign investors.

(1) There is obviously no guarantee that a set of multilateral investment rules would result in an increase in FDI inflows in any individual country. There is no reason to believe that all countries would behave identically with respect to investment liberalization and other important policy determinants of FDI inflows such as privatization policy, competition policy, macroeconomic policy, and tax policy. As was mentioned above in the section on regional trade agreements, the economic policy framework of each country matters a great deal. States would not lose their policy flexibility by negotiating multilateral rules.

(2) A multilateral investment framework would probably aim at locking in the liberalization achieved at the national level, and may also speed up investment liberalization. A built-in agenda for future liberalization would also encourage this trend. But it is entirely possible that some countries would engage in commitments that widen the gap between bound and

applied levels of market openness, as this has been the case for tariffs at the GATT and the services commitments in the GATS. Although the signalling effects of such decision, particularly in the case of smaller economies, would not be lost on foreign investors, WTO members are free to exercise their sovereignty and decide whether a commitment at the WTO should reflect the status quo, as embodied in their domestic investment regime. It is also possible that the rules enshrined in a multilateral investment regime be less liberal than those of a bilateral or regional agreement.

(3) Apart from the importance of addressing the issue of 'modal neutrality' underlined above, a multilateral framework would ensure transparency, predictability and a degree of legal security of domestic FDI regimes. Moreover, a multilateral investment framework does not negate the ability of countries to enhance their attractiveness to FDI flows by improving their physical infrastructure such as telecommunications, roads, ports, airports, power, human resources, and technology. These economic determinants play a key role in encouraging foreign firms to invest in a country. In fact, a comprehensive multilateral investment framework would draw attention to these factors, and contribute to a more efficient allocation of resources, especially if it addresses, in some ways, distorting practices such as investment incentives and performance requirements.

Comprehensive WTO Agreement on Investment: Scenarios to be Considered

The development of a multilateral investment agreement within the GATT/WTO framework has been discussed since the mid-1940s. The current regime inherited from the Uruguay Round contains few investment provisions but no comprehensive coverage. The next WTO Ministerial Meeting will offer an opportunity for member countries to assess whether to negotiate a more coherent set of investment disciplines. In this regard, Latin American countries and other WTO members may wish to consider a number of scenarios in their reflection on how to expand the scope of investment disciplines at the WTO. Without prejudging the decision that these countries will make, these scenarios are briefly discussed below.

(1) The first issue to address is whether to negotiate a comprehensive agreement that covers investment protection and liberalization or to choose a more modest approach and broaden the current regime. The objective of 'modal neutrality' explained earlier would suggest that there is a compelling case to be made for comprehensive multilateral investment

rules that cover goods *and* services. However, the decision to go ahead on that front, in a post-MAI environment, will be largely influenced by the political economy in member countries at the time of the Ministerial Meeting.

(2) Latin American countries must also decide whether they should primarily focus on a hemispheric investment agreement within the FTAA process, bearing in mind that such agreement could serve as a model for the WTO later, or whether they should adopt a two-track approach, that is to negotiate comprehensive investment rules hemispherically *and* multilaterally. *A priori*, it appears that a hemispheric negotiation on investment matters may be easier to bring to fruition because of the clear commitment from all participants that this issue belongs in the negotiation. Also, as was underlined earlier, common approaches have been adopted in investment agreements signed between countries negotiating the Free Trade Area of the Americas. The 1990s saw the emergence of a new consensus in the Americas over the rules governing foreign investment on issues such as scope and coverage, definitions of investment and investor, general standards of treatment, compensation for losses, transfers, and expropriation.

(3) Should WTO members decide to negotiate a comprehensive agreement on investment, they would need to determine the scope of that agreement and to address its three components.

(a) The *substantive scope* consists of the disciplines of the agreement, including the definition of key terms such as investment and investor, which investment and which investor will be entitled to benefit from the agreement. Countries would need to assess the impact of these definitions on the provisions of the agreement and an eventual liberalization process. Should the definition of investment include FDI, portfolio investment, real estate and intangible assets? Should it be broad enough to allow for the inclusion of new forms of investment, while providing for the definition of what is *not* an investment (in order to exclude short-term capital flows)? Should the definition also apply to commitments made in the GATS? As explained earlier, the definition of commercial presence under GATS Article XXVIII is much narrower but does cover pre- and post-establishment investment.

(b) The territorial scope refers to the territory of the Parties that fall under the agreement, including the application of the provisions at the subnational level. The temporal scope informs on whether the agreement applies to investment made, and disputes that arose, prior to the entry into force of the agreement. The provision on scope may also include economic activities reserved to the state that Parties choose to exclude from the agreement.

(c) The provisions on national treatment and MFN treatment are another key element of a comprehensive agreement on investment. WTO members would need to decide whether to apply the MFN and national treatment provisions across the board to all members and sectors (with reservations), or to adopt the GATS approach, for instance to have an all-encompassing MFN provision with temporary exemptions and a conditional national treatment standard, which would apply to all sectors for which members would make commitments.

Members would also need to assess whether the Agreement on Investment would include commitments to investment liberalization in both goods and services, such as how would the current GATS commitments be affected by this new instrument? In fact, should WTO members adopt the 'positive list' or bottom-up approach of the GATS by identifying which sectors are covered by the agreement? Or, should they embrace a 'negative list' or top-down approach to lock in the liberalization achieved at the domestic level and ensure that all future measures are covered by the agreement? Another relevant question is whether the commitments made by WTO members would reflect the status quo, regardless of the approach adopted. As mentioned earlier, this has proved to be difficult in the GATS.

One of the main components of bilateral and regional investment agreements, investment protection provisions, is essentially absent from the WTO framework. There is no coverage of matters related to expropriation, an issue that has become politically very sensitive 'in countries with high levels of regulatory and NGO activism'.[20] A comprehensive agreement on investment at the WTO could address this issue and define the concept of indirect expropriation in such a way as to reaffirm the rights of sovereign countries to regulate. WTO members could also decide to ignore this issue altogether and rely on their network of bilateral investment treaties and regional agreements.

Although payment and transfers, an important component of the provisions on investment protection, are covered in the GATS, the provision on this issue is commitment-specific, which means that it applies only to scheduled sectors and modes of supply. In contrast, the transfer provision in investment agreements is of a general nature. It usually states that the host country must guarantee the free transfer of funds related to investments of investors of another Party. Most agreements include an illustrative list of types of payments that are guaranteed – for example: returns, profits, interests, dividends, and other current incomes; repayments of loans; and proceeds of the total or partial liquidation of an investment. In addition, other types of payments are often listed – for example: additional

contributions to capital for the maintenance or development of an investment; bonuses and honoraria; wages and other remuneration accruing to a
citizen of the other Party; compensation or indemnification; and payments
arising out of an investment dispute. Most agreements also stipulate that the
transfer shall be made without delay in a freely convertible currency or
freely usable currency[21] at the normal rate applicable on the date of the
transfer. Some agreements allow for limitations or exceptions to transfers,
for example in the case of balance-of-payments difficulties and prudential
measures, as long as these restrictions are exercised for a limited period of
time in an equitable way, in good faith and in a non-discriminatory manner.

Investment agreements include two dispute settlement mechanisms. One
deals with disputes between states, and the other allows investors of a
Party to bring a claim against another Party. It appears unlikely for the
time being that investor–state arbitration would be exported to Geneva
because of the burden it would impose on the current system and the political sensitivities it would generate.

A comprehensive agreement would also include provisions on performance requirements and may cover investment incentives. There has been
intense competition among both developed and developing countries in
trying to attract FDI by using investment incentives. Central and sub-
national states (that is, provinces and states) in developed countries make
great use of these instruments. Investment incentives – be they fiscal,
financial, or of other types – often play a significant role in influencing the
location of some specific investments. They may also lead countries to
embark on costly 'grant shopping', resulting in discrimination and distortions in the allocation of production and resources, essentially in rent-
seeking behaviour by investors. Countries with fewer resources may find it
difficult to compete on a level playing field with other states using such
instruments. Countries with federal structures have traditionally been hesi-
tant to tackle this issue in international negotiations. They often feel they
cannot or should not bind their sub-national states.

Provisions on investment incentives could address issues related to their
scope, codification, the prohibition of some types of incentives, and the
principles of transparency and non-discrimination (national treatment and
MFN treatment).

A second scenario is to expand the current WTO investment framework
without negotiating a comprehensive agreement on investment. Several
options are possible. WTO members could focus on investment liberalization
in the GATS and ensure that the commitments reflect more closely the
investment regime in place in each member country. Members could also
elect to develop disciplines on investment in goods to address the market

access component of an investment agreement. Disciplines on investment incentives promoting transparency and non-discrimination, as explained in the previous paragraph, could be added to the SCM, and commitments made in the Plurilateral Agreement on Government Procurement (GPA) could be multilateralized.

A third scenario would be for WTO members to negotiate a Plurilateral Agreement on Investment, which would be comprehensive in nature. The European Commission floated this idea in December 2000.

CONCLUSION AND RECOMMENDATIONS

Challenges Ahead for Latin America

Latin American countries must reflect on the role that an investment agreement should play, and what they want to achieve at the WTO and in the FTAA agreement. A lot of progress has been made with respect to the rules and disciplines governing investment in the region, and in the Americas as a whole. In fact, there are more commonalities at the regional level than multilaterally. By building on the existing consensus in the FTAA, countries of the Americas will strive for a balanced framework that will ensure mutual advantage and increased benefits for all participants. In so doing they may wish to review their recent experience with their own investment instruments and draw lessons to be applied in their negotiations. On investment matters, the FTAA offers an opportunity to show how regional agreements can contribute to building a stronger multilateral trading system.

More broadly, Latin American countries face numerous challenges at the beginning of the twenty-first century. A first challenge is to ensure that their market-oriented reforms implemented during the 1990s are sustained in the long run. A sudden change in policy towards protectionism could lead to massive capital outflows. A second challenge is to include in trade and investment agreements the liberalization achieved unilaterally. Both developed and developing countries benefit from the signalling effects of a negotiated agreement that provides legal security to international investors. Countries also gain in credibility if there is no gap between bound and applied commitments to market access. In the context of a hemispheric investment agreement, Latin American countries must decide, along with the United States, Canada, and the Caribbean, whether the FTAA investment chapter will represent a commitment that reflects the status quo or go beyond the current level of liberalization. They must also discuss whether the agreement should aim at progressive liberalization with a built-in agenda for future liberalization. But more important, Latin American countries need to identify their objectives, priorities and interests in negotiating investment agreements, be they at the regional or multilateral level.

Notes

1. UNCTAD (2000, p. 16).
2. See Ocampo (1989).
3. UNCTAD (2000, pp. 62–3).
4. Edwards (1999, pp. 18–19).
5. WTO (2000, p. 13).
6. Low and Subramanian (1996, pp. 390–1).
7. Sauvé (1994, p. 9).
8. WTO (1996, p. 71).
9. Sauvé (1994, p. 12).
10. WTO (1996, pp. 72–3).
11. Since Congress is vested with authority over foreign commerce under the US constitution, a mechanism was engineered in the Trade Act of 1974 to allow the executive branch to fashion trade deals without having Congress pick them apart piece by piece thus requiring re-negotiation with foreign partners. The fast-track authority, now known as Trade Promotion Authority, gives the executive branch the leeway to negotiate a trade agreement, which is then accepted or rejected as a whole and without changes by Congress.
12. For more on the MAI, see Dymond (1999) and Graham (2000).
13. For an excellent discussion on this issue, see WTO (1996), pp. 52–5.
14. UNCTAD (1996, p. 97).
15. UNCTAD (1998, p. 118).
16. The free trade agreement between Chile and Central American countries was signed on 18 October 1999. Article 10.02 states that Parties may at any time decide – but must within two years of the entry into force of the agreement analyze the possibility – to broaden the coverage of the investment rules in the bilateral investment treaties between Chile and each Central American country.
17. UNCTAD (1998, p. 125).
18. The Trade Negotiations Committee (TNC), which is composed of trade vice-ministers, has the responsibility of guiding the work of the negotiating groups. A consultative group on smaller economies, a joint government–private sector committee of experts on electronic commerce, and a committee of government representatives on the participation of civil society, also meet regularly. The Administrative Secretariat of the FTAA and the Tripartite Committee institutions (Organization of American States (OAS)); Inter-American Development Bank (IADB); and UN Economic Commission for Latin America and the Caribbean (ECLAC) provide respectively administrative and technical support to the FTAA process. The Administrative Secretariat is located at the same venue as the meetings of the FTAA entities

in Miami from May 1998 to 28 February 2001; Panama from March 2001 to 28 February 2003; and Mexico City from March 2003 to 31 December 2004.

19. See OAS Trade Unit (1999).
20. Sauvé and Wilkie (2000, p. 341).
21. There are five currencies, as defined by the International Monetary Fund, as freely usable: dollar, yen, DM, FF, pound sterling. See US Bilateral Investment Treaties, the NAFTA, the Canada–Chile and the Mexico–Chile free trade agreements.

Bibliography

DYMOND, WILLIAM A. (1999) 'The MAI: A Sad and Melancholic Tale', in *Canada Among Nations 1999*, ed. Fen Hampson, Michael Hart and Martin Rudner (Oxford: Oxford University Press).

EDWARDS, SEBASTIAN (1999) 'Capital Flows to Latin America', in *International Capital Flows*, ed. Martin Feldstein (Chicago: University of Chicago Press.)

GRAHAM, EDWARD M. (2000) *Fighting the Wrong Enemy: Antiglobal Activists and Multinational Enterprises* (Washington, D.C.: Institute for International Economics).

GRAHAM, EDWARD M. and PAUL R. KRUGMAN (1990) 'Trade-Related Investment Measures', in *Completing the Uruguay Round: A Results-Oriented Approach to the GATT Trade Negotiations*, ed. Jeffrey J. Schott (Washington, D.C.: Institute for International Economics).

LOW, PATRICK and ARVIND SUBRAMANIAN (1996) 'Beyond TRIMs: A Case for Multilateral Action?', in *The Uruguay Round and the Developing Countries*, ed. Will Martin and L. Alan Winters (Cambridge: Cambridge University Press).

OAS Trade Unit (1999) *Investment Agreements in the Western Hemisphere: A Compendium* (Washington, D.C.).

OCAMPO, JOSÉ ANTONIO (1989) 'Colombia and the Latin American Debt Crisis', in *Debt, Adjustment and Recovery*, ed. Sebastian Edwards and Felipe Larrain (Oxford: Blackwell).

SAUVÉ, PIERRE (1994) 'A First Look at Investment in the Final Act of the Uruguay Round', *Journal of World Trade*, 28 (October), pp. 5–16.

SAUVÉ, PIERRE and CHRISTOPHER WILKIE (2000) 'Investment Liberalization in GATS', in *GATS 2000: New Directions in Services Trade Liberalization*, ed. Pierre Sauvé and Robert M. Stern (Washington, D.C.: Brookings Institution Press).

UNCTAD (1996) *World Investment Report 1996: Investment, Trade and International Policy Arrangements* (Geneva).

UNCTAD (1998) *World Investment Report 1998: Trends and Determinants* (Geneva).

UNCTAD (2000) *World Investment Report 2000: Cross-border Mergers and Acquisitions and Development* (Geneva).

WORLD TRADE ORGANIZATION (1996) *Annual Report, Special Topic: Trade and Foreign Investment* (Geneva).

WORLD TRADE ORGANIZATION (WTO) (2000) *Report (2000) of the Working Group on the Relationship between Trade and Investment to the General Council.*

9 WTO Negotiations and Agricultural Trade Liberalization in Latin America

Alberto Valdés

INTRODUCTION

A new round of WTO negotiations will probably be launched sometime during 2001. In preparation, each WTO member was due to submit negotiation proposals by December 2000. For Latin American countries, the negotiation scenarios stand to be markedly more difficult than those under the Uruguay Round (UR) due to the pressure of domestic lobbying groups who will intensely scrutinize the negotiating agenda. Whereas in the UR negotiations Latin American and Caribbean (LAC) countries found themselves facing relatively few mandated changes due to the previous period of unilateral liberalization, which in some cases went beyond the GATT/World Trade Organization (WTO) requirements, we can now expect a more active and aggressive participation in the discussions in response to sectoral pressures. This would come specifically from producers of import-competing goods, bound to be the net losers of the liberalization process. This chapter presents an overview of agricultural trade policy issues in the LAC region and attempt to identify the region's major interests in the forthcoming WTO negotiations. It is relevant to discuss here the relationship between agricultural trade liberalization and food security. Food security is considered by some food-importing countries as one of the non-trade concerns to be taken into account in the new WTO negotiations. Furthermore, in future negotiating statements in the WTO, some governments (primarily from South Asia, Africa and North Africa/Middle East) will argue that further trade liberalization would threaten food security in their countries. By contrast, others hold that trade liberalization can contribute to improving the efficient allocation of world food supply, enhancing food security at the country level. In most of Latin America – a land-abundant region and where except for Nicaragua, Honduras and Haiti, which are low-income economies, all other countries in the region are classified by the World Bank as middle-income economies – the nexus between food security and trade reforms does not hold. Their concerns are different from those of the net food-importers in the least developed countries.

In this chapter, I first present a brief discussion on the patterns of agricultural trade for individual Latin American and Caribbean (LAC) countries, discussing their net agricultural and food trade position in recent years, the product composition of their agricultural trade, and the patterns on intra- and extra-regional trade. This is followed by an overview on the state of agricultural trade reforms in Latin America. The following section discusses the performance of agriculture following unilateral trade liberalization programmes in the region, with a comparison between early and late reformers. The next section examines the issue of trade liberalization and food security: can one argue that such liberalization is a potential threat to food security in this region? In the last section I attempt to identify the region's main interests in the forthcoming WTO negotiations, stressing the differences in the priorities of producers of importables vis-à-vis exportables.

PATTERNS OF AGRICULTURAL TRADE IN THE LAC REGION

As a starting point from which to identify the interest of the LAC countries in the forthcoming WTO negotiations, it is useful to present their net agricultural and food trade position and to identify their principal agricultural exportables and importable markets.

Food Trade Position

Of the 32 countries in the region, 13 are actually net importers of food and agricultural products and 17 are net importers of food; of which 10 are Caribbean countries.[1] Comparing the 1992–93 and 1996–97 ratios, we observe that 11 countries are characterized by increased import/export ratios. This dispels the commonly held belief that Latin America is a pure agricultural exporting region. The dominant net export position of Mercosur (the Southern Common Market) and the Central American Common market (CACM) members is in sharp contrast to the high import dependence of the majority of Caribbean countries.[2] Three strong export-oriented countries, Colombia, Ecuador and Bolivia, characterize the Andean region. However, two members – Peru and Venezuela – are both net agricultural importers.

Product Composition

Exporters of tropical products are concentrated in Central America and the Caribbean region, whereas in the temperate zone, Mercosur member countries dominate temperate export products. Then there is the case of sugar, which is exported primarily by tropical regions but faces intense competition from subsidized producers in Europe and North America.

What is striking is the growing importance that fruit and vegetable exports are acquiring within the product export composition of several otherwise heterogeneous countries across the region, for instance from Chile in the South, to Costa Rica and Panama in the Centre, to St. Lucia and Dominica in the Caribbean, and Mexico in the North. Despite the fact that traditional fruit and vegetable exports continue to be important (such as bananas for Ecuador, Costa Rica, and Panama), non-traditional sector exports are growing substantially (such as asparagus in Peru, and tomatoes in Mexico). Summing up on the net exporters' side, a subset of countries exporting temperate-zone products – Argentina, Uruguay and Chile – are associated with the position of the Cairns Group. Then there are two other sub-regions which typically export tropical products, one of which is the Caribbean, exporting primarily under preferential arrangements, the Lomé Agreement; and the Central American countries under the Caribbean Initiative for the Americas.

Patterns in Intra- and Extra-Regional Trade

Table 9.1 presents the pattern of agricultural and non-agricultural trade between the principal groups in the LAC region. This table indicates that:

- In absolute terms the share of extra-regional exports dominates in LAC as a whole (on average) and in each of the regions, so gains in market access remain a critical objective for all LAC trading groups;
- The growth rate in the share of intra-regional trade has been growing faster (except for CACM), albeit from a lower base compared to the value of extra-regional trade.

STATE OF AGRICULTURAL TRADE REFORMS
IN LATIN AMERICA

The process of trade liberalization in Latin America pre-dates the Uruguay Round (UR). A few years before, most countries in the region implemented

Table 9.1 LAC: exports of agricultural and non-agricultural products, intra-regional and total (in billions of US$)

Commercial group	1992	1993	1994	1995	1996	1997[a]	Annual growth rate[d]
MERCOSUR							
Intra-subregional	7.2	10.0	12.0	14.4	17.0	20.0	22.7%
World	50.5	54.2	62.1	70.3	75.0	82.3	10.3%
Mercosur/world (%)	14.3	18.5	19.3	20.5	22.7	24.3	
ANDEAN COMMUNITY							
Intra-subregional	2.2	2.9	3.5	4.8	4.7	5.4	19.7%
World	28.3	29.8	34.8	40.2	44.7	48.2	11.2%
Andean Group/world (%)	7.8	9.7	10.1	11.9	10.5	11.2	
CACM							
Intra-zonal	1.0	1.1	1.2	1.5	1.6	1.6	−2.4%
World	4.6	5.1	5.5	6.9	7.3	8.2	13.8%
CACM/world (%)	21.7	21.6	21.8	21.1	21.2	19.6	
CARICOM[b]							
Intra-zonal	0.2	0.3	0.5	0.7	0.8	—	9.9%
World	3.7	3.7	3.7	4.5	4.6	—	12.3%
Caricom/world (%)	6.1	7.9	14.0	15.4	16.7	—	
LAC[c]							
Intra-regional	24.5	29.3	35.2	42.8	46.5	—	41.4%
World	146.1	156.4	177.3	216.1	242.0	—	5.6%
LAC/world (%)	16.8	18.7	19.8	19.8	19.2	—	

[a] Preliminary data.
[b] Includes Barbados, Guyana, Jamaica, Trinidad & Tobago.
[c] Includes the Central American Common Market (CACM), Barbados, Guyana, Jamaica, Trinidad & Tobago, Bahamas, Belize, Haiti, Panama, Dominican Republic, Suriname.
[d] Mercosur, Andean Group, LAIA and CACM (average annual rate 1992–97; Caricom 1992–96).
Source: The Economic Commission for Latin America and the Caribbean (ECLAC), based on official data.

unilateral economy-wide trade reforms that resulted in significant trade liberalization, including agricultural trade. Trade liberalization occurred in the larger context of an ambitious programme of structural reforms that included privatization, deregulation, and the redefinition of the role of the state. These reforms were implemented in conjunction with macroeconomic stabilization programmes. Trade reforms were initially unilateral, then they were incorporated into regional and bilateral trade agreements like Mercosur, NAFTA, the Andean Group, the Central American Agreement, the Chile–Mexico, Colombia–Venezuela agreement, and others. Trade reforms adopted before the UR were totally consistent with what was later agreed upon in the UR agreement, and therefore Latin America came out of the negotiations with relatively few mandated policy changes.[3] The most important aspects of trade reform programmes were: (i) the replacement of most quantitative restrictions on imports with tariffs, and a reduction in both the level and dispersion of tariffs; (ii) the removal of all export taxes, quotas, and licences; (iii) a lessening in the importance of food self-sufficiency as a policy objective; and (iv) a reduced or limited level of state-trading.

At the risk of oversimplification, one could distinguish among three different subgroups within the LAC region. One is the South American block represented by the Cairns Group, while the opposite position is held by the Caribbean countries that favour a much slower pace of trade liberalization. Central America and Mexico are somewhat in between, though closer to the Cairns Group. As a rough outline of the current state of affairs on tariffs and non-tariff barriers (NTBs) affecting agricultural import-competing activities in Latin America (excluding the Caribbean) and regarding other WTO commitments in agriculture, I would highlight the following features:[4]

- Binding tariffs are on average three times larger than applied tariffs (see Table 9.2);
- Average tariffs applied to agricultural imports are higher than those applying to non-agricultural imports;
- In most countries there is a substantial variation around the average tariff, thus a major challenge for the next Round would be a reduction in tariff peaks in several products (see Table 9.3);
- Before the UR, there was already a low incidence of import bans, quotas, and import licences. Several countries had eliminated non-tariff barriers (NTBs) altogether. What remains in terms of NTBs, other than sanitary and phytosanitary (SPS) related measures, are tariff quotas, variable tariffs (surcharges) below the level of tariff bindings, and some non-automatic licences;
- WTO commitments on domestic support for most countries in the region are not binding;

Table 9.2   Applied and bound tariffs in Latin American countries[1]
(% ad-valorem CIF)

Country	Total products		Agricultural products		Index[2] B/A
	Applied	**Bound**	**Applied**	**Bound**	
Argentina	14.0	35.0	4.5	30.4	**6.8**
Bolivia	10.0	40.0	10.0	40.0	**4.0**
Brazil	12.0	32.0	11.0	36.0	**3.3**
Chile	11.0	25.0	11.0	32.0	**2.9**
Colombia	13.0	52.0	14.0	85.0	**6.1**
Costa Rica	12.0	44.0	17.0	44.0	**2.6**
Dominican Republic	20.0	40.0	21.0	40.0	**1.9**
El Salvador	10.0	37.8	14.0	47.0	**3.4**
Jamaica	19.6	38.0	29.7	95.6	**3.2**
Mexico	14.0	49.0	22.0	47.0	**2.1**
Paraguay	11.0	35.0	10.0	35.0	**3.5**
Peru	19.0	32.0	18.0	38.0	**2.1**
Uruguay	12.0	31.0	13.0	35.0	**2.7**
Venezuela	14.0	39.0	15.0	50.0	**3.3**
Average	**13.7**	**37.8**	**15.0**	**46.8**	**3.1**

[1] Corresponds to simple averages of applied and bound tariffs for total and agricultural products.
[2] Ratio of bound to applied agricultural tariffs.
Sources: Michalopoulos, C. (1999) 'Trade Policy and Market Access Issues for Developing Countries', mimeo; and the information on Jamaica in Michael Finger *et al.*, *The Uruguay Round: Statistics on Tariff Concession Given and Received* (Washington, D.C: The World Bank, 1996).

- Export subsidy commitments are not binding; few LAC countries have non-zero commitments on export subsidies under the UR agreement.
- In the UR, Brazil notified export subsidies for 16 products amounting in the base period to an annual average of US$96 million, to be reduced by 24 per cent to a level of US$73 million by 2004. However, despite its option to apply export subsidies, Brazil has not granted any subsidies to agricultural exports in the implementation period. As a member of the Cairns Group, Brazil has taken an active role, stating that it would like to see an end to export subsidies and expressing concern over the practice of rolling over unused export subsidies to the following year. In January 1995 Mercosur moved the process of tariff reduction further.

Table 9.3 Tariffs of LAC countries in 1998, by section of the 1996 harmonized system (% ad-valorem CIF)

Countries	Livestock products			Crops			Oilseeds			Processed foods/tobacco		
	Min	Max	Average	Min	Max	Average	Min	Max	Average	Min	Max	Average
Mexico	0.0	260.0	32.7	0.0	198.0	14.5	0.0	260.0	21.1	0.0	141.0	19.3
Chile	11.0	11.0	11.0	11.0	11.0	11.0	11.0	11.0	11.0	11.0	11.0	11.0
MERCOSUR												
Brazil	0.0	27.0	11.9	0.0	21.0	10.2	7.0	15.0	12.2	5.0	36.0	18.1
Argentina	0.0	19.5	12.3	0.0	17.5	10.6	7.5	15.5	12.9	5.5	23.5	18.3
Uruguay	0.0	24.0	11.8	0.0	17.0	10.4	6.0	16.0	12.1	3.0	23.0	17.9
Paraguay	0.0	22.0	9.9	0.0	20.0	8.1	4.0	20.0	10.4	2.0	30.0	14.6
ANDEAN												
Bolivia	5.0	10.0	10.0	10.0	10.0	10.0	10.0	10.0	10.0	10.0	10.0	10.0
Colombia	5.0	20.0	16.9	5.0	20.0	12.8	5.0	20.0	17.0	5.0	20.0	18.2
Ecuador	0.5	50.5	17.2	0.5	20.5	12.8	5.5	20.5	17.2	5.5	20.5	18.6
Peru	12.0	25.0	16.0	12.0	25.0	17.2	12.0	12.0	12.0	12.0	25.0	17.3
Venezuela	5.0	20.0	16.7	5.0	20.0	12.9	5.0	20.0	16.9	5.0	20.0	18.1
CARIBBEAN												
Antigua & Barbuda	0.0	40.0	19.2	0.0	40.0	16.2	0.0	40.0	23.2	0.0	45.0	16.2
Barbados	0.0	45.0	21.1	0.0	40.0	18.9	0.0	40.0	24.7	0.0	40.0	15.2
Belize	0.0	45.0	27.4	0.0	45.0	18.8	0.0	40.0	22.5	0.0	45.0	19.5
Dominica	0.0	40.0	19.9	0.0	40.0	19.1	0.0	40.0	24.7	0.0	40.0	15.3
Grenada	0.0	40.0	23.7	0.0	40.0	19.4	0.0	40.0	24.7	0.0	40.0	19.4
Guyana	0.0	45.0	26.1	0.0	40.0	19.0	0.0	40.0	24.7	0.0	100.0	24.2
Jamaica	0.0	40.0	24.2	0.0	40.0	18.9	0.0	40.0	24.7	0.0	0.0	40.0
St. Lucia	0.0	40.0	19.9	0.0	40.0	19.6	0.0	40.0	24.7	0.0	45.0	19.6
Suriname	0.0	40.0	22.5	0.0	40.0	18.7	0.0	40.0	24.7	0.0	50.0	18.9
Trinidad & Tobago	0.0	40.0	23.7	0.0	40.0	18.6	0.0	40.0	24.7	0.0	40.0	15.7

Note: Corresponds to Sections I – II – III – IV of the 1996 Harmonized System.
Source: Inter-American Development Bank, 1999, with data from the Statistics and Quantitative Analysis Unit of the LAIA Secretariat and Caricom.

On the whole, Brazil has not had major difficulties in complying with the UR Agreement on Agriculture and honouring its own tariff commitments. One difficulty though was the Common External Tariff (CET) rate of Mercosur for some products that was higher than Brazil's WTO bound rate. Brazil undertook to renegotiate these tariffs with WTO members interested in doing so, indicating that the higher CET would not be applied where it exceeded Brazil's WTO bound rate.

AGRICULTURAL PERFORMANCE AFTER UNILATERAL TRADE LIBERALIZATION REFORMS

The LAC region is like a laboratory for the analysis of the impact of bold economy-wide reform programmes in several countries, of which trade liberalization was a central component and implemented early in the reform process. There are several valuable sources available examining the response of agriculture reform during the last decade; the most comprehensive studies report performance of the evolution for specific countries – for Argentina, Colombia, see Jaramillo (1998); for Chile, see Hurtado, Muchnik and Valdés (1992); for Brazil, see Helfand and Castro de Rezende (2000); for Nicaragua and Peru, World Bank (2000).

But there are also other courageous attempts to synthesize lessons learned for the region as a whole. The study by J. Quiroz (2000) is exceptionally valuable and thus I draw on some of his findings. The degree and depth of reform efforts varied widely across the LAC countries. One can distinguish a group of 'early reformers', that have persisted until today. This group includes Argentina, Bolivia, Chile, El Salvador, Mexico and Peru. As discussed in Quiroz there is little doubt that in the 1990s macroeconomic performance in LAC countries in general, and of the 'early reformers' in particular, was substantially better than in the 1980s. Early reformers increased their average annual GDP growth rates from 0.5 per cent to 4.8 per cent (7 per cent for Chile during 1984–97), while 'late reformers' increased it from 1.2 per cent to only 2.6 per cent.

What is recognized today is that market and structural reform efforts have proven capable of generating sustainable higher GDP growth rates, agriculture included. But not all of agriculture has performed well. Evidence suggests that in the 1990s, known by some as the 'golden decade' for agricultural export growth, rates were relatively higher among early reformers. On average, agricultural GDP growth doubled in the 1990s compared to that in the 1980s (from 1.2 per cent annually in the

1980s to 2.4 per cent during the 1990s), for both 'early reformers' and 'late reformers'. But early reformers achieved higher growth rates in agriculture than the rest (3.1 per cent and 2.4 per cent, respectively, during the 1990s).

Evidence also suggests that import-competing activities in agriculture have faced severe difficulties. Farm sectors producing traditional import-competing products such as cereals, oilseeds, and dairy products (in most countries except Argentina and Uruguay where these products are exportable) not only face much lower levels of protection, but also in addition lower world market prices which during the late 1990s further eroded their margins. Thus within each country, there are considerable differences in terms of policy priorities among producers of export versus import-competing products. In fact, in countries like Chile, there is currently considerable tension in the domestic farm policy debate, centred primarily on problems faced by producers of import-competing products.

For all these reasons, I conclude that what some refer to as 'import relief' is becoming a politically sensitive issue in the region. It is tempting to press for higher border protection, not on arguments of self-sufficiency or 'excessive' import dependence, but as part of a solution to deal with a farm income problem in some regions; those that do not have much flexibility to switch to a different cropping pattern. This problem is one of the reasons why there is so much interest today in promoting alternative non-farm employment opportunities in rural areas. The constraints and options regarding its development are today being discussed in practically every country.[5]

Higher border protection is not the only way out, however; it is a difficult route to follow if one considers that it is not only a question of MFN tariff levels, but also the pressure from preferential access under bilateral and regional trade agreements such as Mercosur which is reducing domestic farm prices for importables. Other possible routes to assist this sub-sector include improvements in roads, further developments in the financial sector, training, agricultural research and technology transfer, which would enhance the sector's competitiveness.

Why the export sector did better than the import-competing sector in agriculture is easily explained by the removal of export taxes and quotas simultaneously with a reduction in tariff barriers on imports. Relative to most other countries in the world, LAC countries were among those with the most significant reduction in agricultural protection.[6] Thus, during the 1990s a substantial change in domestic relative prices occurred within agriculture, favouring exports. However, relative to the price of home goods – a measure of competitiveness in the domestic market – or to a general price index, the prices of exportables did not increase much and those of importables generally declined.

In addition to being determined by the evolution of world market prices, these price ratios are directly and significantly influenced by the evolution of the real exchange rate (RER) (defined as the ratio of the prices of tradeables to those of non-tradeables). The pattern in Latin America following reforms, shows that countries that achieved higher annual growth rates – the early and consistent reformers – also experienced larger declines in RER, in other words a currency appreciation, which reduced the competitiveness of tradeables. The effect of the appreciation of the currency on agricultural incentives and growth was profound. In this context we have to remember that the real exchange rate is not just driven by the evolution of the nominal minimum exchange rate, but also by the evolution of foreign capital flows, the overall level of protection, the level and composition of government expenditure, and real wages (influenced by a now more dynamic non-agricultural sector), and external factors including foreign terms of trade and interest rates.

The main effect of the trade liberalization programme has been the significant change in relative incentives between exportables and importables, the fast growth of agricultural trade, both imports and exports (with ambiguous effects on the trade balance), and the remarkable output and export response to the changing incentives. For the early reformers, agricultural exports expanded at an average of about 12–14 per cent per annum during 1986–98. Agriculture has become a sector which is highly 'tradable'. The ratio of agricultural trade (exports plus imports) over agricultural GDP has reached an average of 87 per cent in 18 countries in the region, and approximately 80 per cent for Mexico, Chile, and Uruguay, reaching 89 per cent in Ecuador, 99 per cent in Honduras, and more than 100 per cent in Costa Rica.[7]

But as mentioned above, market reforms including trade liberalization had a highly differentiated impact in the agricultural sector. For example for a large country such as Brazil, recent analysis of the impact of policy reforms shows that the impact differed between import-competing and exportables, geographic regions, farm sizes, and sub-periods.[8] Partly as a result of a reduction in the levels of protection and credit subsidies, and also influenced by the appreciation of the exchange rate (before 1998) and lower world prices for cereals and for several other commodities, the import-competing sector has experienced a decline in farm profits. And in some countries (such as the Dominican Republic, parts of Brazil, Chile in the mid-South, the Sierra in Ecuador), it happens to also be a sector formed by a large fraction of the small farm sub-sector, which makes it a social problem as well.

For middle-income countries, which cover most of the LAC region, the issue is not trade liberalization versus poverty. Trade liberalization is a critical component of a policy package to accelerate growth, but its impact on the poor is not independent of the rest of the package. Safety-net schemes, income transfers such as the Pro Campo programme in Mexico, price bands for the most sensitive products, and others, are options to consider during the transition period immediately after the opening of trade. Ideally they should be targeted to the low-income farmers producing import-competing products only.

A useful way to understand the impact of trade liberalization in agriculture is to differentiate between the effects on the producers of exports vis-à-vis those of important-competing products, and on subsistence farmers producing home goods. Trade liberalization has improved the performance of the exports sub-sector, and indirectly of wage earners in agriculture because export products tend to be the most labour-intensive sector in agriculture. However, it does not necessarily improve the situation of producers of import-competing goods; in fact in the short run they are likely to lose. In the longer run, their fate depends on their capacity to raise factor productivity and/or switch cropping patterns to more remunerative products. Many can do it, but there are some regions where farmers lack flexibility to adjust their output mix. These subsets of producers are critical to trade liberalization. It is not so much a *poverty* problem: it is a *profitability* problem. On the other hand, consumers who are poor (in urban and rural areas) will benefit from trade liberalization because lower protection has lowered the price of food relative to wage rates. We have clear evidence of this phenomenon for Brazil, and Chile.

To sum up, a fundamental lesson of the experience with the implementation of a programme of economic reforms in most of the LAC region during the last 10–15 years, of which trade liberalization was an essential component, is that it contributed to accelerating economic growth. Economic growth is one of the best anti-poverty measures, because it reduces unemployment and, after some lags, raises real wages, and because it increases government revenues which can be allocated to targeted poverty alleviation programmes to help the poorest households (rural and urban). Whether or not rapid growth trickles down to the poor is an empirical question and it depends on domestic policies. In the LAC countries which had a sustained rate of high growth (5 per cent or more) for several years, there is no question that poverty declined significantly in those countries where governments had the political will and capacity to implement targeted safety-net programmes.

AGRICULTURAL TRADE LIBERALIZATION: A POTENTIAL THREAT TO FOOD SECURITY?

There is no universally accepted definition of food insecurity. In my view, most of the food policy debate on food insecurity is consistent with a definition that states that food security is the ability of food deficit countries, or regions, or households within these countries, to meet target consumption levels on a year-to-year basis. Whose ability to maintain consumption is referred to? Although we should never lose sight of the fact that the most severe impact of short-term food supply instability is felt by the poor, chronic malnutrition that is caused by persistent poverty constitutes a long-term problem whose dimensions and solutions lie beyond the question of food insecurity.

The second issue is whether to analyze the problem in terms of the household's, the region's or the nation's ability to attain food security. Stable food supplies in the aggregate, including self-sufficiency, are not necessarily synonymous with consumption stability for large segments of the population if the nation does not have the means to deliver food to regions or households exposed to food insecurity.

Third, we naturally tend to associate food insecurity with either the fluctuations in food production or with changes in its prices. Actually, fluctuations in non-food prices and production (or exports) also have considerable impact on food insecurity. Ultimately, these various sources of insecurity will result in fluctuations in real income, which have an impact on household food consumption, particularly for the poorest households.

Traditional basic food products (cereals, pulses and edible oils) are import competing rather than exportables in most of the LAC countries. Exporters of grain such as Argentina and Uruguay are exceptions. However, recent trends in consumption patterns in Latin America suggest that the composition of basic food is changing rapidly and the share of meats and dairy products, fruits and vegetables in household expenditure has risen significantly and hence the tradability of food products has become quite diverse across the region.

In most of the LAC region, self-sufficiency as a policy objective is a less and less influential consideration, and discussions about grain reserves and food security stocks are rapidly disappearing from the informed policy debate in practically all the LAC region, notwithstanding occasional emotional warnings by (primarily) some agricultural scientists about the risk of dependence on food imports. For example in Brazil, with its elaborate system of market intervention (grain reserves, minimum price scheme, subsidized credit, and so forth) until the late 1980s, the role of the government in guaranteeing an adequate supply of food, which had a rationale in the context of a semi-closed economy, has withered.[9] And, unlike the case of India and China, one should keep in mind that practically in all import commodities, LAC countries are price-takers in world markets. The exceptions could be white maize in Central America, and some types of beans in Brazil, cases which correspond to very thin markets.

Relative to most other regions in the developing world, Latin America has a lower share of its population in agriculture (less than 50 per cent), it is relatively more land-abundant and has a lower population density relative to the supply of arable land. There are of course exceptions and Haiti is the most dramatic exceptional case. At the country level, we also observe the quasi-non-tradable nature of some food production, which expands and contracts in parallel with changes in domestic demand – driven by income growth. Thus, the small domestic market and constraints and barriers to export competitiveness are often the most pressing concerns. Rather than a genuine concern about adequate food supplies, the real question is how to raise household incomes. Some of these are semi-subsistence farmers, but high proportions of them are net buyers of food in both the urban and rural areas.

In my view, trade policy interventions should not be high on the list of adequate policy instruments to deal with the goal of increasing income and food consumption, for two reasons. First, because raising border protection on food imports raises the domestic price of food for everybody, including the poor. This is so evident in some countries that this negative income effect is today the most valid criticism against the implementation of price bands and their effect of raising the average price. Second, because international trade in farm products is practically everywhere in the hands of the private sector (except for food aid) and price controls at retail and wholesale levels have been eliminated.

In addition to the emphasis on education and health, which represent the two principal social policies of most governments in the region, the direction of policy action in the LAC region to deal with basic needs is shifting rapidly to (a) technology transfers and rural finance for small farmers, and (b) the implementation of targeted safety-net schemes based on an integrated approach to food and health assistance, including schemes such as food-stamp-type programmes, school lunch programmes and, increasingly more influential, direct cash transfers (e.g. Progresa and Pro Campo in Mexico previously mentioned, a very innovative rural pension plan in Brazil, various cash and in-kind transfer programmes in Chile, and others in Peru, Colombia, and Honduras). Small farmers currently producing importables in most cases qualify as recipients of these cash and in-kind transfers, but much needs to be done to improve the delivery of social programmes to distant rural areas.

I would venture to conclude that with 'good' domestic policies, trade liberalization is not in conflict with food security; in fact it is quite the contrary. Furthermore, trade liberalization in the rest of the world would certainly be beneficial for most countries in the LAC region, most of which have a strong export orientation in agriculture.

WTO NEGOTIATIONS: MAIN ISSUES FOR THE REGION

(1) For net *agricultural exporters*, at the next WTO negotiations a strong push for further liberalization of border measures, reduction of domestic support, and reduction in export subsidies in industrial countries is expected. Latin American countries are likely to insist on the following priorities, although this list does not reflect a consensus among many countries:

- substantial reduction of tariff peaks;
- continuation of tariff reductions during the negotiation period at a pace similar to that agreed for the period 1995–2000;
- significant reduction of export subsidies and restrictions on the use of subsidized export credit;
- continued expansion of tariff-quotas (say 10 to 15 per cent annually);
- further reductions of domestic support measures in the amber box, elimination of the blue box, a revision of the green box, and a reduction of the 'de minimis' levels;
- elimination of the Special Safeguard at the end of the transition period;
- further reduction of protection to processed and semi-processed products (tariff escalation);
- revision of antidumping and countervailing duty provisions.

A crucial point here is that, in some important areas, the agenda for the sector producing import-competing products within countries is quite different from that of exportables. However, there is also total agreement on one critical aspect, which is that both groups of producers will press for a substantial reduction in protection and export subsidies in industrial countries. The high levels of agricultural support to agriculture in industrial countries are today the most common and politically most influential argument for requesting exemptions and special treatment (such as higher tariffs) for the agricultural import-competing sector in LAC countries.

(2) The case of producers of *import-competing* agricultural products is the most sensitive farm problem today, and prompts the request by many countries for more flexibility to pursue their domestic development objectives, particularly through their green-box commitments, and more time to adjust their tariff reductions for sensitive products, which in fact today have relatively low tariffs, compared to those in the EU, Japan and India for example. There is today a real concern about low returns in farming, particularly but not exclusively in the production of importables.

Since about 1997, in several LAC countries low returns in farming is the consequence of exceptionally low world prices for some importables, reinforced by the appreciation of the exchange rate in some countries, and aggravated by the implementation of regional and bilateral trade agreements reaching a stage where preferential tariff rates under the agreements are substantially below most-favoured-nation (MFN) rates. And, what makes this issue more politically sensitive is that the problem sub-sectors are typically concentrated in certain regions, with fairly limited employment alternatives (farm and off-farm), and where labour immobility due to aging of farmers and lack of training to compete in the non-farm labour market reduce the employment alternatives for farmers and farm workers. The domestic debate begins to sound worryingly similar to 'multifunctional' issues raised in parts of Europe. Will some regions become depopulated? Will many rural towns lose their economic sustainability?

Thus, regarding the demands from producers of import-competing products at the WTO negotiations I would anticipate emphasis on more flexibility to apply import relief measures, including:

- the flexibility to make use of price floor schemes, and more flexibility to use safeguards and antidumping measures for sensitive products at the time of exceptionally low border prices;
- the allowance for continued use of 'price band' schemes that apply today for some importables in all Andean countries, Chile, and some other countries. This is essentially a variable tariff system based on a moving

average of border prices and not linked to a domestic target price. As long as the basic tariff plus the (variable) surcharge does not exceed the binding tariff, such type of instruments could remain WTO legal;
- maintaining the Special Safeguard and press for its extension to LAC countries which had unilaterally applied tariffication prior to the UR agreement;
- the need to reevaluate measures of domestic support.

RECOMMENDATIONS AND CONCLUDING COMMENTS

The market and structural reforms implemented in the region, of which trade liberalization has been a critical component, has proven capable of generating relatively high growth rates compared to previously low growth rates. However, evidence also suggests that the impact of reforms varied across products, specifically between export and import-competing products. In contrast to the good performance of the export sector, the difficulties with the import-competing sector in some countries tends to dominate the current agricultural trade policy debate. In the context of most Latin American countries today, there are no major conflicts between food security objectives and trade liberalization.

The main contribution of the next WTO Round negotiations towards enhancing rural income (and thus food security) will depend on what it delivers in terms of economic growth and job creation opportunities in farming and agro-processing activities. But some subsectors are likely to lose out. The domestic policy challenge is to be able to implement adjustments problems and policies to assist them during the transition period as opposed to implementing or increasing protectionist practices.

Notes

1. Valdés and McCalla (1999), based on trade flows during 1996–97.
2. Paz and Valdés (1999).
3. Valdés (1998).
4. Paz and Valdés (1999).
5. Berdegue, Reardon and Escobar (2000).
6. Imgco (1995).
7. World Bank (1999).
8. Helfand and Castro de Rezende (2000).
9. Helfand and Castro de Rezende (2000).

Bibliography

BERDEGUE, J., T. REARDON and S. ESCOBAR (2000) 'Rural Nonagricultural Employment and Income in Latin America and the Caribbean', presented at the Annual Meeting of the Inter-American Development Bank, March 2000, New Orleans.

BLANDAO, SALAZAR, ANTONIO (2000) Chapter 3 in FAO *Agricultural Trade and Food Security, Vol.2, Country Case Studies* (Rome: FAO, Commodity and Trade Division).

FAO (2000) *Agriculture, Trade and Food Security, Issues and Options in the WTO Negotiations from the Perspective of Developing Countries* (Rome).

HELFAND and CASTRO DE REZENDE (2000) 'Brazil Agriculture in the 1990s: Impact of policy Reforms', presented at the XXIV International Conference of Agricultural Economists (IAAE), August 2000, Berlin.

HURTADO, H.E. MUCHNIK and A. VALDÉS (1992) 'The Political Economy of Agricultural Pricing Policies: The Case of Chile', in A.O. Krueger, M. Schiff and A. Valdés, *The Political Economy of Agricultural Pricing Policies in Developing Countries* (Baltimore: Johns Hopkins University Press).

IMGCO, M. (1995) *Agricultural Trade and Liberalization in the Uruguay Round – One Step Forward, One Step Back* (Washington, D.C.: World Bank, International Trade Division).

JARAMILLO, C.F. (1998) *Liberalization, Crisis, and Change in Colombian Agriculture* (Colorado: Westview Press).

PAZ, J. and A. VALDÉS (1999) 'Interest and Options in the WTO 2000 Negotiations: Latin America and the Caribbean', World Bank Conference, Geneva.

QUIROZ, J. (2000) 'Agriculture and the Macroeconomy in Latin America During the Nineties', presented at the Annual Meeting of the Inter-American Development Bank, March 2000, New Orleans.

TOMICH, T., P. KILBY and B. JOHNSTON (1995) *Transforming Agrarian Economies – Opportunities Seized, Opportunities Missed* (Ithaca, New York: Cornell University Press).

VALDÉS, A. (1998) *Implementing the Uruguay Round on Agriculture and Issues for the Next Round: A Developing Country Perspective*, PSIO Occasional Paper No. 10, WTO Series, Geneva.

VALDÉS, A. and A. McCALLA (1999) 'Issues, Interests and Options of Developing Countries', presented at the World Bank Conference on Agriculture and the New Trade Agenda from a Development Perspective, October 2000, Geneva.

WORLD BANK (1999) *World Development Report* (Washington, D.C.).

WORLD BANK (2000) *Nicaragua – Poverty Assessment Report 2000* (Washington, D.C.).

10 Trade and Environment: A Challenging Agenda for Latin America

Anabelle Ulate

INTRODUCTION

It is indisputable that the decade of the 1990s encountered a proliferation of initiatives to use economic instruments to achieve environmental goals, a broader research agenda to address the interpellations of the environmentalists and a greater experience on the use of new instruments to confront environmental problems. At the same time, a greater number of countries were joining the World Trade Organization (WTO), a wider spectrum of issues were introduced into the international agenda and the qualitative form of participation was also changing. All of these factors were reinforcing the multilateral trade system.

In November 1971, the GATT Council established a Group on Environmental Measures and International Trade (EMIT Group) to examine upon request, specific matters relevant to trade policy aspects of measures to control pollution. However, the EMIT Group was not requested to meet during the twenty years after its creation, and it met for the first time in November 1991.[1] This came about as a result of a new European initiative in 1990 placing again the environmental issue into the GATT agenda.

The six countries integrating the European Free Trade Area[2] (EFTA) presented a proposal to the Ministerial Meeting requiring the contracting parties (a) to undertake a study on the relationship between environmental policies and the rules of the multilateral trading system; (b) to consider the implications of preparatory work for the 1992 United Nations Conference on Trade and Development (UNCTAD), and submit a GATT contribution to that Conference; and (c) to develop an updated mandate to the EMIT Group in order to provide contracting parties with a forum for these issues.

At the time the Emit Group was created, only 13 Latin American and Caribbean economies were GATT signatories. By 1999, 32 countries were members of the WTO. During this period Latin America and especially the small Caribbean and Central American economies were liberalizing their

trade regimes, entering the multilateral system, attracting foreign invest-
ment and handling a revived global environmental agenda. Most Latin
American countries had lowered their tariff rates before the end of the
Uruguay Round and creation of the WTO. Argentina, Chile and Mexico
had already reached an average tariff rate of around 10 per cent by 1993.[3]
Meantime, foreign direct investment to the Latin American and Caribbean
region had tripled over the previous fifteen years in real terms,[4] from
US$6.632 million dollars in 1980 to US$23.172 million dollars in 1995.

In April 1994 the General Council of the WTO at the Marrakesh
Ministerial meeting decided to establish a Committee on Trade and
Environment (CTE) with an agenda of ten items that highlighted market
access problems, institutional interdependence and, information and participation issues. Some of the market access problems dealt with environmental benefits of removing trade restrictions, the use of taxes, charges
and product requirements for environmental purposes, transparency and
trade consequences of environmental and trade measures.

Parallel to the increasing participation in GATT membership and the
introduction of the environmental controversy into its agenda, another
trend took place during the 1980s and prospered during the following ten
years: preferential trade arrangements (PTAs). Since the creation of
GATT until 1979 there were 61 preferential trade arrangements worldwide. During the 1980s another 14 PTAs were signed and from 1990 until
1998 another 82 PTAs came into force.[5] That is to say, the last decade
gave birth to a new multilateral system, but also to more preferential trade
agreements than ever existed during the previous forty-three years of the
GATT. The Latin American and Caribbean countries were very active
actors in the race to endorse regional trade agreements. The outcome of
this 'open regionalism', as has been defined by the Economic Commission
for Latin America and the Caribbean (ECLAC), is that in addition to the
ongoing negotiations for the creation of the Free Trade Area of the
Americas (FTAA) during the 1990s, at least 20 preferential trade agreements[6] were signed amongst the Latin American and Caribbean countries
themselves, with North America and the European Union.

While Mexico was negotiating the NAFTA (North American Free Trade
Agreement) with the USA and Canada, the environmental debate was in
crescendo. Greater participation of the Latin American and Caribbean
economies in the world markets raised many questions within the already
environmental concerned OECD countries. It unfolded a wide discussion
and research within the WTO, the World Bank and other national and
international fora. The research agenda includes, amongst others: (a) the
measurement of the environmental damage due to the increasing volume

of trade; (b) the effects of higher abatement costs and the environment of the OECD countries on the firm's competitive advantage; (c) the migration of firms towards developing countries with lesser environmental standards; (d) the relation between economic growth and the improvement of the environment; (e) eco-labelling and trade policy; subsidies and environmental compliance; and (f) the relation between new patterns of specialization and the environment. All these issues will be addressed in this chapter.

The rate at which new evidence comes to light with regard to the efficiency of instruments to achieve environmental and trade goals, the increased number of preferential trade agreements, the wide range of multilateral environmental agreements, and the speed by which new initiatives on environmental policy are being implemented, keeps the environmental debate open, the institutional framework at stake and the international political arena complex.

This chapter will draw attention to the areas of controversy in trade policy and the environment, and the most pressing issues that need addressing under WTO discussions and whether environment issues should be part of the WTO agenda. In closing, it will follow with policy recommendations for Latin America.

TRADE LIBERALIZATION AND ENVIRONMENTAL PROTECTION: PRESSING ISSUES

(1) There are concerns from environmental groups, who argue that trade liberalization increases the volume and changes the composition of trade towards natural resources and an increase in primary products and 'dirty industries'. In all countries except for Mexico, trade specialization caused a greater intensive use of natural resources, and Brazil even increased its specialization in the 'dirty industries' sector. Furthermore, Nordström and Vaughan (1999),[7] studying the effects of the Uruguay Round on air pollution, conclude that pollution is expected to increase in Latin America and other developing countries as the volume of trade increases. This is because the introduction of new and cleaner technologies and the increase in income (technique effect) may not offset the increase in pollution due to a higher economic activity (scale effect) and a reallocation of resources from highly regulated activities to less regulated or pollution intensive activities (composition effect).[8] To avoid this unwanted outcome, there is a need to combine trade and environmental reforms.

(2) Governments should avoid the use of trade restrictions to protect the environment, since trade policy is not created for punishment or inducement

of green behaviour.[9] Trade restrictions will have negative effects on welfare and it may not contribute to improving the environmental behaviour of economic agents since in general it acts indirectly on environmental problems.

(3) Environmental problems should be tackled directly at their source; otherwise it may impose unnecessary costs to society. The polluter-pays principle (PPP) as a domestic policy is an effective way of handling the problem. The PPP measure was introduced in 1972 by the OECD countries as an efficient instrument to internalize social costs and increase the efficiency in the allocation of resources.[10] According to Low and Safadi (1992)[11] it favours prevention against compensation for the damage that has been done. It prevents trade frictions since it internalizes environmental externalities as a cost of *production* instead of using *subsidies* to cover abatement costs.

(4) Environmental subsidies may serve to improve the environment but not for gaining a comparative advantage. In this sense, environmental subsidies in the energy, agriculture and fishing sectors will achieve trade and environmental goals simultaneously, since evidence[12] shows that these sectors pollute the environment and deplete resources. Subsidies continue to be a relevant issue in the WTO since the discussions within the CTE have focused its attention onto other sectors such as forestry, nonferrous metals, textiles and clothing, leather and environmental services.[13] The Agreement on Subsidies and Countervailing Measures allows for the use of 'actionable and non-actionable' subsidies granted to producers by governmental programmes that are intended to cover for extra costs or loss of income due to environmental compliance.

(5) Standards should not be harmonized and hence lower standards should not be subjected to countervailing duties. According to Bhagwati and Srinivasan (1997)[14] the objections against the existence of a diverse set of standards may be grouped into four main categories: (a) it is unfair trade; (b) it may result in developed countries losing their higher standards; (c) it involves conflicting ethical preferences; and (d) it introduces vulnerability for international institutional arrangements.

It has been argued that industries based on locations with lower environmental standards were receiving environmental subsidies that should be 'subject to the imposition of countervailing duties to correct their perceived impact on trade'[15] or else be eliminated by harmonizing environmental standards across borders. This controversy led to a very rich debate on the use of trade measures to achieve environmental goals, the definition and rationale for seeking harmonization of standards and the economic and environmental meaning of enforcing the same environmental measures amongst nations.

(6) Countervailing duties are not efficient instruments. The literature refers to Pearson's (1987)[16] assertion that countervailing duties are not efficient for two reasons: (a) countries have different assimilative capacities and hence show different benefits and costs of abatement, so that standards should be determined domestically, and (b) abatement costs seem to be quite small for affecting trade patterns. There should be different pollution tax rates across countries to deal with domestic pollution problems, so that imposing one's own set of standards on another country is a harmful and inefficient solution.

(7) Cooperation and transfer payments are necessary for improving environmental policy in developing countries. In this case, cooperation is a non-market mechanism essential for trade liberalization and environmental protection. Trade agreements have proliferated over the past ten years as was pointed out before, but so have agreements related to the environment. The growing number of multilateral environmental agreements, around 216, could be interpreted as an indication that governments may find it difficult to act individually and hence are seeking international cooperation to address environmental problems, or that organized groups are exerting pressure to confront this issue.

Nonetheless, to avoid non-compliance by any of the parties, international agreements require enforcement provisions as retaliatory or punishment mechanisms. NAFTA, with its Environmental Side Agreement (ESA), is a good example. The agreement introduces trade sanctions to ensure enforcement of domestic environmental laws although in a milder version as originally proposed by the United States, due to the opposition of Canada and Mexico. Up to now, on environmental matters the NAFTA and the ESA have proved, as intended, to be a bridge for cooperation rather than an instrument for sanctions. Indeed a study done by Dasgupta, Hettige and Wheeler (1997) for the Mexican industry and quoted by the World Bank (2000b) found that 86 per cent of plants with a strong environmental management system (EMS) comply with environmental regulations, while only 24 per cent of the firms with a weak EMS, comply. (Canada and Chile Trade Agreement and its Agreement on Environmental Cooperation, which came into force three years after NAFTA, does not have trade sanctions as a retaliatory instrument.)

(8) A well-established proposition is that feasible solutions to problems of environmental degradation with international repercussions may require side payments.[17] This is particularly important for countries with lower capacity to pay for abatement costs. In 1989 the Central American Common Market (CACM), one of the first trade agreements established in Latin America, established the Central American Commission for the

Environment and Development (CCAD) as an agreement for cooperation to achieve environmental goals. In 1994 at the Summit of the Americas the United States signed an Agreement with Central America (CONCAUSA), which included technical and financial assistance for the conservation of bio-diversity, energy and environmental legislation.

The Fear of Losing Competitiveness

The idea of losing industries due to the existence of lax environmental measures elsewhere, aroused strong fears with respect to the existing environmental measures in the OECD countries. It was argued that they could react by relaxing their own environmental standards. Higher abatement costs required by more stringent environmental policies of the OECD countries were perceived as a relative disadvantage and would drive the polluting-intensive industries towards less stringent environmental locations. Notwithstanding, empirical evidence shows that between 75 per cent to 80 per cent of polluting industries have been located in developed countries during recent decades, so this does not seem to confirm that industries are migrating to developing countries.[18]

Economic Growth is Not Enough

Putting aside any questions concerning the sources of economic growth, the issue of whether economic growth is a sufficient condition to induce necessary improvements in the environmental system of developing countries, remains open. To answer the question one has to take into account the relation between income and pollution levels, that is the Kuznets environmental inverted-U shaped curve. Nordström and Vaughan (1999) reviewed extensively the empirical findings on this relationship and they concluded that the results are mixed: those indicators that appear to demonstrate some characteristics of an inverted U-shaped pollution path are certain types of local, primarily urban, air and water pollutants. Conversely, pollutants of a more global nature do not seem to accord with the Environmental Kuznets Curve (EKC) hypothesis, notably CO_2 emissions.

When the evidence supports the existence of a turning point in income that will allow pollution to decline, there still remains a concern on the environmental consequences of waiting until the countries reach that estimated income level. For example, deforestation does present an inverted U-shaped curve and the estimated turning point for Latin American countries is estimated at $5,400 income per capita.[19]

According to the data of the World Bank (2000a), there were 12 Latin American countries[20] with an annual deforestation rate greater than unity during the 1990–95 period. Of these countries, only Costa Rica and Panama had in 1998 a GNP per capita higher than the estimated turning point. The issue here is whether the environmental consequences of waiting until these countries reach the adequate income level to begin with the full environmental measures to tackle the problem is recommendable. Central America is a biological bridge between the northern and southern part of the American Continent and the depletion of these environmental assets may be irreversible. From the environmental point of view the issue is not economic since there could be irreversible ecological damage done in the present that later higher-levels of income will not be able to amend.

In sum, empirical findings suggest that the Latin American and Caribbean economies are facing higher environmental problems due to changing patterns of trade and the increase of its volume. If one includes the welfare of present and future generations, environmental policy must be a complementary element of trade liberalization. The challenge is to identify which instruments may be complementary and to define the way they may accomplish environmental goals without restricting an open trading system.

There is now recognition amongst WTO members that governments 'have the right to establish their national environmental standards in accordance with their respective environmental and development conditions, needs and priorities and it would be inappropriate for them to relax their existing national environmental standards or their enforcement in order to promote trade'.[21] Furthermore, there is reasonable evidence to conclude that countries will not embark on a race to relax their environmental regulations, that economic growth is not a sufficient condition to improve the environment and that more community participation and information disclosure are new instruments to improve environmental compliance.

Information Disclosure is an Efficient Instrument

Information disclosure is a very powerful instrument. In financial markets it may affect the value of assets such as stocks. There seems to be enough evidence to show that financial markets tend to reward companies with a leadership in environmental management, and punish, with lower share prices, those firms where poor environmental management is revealed. In Canada and the United States the lessening of stock values due to lax environmental management may range on average between 0.3 per cent and 2 per cent, and in Mexico and the Philippines gains may be as high as 20 per cent and average losses between 4 per cent and 15 per cent.

SHOULD WTO INSTRUMENTS INCLUDE
ENVIRONMENTAL GOALS?

One of the most controversial issues under discussion is whether GATT instruments should be broadened to include environmental goals or if there should be a specific agreement on environment issues within the WTO. The main concern regarding environmental policy is the introduction and design of institutions that provide the right incentives for protecting the resilience of ecological systems.[22] This outcome depends on the market system that is well identified within political boundaries and according to its structure of property rights, laws and cultural beliefs. In the environmental system, incentives (costs and benefits) are mainly external to the market or are the outcome of ill-defined property rights within ecological systems that are not defined by political boundaries and go beyond domestic cultural values.

Multilateral trade policy seeks to reduce trade protection and enhance liberalization of trade flows across borders so as to increase welfare of current citizens of the interacting nations. Meantime, environmental policy seeks to increase protection and reduce the liberal use of resources to safeguard the resilience of ecological systems in order to increase welfare of current and future generations around the globe. The two goals require more cooperation amongst nations not only to finance but also to assess with transparency and predetermined mechanisms the direction and effectiveness of efforts made to enforce the local and international green obligations. The WTO is well designed to safeguard and improve the multilateral trade system but it knows very little about the workings of ecological systems and the magnitude of resilience capacity. These should be assessed by a different international forum and is an issue yet to be solved.

A second controversial issue is that the 'greening process' of the incentive structure has been intense, diverse and asymmetric. *Intense*, since the process hastened during the last decade of the twentieth century. *Diverse*, because new instruments go beyond tax and subsidies to include product environmental standards and production process methods. *Asymmetric*, because the upper hand is on the side of the OECD countries. These new instruments may be voluntary or mandatory, they may well result from a private initiative or from a governmental decision, they could come from a domestic or international organization, and they may be agreed upon by cooperation through international agreements.

A clear example is the setting of standards for products and production process methods (PPMs) to address environmental externalities in consumption and production. This makes trade and environmental policy two interdependent processes, because these new instruments should comply at the same time with trade and environmental goals and hence may affect trade flows. 'The majority of trade-related environmental measures have been notified under the Technical Barriers to Trade Agreement. Since the entry into force of the Agreement, on January 1995, about 2,300 notifications have been received, of which some 11 per cent are environmental related.'[23]

The 1991 tuna–dolphin dispute between the US and Mexico captures the essence of trade and environmental controversy. It represents the confrontation of an OECD country, the United States, with a developing country, Mexico. This dispute is a clear example of the application of unilateral trade restrictions by a country, the US, seeking to change production methods (fishing methods) used by a foreign country, Mexico. GATT decided against the United States as a 'GATT-inconsistent application of extraterritorial trade policy'. However, this decision did open a debate on whether this GATT principle should be amended in order to achieve environmental goals.[24]

Eco-Labelling and Trade Policy

Eco-labelling is an issue that has been reviewed by two WTO Committees: the Committee on Trade and Environment (CTE) and the Technical Barriers to Trade (TBT) Committee. It is a voluntary instrument that appeals to consumers' 'green' preferences, offering them additional information about the environmental characteristics of the product. The label can be awarded by a private or governmental agency. The oldest experience is the German Blue Angel created in 1977. At the beginning, the programme covered 45 products and in 1997 this number increased to 4,500 products.[25] Meantime, in 1988 the Canadians created the Environmental Choice Program. In 1989 Japan introduced the EcoMark, the Nordic countries created the White Swan and the United States the Green Seal.[26] During the 1990s even more programmes were established around the world; worth mentioning are the European Flower in the European Union and the Environmental Choice in Australia and New Zealand. Altogether, there are around 26 eco-labels of the Type I.[27]

Although the level of government intervention varies between programmes, the industry involvement is generally high, because it is in their interests to be involved in the selection of product categories in determining the criteria and thresholds for eco-labelling and in the boards or juries that decide upon the criteria. Taking into account the number of programmes that already exist in the OECD countries, one could conclude that this type of instrument introduces three problems for developing countries. (a) There is an asymmetry in the design of the instrument, the 'cradle-to-grave' approach may discriminate against foreign producers and there are compliance and certification costs that must be considered by the firm before entering an OECD market. For example, the German textile industry has already proposed a product label and a process label, and the EU appointed Denmark for the development of eco-criteria for T-shirts and bed linen, and the Netherlands to develop parameters for eco-labelling for footwear.[28] (b) All the above initiatives apply the 'life-cycle principle'. This principle introduces criteria and standards that cover five stages of this cycle and relate to the use of renewable and non-renewable raw materials, energy consumption, discharges and emissions of unhealthy and environmental hazards, wastes, and with different emphasis in the reutilization of the final product and its parts.[29]

The application of environmental standards to the process and production methods based on the life-cycle principle is a controversial issue, since it opens the debate on the extraterritoriality of these measures, and the introduction of additional costs to access the market. The unilateral decision to apply the importing country's regulations does not take into account that environmental effects differ between ecological systems, and that countries have different environmental priorities. Moreover, local producers may benefit indirectly from the measure, since they may have the technology, raw materials and inputs necessary to comply with the standards.

In order to comply with the standards and regulations required by the eco-label, the firm has to disburse money. It has to pay a fee for the use of an eco-label. In the European Union this amounts to 0.15 per cent of the factory price.[30] The Green Seal Program charges a fix fee of $10,000 to those companies that request product criteria, even though the company may not get the label. The Canadian Program charges an annual licence fee that ranges between 0.05 per cent and 0.1 per cent of sales to use the label.[31] If the label requires a third-party certification, another cost is added to the process. For example, the Canadian Program charges between $7.50 and $2,500 per site of production for auditing and verification. Finally there are compliance costs since the firm will probably need to invest in new equipment, infrastructure, know-how, and a procurement policy for input and raw materials.

If successful, all these costs will translate into an eco-label and a possibility to access the market. So far, estimates of a green premium that will compensate for these costs do not show a clear economic advantage. For example, Varangis *et al.* (1995) estimated that tropical timber certification may imply revenue equivalent to 4 per cent of all timber revenues of developing countries. On the other hand, if the firm later decides to leave the market it cannot recuperate all of the costs because the eco-label cannot be sold or used in another market. Hence, the proliferation of these schemes across countries will make this problem worse especially for developing countries. These initiatives would limit possibilities to access OECD markets, and therefore are better handled under a multilateral setting.

ISO Certification

The ISO 1400 standards to manage the environment are another example of voluntary measures, but in this case they come from a multilateral organization: the International Organization for Standardization (ISO) introduced in the middle of 1996. In order to achieve ISO certification, firms must follow several steps that deal with a signed commitment to comply with environmental regulations, pollution prevention and continuous improvement, to develop performance targets, to implement a well-defined procedure and responsibilities management system, and conduct management audits. At the end of 1997 the World Bank awarded approximately 5,000 certificates to 55 countries,[32] dividing each country's total certification by its GDP and standardizing the result on a scale from 1 to 200.

Western European countries are the leaders: out of 16 European countries with ISO certifications, twelve of them have an index equal or greater than 20 points. Denmark, Sweden, Ireland and Finland, in that order, are world leaders with an index greater than 100 points. North America lags behind since Canada reached 15 points and the US 3 points. Within developing countries, the Asian countries are the leaders: already twelve countries have obtained ISO certifications and eight of them have an index greater or equal to 20 points with Korea and Malaysia leading the group with 95 and 82 points respectively. In Latin America eight countries have obtained ISO certifications, but only Costa Rica leads the group with 22 points. The implicit assumption is that firms with ISO certification contribute to reducing pollution.

Eco-Labels and ISO Certification Implications on Trade

Although eco-labels and ISO certification are voluntary mechanisms, the logic of the market may turn them imperative. One may refer to the American wooden-doors market as an example of a product category that combines the presence of Green Seal eco-labels and the participation of

Latin American countries. The strongest foreign competitor is Canada which represented 52 per cent of all imports into the United States in 1996, and the biggest Latin American exporters, Brazil, Mexico, Costa Rica, Chile, Bolivia and Guatemala, together represented 28.5 per cent of all imports.[33]

The Costa Rican firm Portico exports wooden doors to this market and was one of the two tropical-wood producers that received certification by the American Scientific Certification Systems (SCS) under their Forest Conservation Program. This firm[34] is owned by three local and three foreign entrepreneurs. All of them are strong national and international entrepreneurial groups. Portico has argued that the learning process and the development of know-how to manage the forest on a commercial scale have been difficult and expensive. Based on this case, it is probable that an exporter planning to enter the Danish market without an ISO certification will be unable to compete with the domestic firms, and that an exporter to the German market without the Blue Angel eco-label in the relevant product categories will find it difficult to survive.

The proliferation of eco-labels has three consequences for trade and international relations. (a) They do increase 'transaction costs for foreign producers' and may increase the difference in costs of certification between domestic and foreign producers as asserted by da Motta Veiga (2000) and hence affect market access. (b)These standards are voluntary and are increasingly coming from the private sector, as it became clear with the above review of the eco-label schemes. The American Society of Testing (AST), a private institution, has issued about the same amount of standards as those recognized by the American National Standards Institute.[35] (c) Standards are endogenous to the market. Standards and eco-labels are specific to each production sector; hence it implies the evolution of two social institutions, a market and a 'club'. The latter provides and finances this public good as an interdependent process to the development of the market, so that one may expect changes in the composition of this 'club' with the evolution of the markets.

COORDINATION OF AN AGENDA ON ENVIRONMENTAL ISSUES

The setting of an agenda depends on the actors involved. The Seattle and aftermath events showed that this point is true even when the actors are not officially recognized. One may conclude that the intense and wide trade negotiations held by Latin American countries over the past 15 years have been an advantage in addressing the environmental issues in the international fora. Nevertheless, out of the 27 preferential trade agreements only three have a specific reference or agreement on environmental cooperation: NAFTA, Canada–Chile, and Mexico–European Union. All of them involved an OECD country. Mercosur does not have a common agreement on environment, and according to Tussie and Vásquez[36] does not hold a high profile on the institutional agenda. Even for the case of NAFTA, Mexico is too involved in complying with environmental requisites of the ESA and may not be giving adequate care to the green issues of the WTO agenda.[37]

Within the negotiation process of the Free Trade Area of the Americas (FTAA) the environmental issue has been losing its profile. In the Miami Summit in 1994, sustainable development was one of the four chapters of the Action Plan, with a long list of environmental themes. But in the second Summit in Santiago de Chile in 1998, the environment issue was included within the chapter on trade and integration but was reduced to cooperation in the energy sector and to joint support of the Kyoto Agreement. It is interesting to underline that the United States has promoted the introduction of the environment issue into the FTAA agenda, at least as a group to study the topic, but Mexico, the Andean Community and the Central American countries have opposed the idea. Meanwhile, Canada, Chile and Mercosur agreed to address this issue, but not as part of the current negotiations.

This attitude seems to ignore the intense evolutionary process of the last ten years. To begin with, one must recall that it was the member countries of the European Free Trade Area (EFTA) that took the initiative to include an environmental agenda within GATT, at the beginning of the 1990s; and also, that the disputes over the use of the instruments provided by GATT and the introduction of standards for environmental purposes have increased during the past two decades. Out of the 115 panel reports issued from 1947 until 1994, 5 per cent were related to human health, animal health or the environment; two of them were issued during the 1980s and four between 1990 and 1994. Since the entry into force of the WTO in January 1995 until December 1998, 16 per cent of the 38 panel reports concerned these same issues.[38]

To Open on Time the 'Green Box' Instruments

Most Latin American countries have increased their volume of trade and changed their pattern of specialization towards natural resources intensive activities. This implies, amongst other things, a revision of its agricultural policy and the use of subsidies allowed within WTO's 'green boxes'. If the OECD countries decide to increase access to agricultural products from the rest of the world, environmental issues need addressing. An opportune and early intervention of governmental policies in combination with the participation of producers and relevant research institutions to enhance the development of environmental friendly techniques in the agricultural sector will make the difference. In as much as the evidence suggests that the market might not reward this effort accordingly, the issue does not seem to be the green premium, but to be left out of the market.

To Join the 'Club' of Evolving Standards

After reviewing the eco-labelling schemes, there is no doubt that standards for eco-labels are an expression of the OECD's preferences, are voluntary and increasingly set by the private sector and are endogenous to the evolution of the market. The challenge to the Latin American economies is to better understand the complexity of these standards, as these Clubs may change with the expansion and recomposition of the markets. Standards and eco-labels are specific to each production sector. From the point of view of the Latin American countries, a necessary condition to join the club is the enrolment of the private sector in this process. This requires a well-organized private sector, with the participation of small and medium-size enterprises, with the resources able to cooperate in any of the national and international organizations that are currently developing product standards and production and process methods.

In this regard, the market access debate is leaving the public realm and entering the private sector sphere. This is an immediate challenging task: how to increase international participation in order to attain public goods that may also reveal Latin America's own preferences.

Domestic Policy

Domestic policy has become a necessary condition for international negotiations. Trade liberalization may be increasing environmental damage and it is reasonable to state that economic growth is not a sufficient condition to achieve environmental protection. Societies need government intervention to ensure environmental protection and accrue the benefits of trade liberalization. It is also clear that governments have the right to set their own national standards, but at the same time it has become more evident that 'foreign eyes' will oversee that the domestic enforcement process is carried out efficiently. Public awareness may involve the local community, the international finance markets, the NGOs, or an international organization.

Institutional Building

Institutional building around environmental cooperation in the region seems to be way behind trade institutions. There is enough evidence to show that the Latin American and Caribbean countries have built experience on trade integration but less so on environmental cooperation. 'This probability of increased regionalism and interdependence among developing countries is not particularly positive in terms of environmental upgrading.'[39] Although these processes should not be mingled, they indeed ought to be complementary. The CCAD in the Central American Common Market is a step forward in this direction.

The specificity of the environmental problems, patterns of growth and social and political institutions of different countries in the region are providing new and diverse instruments and experiences to deal with environmental problems. In order to assess this experience, to interchange information, to build up knowledge and to interact with other international fora, Latin America must strengthen this institutional void.

CONCLUDING COMMENTS

The international fora have become wider and more complex. Trade policy, instruments and institutional building in the multilateral trade system have taken fifty years to reach the current level and are still in the making. The main issue that lies beneath trade negotiations and agreements deals with the use of incentives to guide decision-making across borders in order to achieve a greater liberalized, non-discriminatory and transparent trade system. But environmental goals have placed priorities into new variables: the need of a strong and efficient government intervention in environmental protection, the quality of the political institutions, an active community, private sector participation in setting standards, international cooperation to assure compliance of common goals and an independent process of assessment of environmental protection.

WTO has introduced environmental protection as a complementary issue, but it cannot expect to become one of its main goals. Evolving priorities call for a new international organization that will handle them as its main challenges, leaving trade issues as complementary goals. The issue here is whether the Latin American and Caribbean countries are building capacity to assert and identify their interests, but unfortunately the gap with the OECD countries' experience is still wide and the process of awareness of the problem is even slower.

Notes

1. Nordström and Vaughan (1999) annex I, p. 68.
2. Austria, Finland, Iceland, Norway, Sweden and Switzerland.
3. World Bank (2000a) p. 56.
4. In terms of 1996 US$ million dollars; CFI (1997) appendix 1.
5. World Bank (2000a) p. 54.
6. Information from CEPAL (1999) and www.oas.org
7. Nordström and Vaughan (1999) p. 33.
8. Grossman and Krueger (1991) pp. 4–6.
9. Low and Safadi (1992).
10. Dean (1992) p. 20.
11. Low and Safadi (1992) p. 36.
12. World Bank (1992) and Nordström and Vaughan (1999).
13. Nordström and Vaughan (1999) annex I, pp. 79–80.
14. Bhagwati and Srinivasan (1997) p. 161.
15. Hudson (1992) p. 59.
16. Pearson (1987).
17. Low and Safadi (1992) p. 36.
18. Nordström and Vaughan (1999) p. 4.
19. Nordström and Vaughan (1999).
20. These are Bolivia (1.2), Costa Rica (3.0), Dominican Republic (1.6), Ecuador (1.6), El Salvador (3.3), Guatemala (2.2), Haiti (3.4), Honduras (2.3), Jamaica (7.2), Nicaragua (2.5), Panama (2.1), and Paraguay (2.6).
21. Nordström and Vaughan (1999) annex I, p. 74.
22. Arrow *et al.* (1995) p. 521.
23. Nordström and Vaughan (1999) annex I, p. 79.
24. Tussie and Vásquez (2000a).
25. Nordström and Vaughan (1999) p. 41.
26. Information coming from UNCTAD (1994) p. 7.
27. According to ISO there are three types of eco-labelling schemes. Type I is based on criteria set by a third party. Type II is based on self-declaration by manufacturers. Type III is based on product information, without comparing or weighing the environmental aspects (UNCTAD, 1994, p. 6).
28. Da Motta Veiga (2000) pp. 64–5.
29. Da Motta Veiga (2000) p. 67.
30. Rouan (2000) p. 97.
31. Fredriksson and Chua (2000).
32. World Bank (2000b) pp. 86–7.
33. Fredriksson and Chua (2000) p. 78.
34. The information about Portico comes from Camacho and González (1992) pp. 179–89.
35. Casella (1997) p. 145.
36. Tussie and Vásquez (2000b) pp. 195–9.
37. Schatan (2000) p. 179.
38. Nordström and Vaughan (1999) annex I, pp. 82–5.
39. Tussie (2000) p. 233.

Bibliography

ARROW, K., B. BOLIN, R. COSTANZA, P. DASGUPTA, C. FOLKE, C.S. HOLLING, B.-O. JANSSON, S. LEVIN, K.-G. MÄLER, C. PERRINGS and D. PIMENTEL (1995) 'Economic Growth, Carrying Capacity, and the Environment', *Science*. vol. 268, 28 April.

BHAGWATI JAGDISH and T.N. SRINIVASAN (1997) 'Trade and the Environment: Does Environmental Diversity Detract from the Case for Free Trade?', in Jagdish Bhagwati and Robert Hudec, *Fair Trade and Harmonization: Prerequisites for Free Trade?, Volume I: Economic Analysis* (Cambridge, Massachusetts: MIT Press) (second printing).

CAMACHO, EDNA and CLAUDIO GONZÁLEZ (1992) 'Apertura comercial y ajuste de las empresas', Academia de Centroamérica y Centro Internacional para el Desarrollo Económico, San José.

CASELLA, ALESSANDRA (1997) 'Free Trade and Evolving Standards?', in Jagdish Bhagwati and Robert Hudec, *Fair Trade and Harmonization: Prerequisites for Free Trade?, Volume I: Economic Analysis* (Cambridge, Massachusetts: MIT Press) (second printing).

CEPAL (1999) 'Los bloques comerciales regionales en América Latina y el Caribe: características y efectos estáticos y dinámicos', LC/MEX/R.736, Octubre.

CORPORACIÓN FINANCIERA INTERNACIONAL (CFI) (1997) *Inversión Extranjera Directa*, Serie Experiencias de la CFI, No. 5 (Washington D.C.: World Bank).

DA MOTTA VEIGA, PEDRO (2000) 'Environment-Related Voluntary Market Upgrading Initiatives and International Trade: Eco-labelling Schemes and the ISO 1400 Series', in Diana Tussie (ed.), *The Environment and International Trade Negotiations: Developing Country Stakes*, International Political Economy Series (Macmillan, in association with International Development Research Center, Canada).

DASGUPTA, S., H. HETTIGE and D. WHEELER (1997) *What Improves Environmental Performance? Evidence from Mexican Industry*, World Bank Development Research Group, Working Paper No. 1877, December.

DEAN, JUDITH M. (1992) 'Trade and the Environment: A Survey of the Literature', in Patrick Low (ed.), *International Trade and the Environment*, World Bank Discussion Paper 159 (Washington D.C.: World Bank).

ESTY, DANIEL C. (1996) 'Greening World Trade', in Jeffrey Schott (ed.), *The World Trading System: Challenges Ahead* (Washington D.C.: Institute for International Economics).

FREDRIKSSON, PER and SWEE CHUA (2000) 'El impacto del eco-etiquetado norteamericano en el comercio exterior de los países en desarrollo', in Mónica Araya (ed.), *Comercio y Ambiente: Temas para avanzar el diálogo*, Organization of American States (OEA).

GROSSMAN, GENE M. and ALAN B. KRUEGER (1991) *Environmental Impacts of a North American Free Trade Agreement*, NBER Working Paper No. 3914, National Bureau of Economic Research, Cambridge, Massachusetts.

GUTMAN, GRACIELA (2000) 'Agriculture and the Environment in Developing Countries: The Challenge of Trade Liberalization', in Diana Tussie (ed.), *The*

Environment and International Trade Negotiations: Developing Country Stakes, International Political Economy Series (Macmillan, in association with International Development Research Center, Canada).

HUDSON, STEWART (1992) 'Trade, Environment and the Pursuit of Sustainable Development' in Patrick Low (ed.), *International Trade and the Environment*, World Bank Discussion Paper 159 (Washington D.C.: World Bank).

LEVINSON, ARIK (1997) 'Environmental Regulations and Industry Location: International and Domestic Evidence', in Jagdish Bhagwati and Robert Hudec, *Fair Trade and Harmonization: Prerequisites for Free Trade?, Volume I: Economic Analysis*. MIT Press. (Cambridge, Massachusetts: MIT Press) (second printing).

LOW, PATRICK (ed.) (1992) *International Trade and the Environment*, World Bank Discussion Paper 159 (Washington D.C.: World Bank).

LOW, PATRICK and RAED SAFADI (1992) 'Trade Policy and Pollution', in Patrick Low (ed.), *International Trade and the Environment*, World Bank Discussion Paper 159 (Washington D.C.: World Bank).

NORDSTRÖM, HÄKAN and SCOTT VAUGHAN (1999) *Trade and Environment*, Special Studies 4 (Geneva: WTO).

PEARSON, CHARLES (1987) '*Multinational Corporations Environment and the Third World*' (Durham: Duke University Press).

ROUAN, CLAUDE (2000) 'La Ecoetiqueta de la Unión Europea', in Mónica Araya (ed.), *Comercio y Ambiente: Temas para avanzar el diálogo* (OEA).

SCHATAN, CLAUDIA (2000) 'Lessons from the Mexican Environmental Experience: First Results from NAFTA', in Diana Tussie (ed.), *The Environment and International Trade Negotiations: Developing Country Stakes*, International Political Economy Series (Macmillan, in association with IDRC).

TUSSIE, DIANA (ed.) (2000) *The Environment and International Trade Negotiations: Developing Country Stakes*, International Political Economy Series (Macmillan, in association with International Development Research Center, Canada).

TUSSIE, DIANA and PATRICIA VÁSQUEZ (2000) 'The International Negotiation of PPMs: Possible, Appropriate, Convenient?', in Diana Tussie (ed.), *The Environment and International Trade Negotiations: Developing Country Stakes*, International Political Economy Series (Macmillan, in association with International Development Research Center, Canada).

TUSSIE, DIANA and PATRICIA VÁSQUEZ (2000) 'Regional Integration and Building Blocks: The Case of Mercosur', in Diana Tussie (ed.), *The Environment and International Trade Negotiations: Developing Country Stakes*, International Political Economy Series (Macmillan, in association with IDRC).

UNCTAD (1994) *Eco-Labelling and Market Opportunities for Environmentally Friendly Products*, Report by the UNCTAD Secretariat, United Nations Conference on Trade and Development, TD/B/WG.6/2, Geneva.

VARANGIS, PANAYOTIS, RACHEL CROSSLEY and CARLOS A. PRIMO BRAGA (1995) 'Is There a Commercial Case for Tropical Timber Certification?', Policy Research Working Paper 1479, The World Bank, June.

WILSON, JOHN DOUGLAS (1997) 'Capital Mobility and Environmental Standards: Is There a Theoretical Basis for a Race to the Bottom?', in Jagdish Bhagwati and Robert Hudec, *Fair Trade and Harmonization: Prerequisites for*

Free Trade?, Volume I: Economic Analysis (Cambridge, Massachusetts: MIT Press) (second printing).

WORLD BANK (1992) 'Development and the Environment', *World Development Report 1992* (Washington D.C.: Oxford University Press).

WORLD BANK (2000a) 'Entering the 21st Century', *World Development Report 1999/2000* (Washington D.C.: Oxford University Press).

WORLD BANK (2000b) *Greening Industry: New Roles for Communities, Markets, and Governments*, a World Bank Policy Research Report (Washington D.C.: Oxford University Press).

11 Labour Markets and Trade Reform in Latin America: The Challenge for the Future

Luis A. Riveros

INTRODUCTION

The opening of the economy constituted a fundamental change in Latin America in the post-1970s and marked a dramatic reversal of the protectionist policies that had been pursued for decades at the cost of serious distortions and intractable macroeconomic imbalances. Protectionism had been seen as an effective tool for dealing with chronic poverty and unemployment in the region and for coping with the consequences of slow economic growth. Accordingly, labour-market policies in most Latin American countries (LACs) in the post-1945 era were designed to fit in with an inward-oriented development process entailing large-scale state intervention in the economy and broad-spectrum welfare policies. Thus, in keeping with the ideological conviction that labour is in permanent need of legal or institutional protection, wages and employment were heavily regulated.

The wave of structural economic reforms that began to gather momentum in the 1970s has swept over the entire region since the mid-1980s. These reforms, that resulted in a significant liberalization of most markets, have led to a substantial economic downsizing of the state and, through the elimination of tariff and non-tariff barriers, have opened the economy up to trade and financial flows.[1] However, while the economic reform process has been both comprehensive and profound in most areas, an insufficient degree of labour-market flexibilization is still to be found throughout the region. Reform in this sphere has generally been regarded as a thorny political issue, and this perception has prevented progress from being made as rapidly as in other areas. A convincing argument can therefore be made that more than twenty years after the reform process began, labour-market rigidities are still one of the key constraints hampering efforts to attain a more rapid and successful integration of the Latin American economies into world trade. This argument will be explored more fully in this chapter.

STRUCTURAL REFORMS AND TRADE OPENING

The extent and results of the economic reforms implemented by LACs since the 1980s are summarized in Table 11.1 (see Stallings and Perez, 2000), which shows the average reform indices for 17 countries.[2] These indices, which nearly doubled between 1970 and 1995, denote the degree to which reforms have been made in such areas as trade, capital markets, state ownership and taxation. The substantial changes that have clearly been made in the areas of import liberalization and tax reform have primarily taken the form of greater fiscal restraint and tax cuts.[3] In the case of financial reforms, the average reform index (Stallings and Perez) almost tripled between 1970 and 1995, but reforms relating to the privatization of public-sector firms and the opening of the capital account have been relatively sluggish (see Table 11.1, columns 3 and 4). Clearly, if a similar index were to be constructed for labour-market reforms, it would show a flat trend over the past 25 years, given the lack of any substantive institutional reforms in traditional interventionist policies.

Naturally, trade liberalization has been a vital component of the structural economic transformations undertaken by LACs. Most of these countries have either dramatically reduced the coverage of non-tariff barriers or have eliminated them altogether within a comparable time period as well as reducing the range of import duties, which have traditionally been in the zero-100 per cent or even zero-200 per cent range. According to Edwards

Table 11.1   Reform indexes, 1970–95

	Import liberaliz.	Financial reform	Capital account opening	Privatization	Tax reform	Average
1970	0.501	0.315	0.588	0.773	0.198	0.472
1975	0.567	0.329	0.543	0.773	0.269	0.493
1980	0.662	0.439	0.567	0.745	0.307	0.548
1985	0.652	0.448	0.545	0.696	0.348	0.541
1990	0.803	0.725	0.683	0.722	0.445	0.638
1995	0.946	0.927	0.848	0.804	0.573	0.821

Source: Taken from Stallings and Perez (2000).

(1994), the four main elements in Latin America's trade reforms have been: (i) a reduction in the coverage of non-tariff barriers, including import quotas and bans; (ii) a reduction in the average level of import duties; (iii) a reduction in the tariff structure's degree of dispersion; and (iv) the frequent use of exchange-rate policies to maintain a competitive real exchange rate in order to backstop the reduction of export taxes.

Trade Reforms and Political Resistance

Unilateral trade opening and recent trade negotiations with both industrial nations and less developed countries (LDCs) have been surrounded by heated political disputes in most LACs. Disputes regarding the strategy and pace of further efforts to open these economies up to trade have generally involved governments, business associations in various branches of industry and labour unions. Discussions have centred on the costs of transition in terms of the relevant firms' financial performance, the macroeconomic outcome or unemployment and wage levels. Mexico, Chile and Costa Rica provide good examples of the political economy that has surrounded the trade opening process at different stages. In general, the friction generated by the reallocation of production resources from contracting to expanding industries in order to make full use of comparative advantages has been associated with political and social disruptions in most LACs. These problems, which have not been unrelated to the countries' poor record in respect of labour-market reform, have been manifested in a sharp contraction of industries that had previously been protected under the import-substitution scheme, followed by the sluggish takeover of industries favoured by the new trade regime. This process has led to high unemployment and the bankruptcy of entire branches of industry.

In general, the labour-market adjustment that has been made in most LACs in response to structural economic reforms has sparked political unrest. Persistently high unemployment levels, declining real wages and a deterioration in income distribution have been prominent factors in this unrest. Countries having weak social safety nets (including an inadequate capacity for retraining displaced workers from contracting industries) and notable rigidities in relocating labour across industries have in many cases considered any further trade opening to be politically unwise.

Although Latin America's political and economic efforts to reform its economies and open them up to world trade have been applauded in the international arena, they have not been reciprocated by industrial countries. Protectionist practices in industrial countries remain common; even after seven rounds of GATT-sponsored negotiations, most industrial countries

have continued to employ an extensive array of non-tariff barriers that effectively block freer trade. These barriers have actually increased recently, in
spite of significant tariff reductions in developing countries.[4] Any effort to
pursue further trade reforms will have to address this political reality in most
LACs, particularly within the framework of any multilateral strategy formulated under the aegis of the WTO. The possibility of concluding free trade
agreements (FTAs) with specific partners, either in the same region or elsewhere, constitutes a promising option for the negotiation of the terms called
for by the political economy of transition.

At the same time, and in a more positive context, these political developments have cleared the way for Latin America to enter into preferential trading agreements, which are seen as a more amenable strategy for these
economies' entry into the globalization process than a multilateral approach
would be. In addition, this is viewed as the basis for a more proactive sort of
export promotion policy that would gain support among politicians and
social leaders. However, as noted earlier, in order to achieve positive results,
the Latin American countries need to introduce reforms aimed at giving
labour markets greater flexibility. Notwithstanding the importance of the
debate as to whether regional integration and bilateralism may or may not
serve as intermediate steps on the path towards a more perfect GATT/WTO-
based multilateral system,[5] trade negotiations and the formation of regional
blocs are what will determine the future trade policy of Latin America.

LABOUR MARKET POLICIES IN LATIN AMERICA

Intervention in the labour market was the rule rather than the exception in
most Latin American countries in the aftermath of the Second World War.
The goal of providing protection for labour was usually achieved by means
of a profuse legal structure that included numerous regulatory agencies
and a vast array of specific regulations which government officials were
supposed to enforce. In addition to policies for protecting labour, labour
unions were exceedingly active, especially in public-sector firms and the
central government, but also in the large private-sector firms that had been
fostered by the inward-looking development model. In general, the political view that labour needed to be 'defended' from what was usually seen
as an undesirable capitalist-dominated scenario of purely market-oriented
outcomes, held sway in most LACs in the era following the Second World
War. This view was also in keeping with trade protectionism and with the
idea that large-scale state intervention in the economy was a necessary
corollary of an inward-oriented development process.

Although labour regulations have undergone changes as part of recent economic reforms, the traditional framework has, for the most part, survived. It is quite striking that the highly interventionist policies implemented in the labour market since the 1940s have been maintained in spite of significant progress in the liberalization of other sectors of the economy.

This has been a major obstacle to further economic liberalization and the integration of LACs into international trade, as is demonstrated by the general reluctance to deal with FTAs, including any explicit addenda on labour policies. In the case of Mercosur, for instance, labour issues have virtually been excluded from the negotiations because they have been seen as providing a dangerous opportunity for transmitting unfair labour practices or shifting 'excess' labour from one country to another. This issue has also been disregarded in the NAFTA treaty and in Chile's current preparations for free trade negotiations.

When subsequent efforts have been made to launch labour reforms, in many countries they have received very little support from politicians because they appear to be 'anti-labour' initiatives. Labour-market rigidities can therefore be expected to remain a major stumbling block to further trade reform. In order to deal with the labour-related costs of the transition, considerable fiscal problems will first have to be overcome. In order to protect wages and employment during the transition, a social safety net would need to be developed, and this would demand a substantial amount of traditionally scarce public resources. This is true regardless of the ultimate outcome of the necessary debate as to what form such expenditures should take in order to achieve maximum effectiveness and equity. At the same time, the need for any LAC to negotiate increased labour flexibility and international mobility (as is the case with trade and capital) has not been clearly signalled in the current search for more active trade agreements.

Labour Standards

There are five spheres in which labour standards have traditionally been applied in LACs. It is worth taking the time to outline these areas, considering their long-standing traditions and their importance for future trade negotiations, including those undertaken within the framework of the WTO. Not all of them apply equally throughout Latin America, but as a rule they are all present in each of the countries:[6]

- Minimum compensation for work;
- Establishment and protection of workers' rights;
- Protection for specific segments of the labour force;

- Regulation of working conditions; and
- Income security.

Minimum Compensation for Work

(a) *Minimum Wages*   One of the most common policy measures applied in Latin America has been the establishment of minimum wages across economic activities and across the labour force. The minimum wage, as pointed out by Paldam and Riveros (1989) and Riveros (2001), has been applied without distinction by gender, age or skill level, although lately exceptions have been allowed in some countries for youth and/or unskilled workers. The real problem is not the concept itself or the belief that minimum wages can protect workers from unfair wage-setting practices. The point at issue is the use of the minimum wage as a *distributive* instrument that can be used to raise the wages of unskilled workers artificially. This would generate a distortion in terms of competitiveness in world markets, since wages would then not be a true reflection of the social opportunity cost of labour. Not surprisingly, this could act as a deterrent to foreign investment that is one of the results of successful trade reforms.

Many politicians in the region still believe that raising the minimum wage does no harm and that, on the contrary, it brings desirable social results. The evidence clearly indicates, however, that the positive impact of such an increase is negligible (since it has no effect on the informal sector or most of agriculture) while a relatively high minimum wage discourages employers from hiring unskilled workers in formal-sector industries and thereby exacerbates wage differentials between industries subject to the minimum wage and those that are not. Furthermore, an active minimum wage policy is regarded as a bad sign by potential investors since it introduces the risk that the local cost of unskilled labour may be increased arbitrarily and therefore encourages the adoption of labour-saving technologies.

(b) *Mandated Non-Wage Benefits*   Mandated non-wage benefits, or non-wage labour costs, are another policy tool that has played an important role in the Latin American labour market. The cost of vacation leave, health-care cover, housing subsidies or allowances, social security payments and so forth normally amount to about 40 per cent of the total wage bill.[7] This figure compares favourably with the percentage – about 50 per cent of costs – for OECD countries (total hourly labour costs in Latin America average about US$2.00, whereas in OECD countries the figure is above US$15.00). Of course, the real issue here is how total labour (wage and non-wage) costs compare with labour productivity. A simple calculation based on the ratio between labour costs and per capita income indicates that while labour productivity is lower in LACs than in industrial economies, LACs are not necessarily at a disadvantage in terms of their position in the competitive ranking.[8]

(c) *Wage Indexation*   Another traditional instrument in LACs has been the indexing of nominal wages to past inflation. Under prevailing conditions of macroeconomic stability, indexation is no longer practised, and the purchasing power of real wages is politically more manageable than before thanks to these economies' lower rates of inflation.

Nonetheless, political resistance to further trade reforms in the region has largely been motivated by a desire to maintain traditional wage and non-wage regulations. As has been noted, these regulations introduce rigidities into the labour market. If the minimum wage is set at a level that does not allow the market to reflect the real social opportunity cost of unskilled labour, then the benefits of trade reforms will be greatly reduced because they will fail to jumpstart growth in competitive sectors. The same thing will occur if wage indexation or non-wage cost regulations undermine the market's ability to reallocate labour based on the various production activities' comparative advantages. The key point here is that governments should use other social policies to protect the poor, but they should not do so by distorting the labour market's allocative functions.

Establishment and Protection of Workers' Rights

(a) *Unionization*   This principle is explicitly upheld in the labour laws of each country. The aim of its incorporation has been to maintain some degree of equilibrium between labour and capital in negotiations on wages and working conditions. In the past, LACs generally had powerful unions, and these unions took on symbolic importance in the cases of the national unions in Mexico, Argentina, Brazil and Chile. Labour unions enjoyed considerable power under the law, which often included provisions making union membership compulsory as well as granting their leaders immunity and the authority to bargain across entire branches of industry. The present situation is quite different. This turnaround has not necessarily been due to legally-mandated changes in traditional precepts, in many cases it is attributable to economic reforms that have weakened trade unions and greatly reduced their sphere of activity.

It is indeed true that trade unions in Latin America are now more closely linked to the public sector. What is more, they have never been effective in rural areas or in small and medium-sized firms. Changes in union rules have altered the regulations that once made membership mandatory and have moderated financial and political support for labour unions. At present, labour unions are no longer considered to pose any major obstacle to further trade reforms, now that their activities are confined to the public and services sectors. From this standpoint, it is easier for governments to pursue trade negotiations either through the WTO or under FTAs. The role of labour unions has become more 'political', rather than being oriented exclusively towards the protection of wages and employment in specific industries. Unions are now concerned with more general issues such as the chronic unemployment or indirect pressure on wages (especially public-sector wages) that trade reforms may bring about.

(b) *Collective Bargaining* Another aspect is that of collective bargaining. In the past, firms were required to negotiate at the level of industrial branches. This significantly increased the unions' power and jeopardized medium-sized and small businesses' profitability. In countries such as Mexico, Chile and Argentina, reforms have been designed to introduce firm-based bargaining and include more 'company-friendly' procedures for dealings with private firms, which in the past were often faced with long and costly legal proceedings. Progress in moving towards a more transparent labour market and a more competitive organizational structure is still slow, however; this may be a serious impediment to new investment in large firms facing stiff competition within the domestic economy. In terms of trade agreements and further negotiations in the WTO, greater transparency in the region's labour markets is a prerequisite for combating unfair labour practices and establishing a wage structure that accurately reflects the social opportunity cost of labour.

(c) *Strikes* A third precept in this area is the right to strike. In the past, there was essentially no limit on the duration of a strike, nor were there rules about the replacement of striking workers, even insofar as it related to the coverage of the agreement in terms of union and non-union members. Although there have been reforms aimed at reducing restrictions in this regard, in most cases there is strong opposition to any further erosion of labour's power.[9] Since, apart from the public and services sectors, labour strikes have traditionally been concentrated in the manufacturing sector, they have thus far been no hindrance to trade activities that are mainly concerned with agriculture, forestry and fishing (although in countries such as Chile, there is a continuing tradition of disputes in the mining industry). In countries with strong manufacturing sectors, such as Mexico, the scarcity of disputes in these industries can be attributed to the fact that they are chiefly made up of medium-sized and small units which rely heavily on their specific competitiveness in terms of internal and external trade connections.

Protection of Labour Force Segments

There are usually two sets of protective regulations in this category. The first concerns the establishment of a minimum working age, which is designed to protect children from exploitation and increase the likelihood that they will remain in school. As fundamental as this aim is, it has clearly not been fully achieved, given the extent of poverty, the region's insufficient educational infrastructure and the large size of its agricultural and informal sectors. Evidently, appropriate enforcement of child labour laws is warranted. The delicate issue of unfair labour practices is associated with a social dumping argument frequently used by interest groups favouring protective polices in industrial countries, including within the WTO. It is true that child labour or other unfair practices – such as unpaid overtime or unrestricted work conditions for pregnant women – are used in many poor countries to reduce total labour costs. However, it is also clear that the cultural and economic realities of these countries are not necessarily the same as those prevailing in the industrial world.

The second set of regulations concerns the protection of women, particularly through maternity leave, special shifts and company-funded childcare systems. This is an important, largely unresolved issue that will need to be addressed in order to arrive at a transparent international agreement on the restriction of certain practices that not only distort the competitiveness of a given country or industry but that may also be inhumane. By no means should this be construed as implying that labour practices and regulations prevailing in industrial countries should simply be reproduced and transferred to the developing world; a careful assessment of the cultural and economic realities of poorer countries is called for. A question of human rights is at stake here, and the issue needs to be addressed more explicitly at the level of international organizations.

Regulation of Working Conditions

The laws in this area normally include minimum health and safety standards, as well as setting mandatory maximum work hours. There does not appear to be any substantial difference between the situations prevailing in most developing and most industrial economies.

Income Security

(a) *Social Security Payments* Two major elements are involved here which normally account for a significant portion of employers' total non-wage labour costs. One is the social security contributions that firms were customarily required to make under the traditional pay-as-you-go system which predominated in the region in the post-Second World War era. However, varying types of reforms carried out in Latin America in the 1980s and 1990s have introduced a wholly worker-financed private capitalization system consisting of individual accounts that can be accessed upon retirement. In general, these reforms have significantly diminished firms' labour costs.[10] This has, of course, greatly improved employment and competitiveness in global markets; in the case of Chile, for instance, there has been a set reduction of more than 10 per cent in total wage costs compared to the amount employers had to pay under the old pension system.[11]

(b) *Job Security Regulations* Regulations on job security are the other major element in this category. As indicated by authors such as Heckman and Pages (2000), job security rules have had a substantial impact on employment levels and distribution in Latin America, reducing overall employment and promoting wage inequality. Table 11.2 shows Heckman and Pages' estimates of the marginal cost of labour dismissals. The indices given in the first column are a measurement of firing costs that sums up the entire tenure severance pay profile using a common set of dismissal probabilities across countries. In other words, this index computes the expected future cost, at the time that a worker is hired, of dismissing him/her at a later date.

As may be seen from the table, severance payments (the largest component of non-wage labour costs in Latin America) amount to anywhere between 15 per cent and 40 per cent of total wage costs. According to Heckman and Pages (2000), LACs' rankings in this index are generally much worse than those of the OECD countries.[12]

As a result of this situation and its obvious implications in terms of impairing competitiveness, several LACs have recently begun working to reduce severance payments and to introduce private unemployment insurance schemes. These schemes would function on the basis of a savings account to which both the employer and the worker would contribute and which the worker could access in the event of his/her dismissal under conditions stipulated by law. However, LACs face important political problems in this regard, since they would have to convince the unions of the wisdom of adopting a private-savings unemployment insurance scheme

Table 11.2   Job security index across Latin America, the
Caribbean and OECD countries, end of the 1990s

Country	Index job security (monthly wages)	% annual wage	Ranking
Brazil	1.785	14.871	1
Jamaica	1.920	16.003	2
Paraguay	2.168	18.068	3
Uruguay	2.232	18.599	4
Trinidad & Tobago	2.548	21.230	5
Nicaragua	2.563	21.358	6
Panama	2.718	22.652	7
Dominican Republic	2.814	23.454	8
Venezuela	2.955	24.625	9
Argentina	2.977	24.808	10
Costa Rica	3.121	26.005	11
Mexico	3.126	26.050	12
El Salvador	3.134	26.116	13
Chile	3.380	28.164	14
Colombia	3.493	29.108	15
Honduras	3.530	29.418	16
Peru	3.796	31.632	17
Ecuador	4.035	33.621	18
Bolivia	4.756	39.637	19

Source: Heckman and Pages (2000).

that, from their viewpoint, would compare poorly with existing firm-financed severance payments, which are cost-free to the employee. Progress in this area has been insufficient, and job security can rightly be described as the area of labour-market regulation that is the most detrimental to international competitiveness at the present time.

Two of the most important consequences of job security regulations are an increase in the total cost of labour and a reduction in labour mobility. In fact, restrictions placed on firing procedures by these regulations usually act as a severe constraint on firms seeking to adjust the size and composition of their staffing levels in response to prevailing technological and market conditions. In this respect, job security constitutes a significant barrier to external investment and improved competitiveness in global markets. Liberalization in the area of job security is still a delicate political issue in these countries. It is important to note that even in Chile, where labour reforms were introduced in the 1980s that restricted job security in terms of its cost to employers, there has been persistent political pressure for the restoration of some of the more stringent regulations that were in place during the greater part of the 1960s and 1970s. From the viewpoint of politicians and the unions, it would be unacceptable, either within the framework of the WTO or under free trade agreements, to negotiate anything that would imply a reduction or elimination of job security regulations.

LABOUR MARKETS DURING THE REFORMS OF THE 1990s

All the above-mentioned policy considerations are important factors in terms of trade policy and the likelihood of carrying out successful trade negotiations. In general, these policy factors influence the allocative functions of the labour market and probably have a pervasive impact on labour costs and on both intra-firm and inter-firm labour mobility. However, recent developments in the labour market are worth examining within the context of an assessment of the level of political willingness to pursue labour reforms designed to permit the implementation of further trade measures. Labour market outcomes are generally regarded as one of the most controversial aspects of the overall results of recent economic reforms.[13] Low employment growth, high open unemployment, declining real wages and a greater dispersion of wage levels all combine to create a situation that discourages the political support needed to push for further reforms.

It may be, however, that prevailing rigidities – particularly those present in the labour market – are actually to blame for unsatisfactory outcomes such as these. It may also be the case that existing regulations and institutions do not necessarily raise the relative cost of labour in LACs excessively and that the observed outcomes are essentially due to failures in other markets (for instance, distortions in industrial economies, in the capital market or in certain key output markets). Another possible interpretation – one favoured by most politicians – is that the economic reforms implemented so far do not necessarily bring any improvement in labour market outcomes or the social situation in general. It is therefore unlikely that undesirable outcomes could be due to imperfections or rigidities in labour markets.

At the same time, political criticism of labour market reforms should draw a clear distinction between short and longer-term outcomes. The most detrimental effects of trade reforms in terms of employment and wages are seen in the short run, while flexible markets should allow for positive longer-term outcomes, such as increased employment and higher wages in industries that are able to compete internationally in the export sector. Politicians' frequent claim that reforms 'do not do any good' for labour markets or the overall social situation disregards this basic and simple differentiation. Moreover, the distinction between shortand longer-term outcomes should provide the underpinnings for a strong argument in favour of reforming labour markets in order to attain the flexibility needed to maximize and accelerate the positive impact of trade reforms. Protectionism in most LACs in the pre-1970s era was prone to slow employment growth relative to the increasing supply pressures generated by intensive internal migration. This policy stance was therefore predisposed to high structural unemployment, a problem that was dealt with by the growth of the urban informal sector and public-sector employment. The introduction of structural economic reforms created higher unemployment because of the downsizing of the state which they involved in most LACs. In addition, the informal sector expanded to cope with the increasing labour supply pressures stemming from the continuation of internal migration. The growth of the informal sector was also conducive to a decline in average real wages during the transition period, together with a drop in the relative wages of unskilled labour.

Two of the most important questions for the future are whether there will be further supply pressures in the labour market and whether there will be sufficient employment growth to cope with them. It is likely that labour supply pressures will be less intense than in the past but, given the increase in the female labour participation rate, they may be considerable. Hence, in order to cope with the implications of this trend, it will be necessary to have flexible labour markets that are able to reallocate labour efficiently on the basis of its 'opportunity cost'. This issue is of vital importance for the continuation of trade reforms in view of their generally critical impact on employment.

The Female Labour Participation Rate

Population growth in Latin America has slowed considerably (see Table 11.3). Despite the consequent decline in supply pressure on the labour market, labour growth has followed more or less the same pattern

Table 11.3 Average yearly growth rates

	1950–80	**1980–90**	**1990–98**
Per capita GDP	2.8	−0.2	1.7
Population growth	2.6	2.0	1.6
Labour force	2.7	2.9	2.5

Sources: Berry (2001); Weller (1999).

since the 1950s, with no more than very small incremental changes over time. Given the region's declining population growth rates, this fact is accounted for by its rising labour force participation rate (the rate of employed persons plus unemployed persons divided by the population aged 15 or older). This ratio rose steadily throughout the 1990s (climbing from 54.8 per cent in 1991 to 56.7 per cent in 1997 as an average for Latin America). To a large extent, this has been due to the increased participation of women in the labour force, since this group's participation rate has jumped from 38.1 per cent to 41 per cent over the same period.

Open Unemployment

One of the significant problems associated with economic reforms has been open unemployment. In countries such as Mexico and Brazil, because of the existence of a large informal market in urban areas, there is considerable debate as to the suitability of the statistical devices now used to measure unemployment. The experiences of Chile, Argentina and Colombia serve to illustrate what has happened in the presence of expanding open unemployment. Since there is no unemployment insurance or any comprehensive fiscal subsidization programme for the unemployed, the existence of relatively high rates of unemployment creates a severe social problem. Unemployment in the region is a political and social issue of major importance that is also linked to the presence of poverty and the exacerbation of this problem during adjustment periods. The persistence of this situation is a cause for concern. In Chile, for example, where a relatively low rate of unemployment was achieved in 1998, jobless levels rebounded to double digits (approximately 11–12 per cent) in 1999 and 2000, and Argentina, Colombia, Peru and Venezuela continue to register high unemployment figures (see Table 11.4).

Stagnation of Real Wages

On average, the Latin American region has seen a stagnation of real wages since 1990 and drop in real terms if 1980 is used as the base year (see Table 11.5). This is the case in Argentina – where unemployment has also been climbing steeply – and Mexico. In Mexico, the decrease in wages has taken place despite relatively low and stable unemployment levels. This decline is associated with employment in the 'maquila' industry, but has been questioned on the grounds of the conceptual suitability of official statistics. In Brazil, wages have been declining since 1985, whereas in Colombia and Chile there has been real growth since the 1980s (despite, in the latter case, high unemployment). In Chile the average annual growth rate of 3 per cent in real wages has in any case been lower than the average growth rate for the same period (more than 6 per cent per year). As mentioned by Robbins (1996), economic growth in countries such as Chile has led to a dispropor-tionately large increase in the wages of skilled labour, which has in turn broadened wage differentials and led to a deterioration in income distribution.

Table 11.4   Urban unemployment rates (selected years)

	1982	**1990**	**1994**	**1998**
Argentina	5.3	8.6	11.5	14.9
Chile	20.0	6.6	8.3	7.6
Brazil	6.3	4.3	5.1	5.8
Colombia	9.1	10.2	8.9	12.7
Mexico	4.2	2.8	3.7	3.9
Venezuela	7.8	10.6	8.9	12.8

Source: Berry (2001).

Table 11.5   Average real wages (1990 = 100)

	1980	**1985**	**1995**	**1998**
Argentina	130.0	135.7	100.9	99.1
Brazil	87.8	101.9	88.0	94.0
Chile	95.4	89.3	123.6	128.1
Colombia	85.0	97.4	105.4	110.2
Mexico	128.3	97.4	111.5	97.2
L. America	116.4	112.0	100.7	99.1

Source: Economic Commission for Latin America and the Caribbean (several yearly issues).

CONCLUDING REMARKS

The picture that emerges from an analysis of recent developments in LAC labour markets justifies many of the concerns expressed by local politicians. A significant unemployment problem has persisted, together with a drop in real wages and a sharpening of wage differentials between skilled and unskilled labour. A further unilateral opening of these economies to international trade is a sensible economic objective, but it may be too costly because of the serious social problems it might generate. Under these circumstances, the negotiation of trade agreements with other countries or groups of countries may be a more promising option because the associated transition period may be easier to withstand. In fact, it is feared that, under a multilateral strategy, LACs may be unable to negotiate on such issues as the continuation or phase-out of pervasive modes of intervention in the labour market. This interpretation is corroborated by an analysis of the failures of successive GATT rounds and the notable levels of trade protection adopted by many industrial economies. LACs' interests may be better served by an FTA strategy, since more of their particular problems and aspirations with regard to the costs of a transition to a freer trade scheme could be included in a negotiating agenda and/or in an addendum to a formal agreement. It could therefore be argued that the best approach for LAC governments would be to step up FTA based negotiations and to work for a more explicit international agreement on transitional costs within the framework of the WTO.

The first conclusion that can be drawn from the above analysis is that the economic adjustment process has played an important role in Latin America and has produced long-lasting results in terms of the shift of labour from contracting to expanding industries. This process has exacerbated transitional open unemployment and this, in combination with rigidities in labour market institutions, constitutes an obstacle to further trade reforms.

A second conclusion is that trade liberalization has been the most visible and important policy reform in the region. However, many experts contend that industrial countries have not supported the unilateral tariff reduction policies pursued in the 1980s and 1990s.

The third conclusion is that LACs are characterized by notable labour market rigidities that are associated with regulations and interventions, especially those that raise total labour costs substantially above the wage cost of labour. These regulations do not differ markedly from those used in industrial countries, with the probable exceptions of job security and strike regulations. Job security appears to be the main cause of poor competitiveness in a world trade context and plays a major role in maintaining labour market rigidities.

The fourth conclusion is that employment growth in LACs has not been rapid enough to cope with the expansion of the labour supply. At the same time, job quality has declined, as demonstrated by the swift expansion of the informal sector. This situation will probably not change substantially in the future. Unemployment has been persistent and is likely to remain high. Real wages have been flat or, at the least, there has been little correlation between wages and economic growth. Within the context of trade liberalization, economic growth has been associated with a deterioration in income distribution. This is because expanding sectors are more intensive in relatively more skilled labour, for which wages have increased substantially in comparison with unskilled workers, who constitute the segment in which poverty and other social ills are the most serious.

This distressing situation is compounded by the fact that productivity gains have mainly occurred in tradable producing sectors rather than in terms of employment. Consequently, the expansion of non-tradable sectors has resulted in higher employment but lower productivity. All the above factors serve to reinforce the arguments of many politicians and policy-makers in LACs who recommend a cautious approach to any further implementation of the reform agenda. It is felt that further trade reforms should be undertaken only if there is a willingness to negotiate transitional costs. This is probably why initiatives relating to sub-regional agreements among countries having fairly similar regulatory systems (for instance, the Mercosur countries, those participating in the Central American initiative or even the Andean Community nations) have been seen as more promising and have gained greater acceptance from a political standpoint. Naturally, in countries that have more ambitious trade reforms already in place, such as Chile and Mexico, the focus is more on the need to find trading partners or associates in industry or the Asia-Pacific region.

At the same time there are serious concerns about the possible negative social and political effects of any effort to dismantle labour market institutions. LACs should focus on building a better human resource development infrastructure, including, in particular, formal education and training facilities; this would be the best way to attract external investment in more sophisticated industries. Nonetheless, while there are still strong labour supply pressures, this could exacerbate the region's unemployment problems.

Negotiations in the WTO, in any case, must be directed towards aligning LACs' labour standards with those of industrial countries although they are, in general, quite similar.

Notes

1. The extent of trade reforms is clearly indicated by tariff reduction in LACs. In 1985, the early reformers (Bolivia, Chile and Mexico) exhibited average tariff charges equivalent to 30 per cent, which were reduced to an equivalent of only 7.7 per cent on average for the period 1991–92. In the case of 'very recent reformers' (including, among others, Brazil, Colombia, Peru and Venezuela) the average tariff in 1985 reached 57.3 per cent, which drastically declined in 1991–92 to only 15.8 per cent. See Edwards (1994).
2. The countries included in the Stalling study, for the purpose of preparing the information contained in Table 11.1 are: Argentina, Bolivia, Brazil, Colombia, Costa Rica, Chile, Dominican Republic, Ecuador, El Salvador, Guatemala, Honduras, Jamaica, Mexico, Paraguay, Peru, Uruguay and Venezuela.
3. In general, and as a result of profound trade and other economic reforms, LACs have become highly integrated into the world trading system. See Michalopoulos in this volume.
4. Edwards solidly raises this argument by illustrating the fact that OECD countries are characterized by non-tariff barriers coverage ratios against exports from Latin America, equivalent on average to 29 per cent reaching as high as 63 per cent and 38 per cent in the cases of Argentina and Brazil respectively.
5. Corden (1984).
6. See, for a more detailed description, the *World Economic Report* of the World Bank (1996).
7. This figure has been estimated by Riveros (1989) and it corresponds to an average for Argentina, Brazil, Colombia, Chile, Mexico and Peru for the period 1970–85. According to more recent estimates, this figure has not substantially changed.
8. If one takes the average per capita income in LACs to be about $4,000, whereas it reaches more than $16,000 in OECD countries, the ratio labour-cost/per capita income is still higher in the case of the latter.
9. Even in the case of Chile, where a very liberal law was passed during the military regime in connection with unionization and strikes, there is a current proposal to modify it in order to restore some of the workers, rights that were previously eliminated.
10. For instance, in the case of Chile, the contribution to social security implied a cost for the firm of about 17 per cent of total wages.
11. In the case of Chile, with an employment-wage elasticity of 0.75, the decrease in total wages would have implied a 7.5 per cent growth in total employment.
12. Twelve OECD countries (USA, New Zealand, Australia, Canada, Norway, Germany, France, Poland, Switzerland, UK, Belgium and Austria) included in the study, rank between 0 and 14.86 per cent, that is, below than the lowest level seen in Latin America in terms of the proportion of job security in annual wages. Only Spain (26.3 per cent) and Portugal (34.7 per cent) are at LACs' levels.
13. Weller (1999).

Bibliography

BERRY, ALBERT (ed.) (2001) *Labor Markets Policies in Canada and Latin America. Challenges of the New Millennium* (Kluwer Academic Publishers).

CORDEN, MAX (1984) 'The Normative Theory of International Trade', in R. Jones and P. Kenen (eds), *Handbook of International Economics*, Vol 1 (Amsterdam: North Holland).

Economic Commission for Latin America and the Caribbean (ECLAC), *Panorama Económico de América Latina* (several yearly issues).

EDWARDS, SEBASTIAN (1994) 'Trade and Industrial Policy Reform in Latin America', NBER Working Paper 4772.

HECKMAN, JAMES J. and CARMEN PAGES (2000) 'The Cost of Job Security Regulation: Evidence of Latin American Labor Markets', NBER Working paper no. 7773.

MICHALOPOULOS, CONSTANTINE (2001) 'Latin America in the WTO', Chapter 2 in this volume.

PALDAM, M. and L. RIVEROS (1989) 'Salarios Minimos y Medios: Analisis de Causalidad. Los Casos de Argentina Brasil y Chile', *Cuadernos de Economia*, no. 73, Universidad Católica de Chile, Santiago.

RIVEROS, LUIS (1989) 'Diferencias internacionales en los costos salariales y no salariales', *Estudios*, XII-51 (83–97), Fundación Mediterránea, Septiembre.

RIVEROS, LUIS (2001) 'Minimum Wages in Latin America: The Controversy About Their Likely Economic Effects' in (2001).

ROBBINS, DONALD (1996) 'Evidence on Trade and Wages in the Developing World', OECD Development Centre, Technical Paper, no. 119, Paris.

STALLINGS, BARBARA and WILSON PEREZ (2000) 'Growth, Employment and Equity: The Economic Reforms in Latin America and the Caribbean', Working Paper, Economic Comission for Latin America (ECLAC).

WELLER, JURGEN (1999) 'Los Mercados laborales en América Latina: su Evolución en el Largo Plazo y sus tendencias Recientes', Serie Reformas Económicas 11, mimeo, Santiago-Chile.

12 The Trade–Labour Nexus: Latin America's Perspective[1]

José-Manuel Salazar-Xirinachs

INTRODUCTION

The Seattle Ministerial Meeting highlighted the diverging positions of industrialized and developing countries on trade and labour. Below I will describe and analyze the main arguments of Latin American and Caribbean (LAC) countries regarding the inclusion of labour issues into the WTO negotiations.

While LAC countries have an agenda for cooperation on labour issues, they are generally united against linking trade and labour issues in trade negotiations and agreements. It might be accurate to say that most LAC countries prefer to cooperate on labour issues globally in the context of the International Labour Organization (ILO), and hemispherically in the context of the Labour Initiative in the Inter-American system, so as to avoid a formal or legal linking of trade and labour issues in the WTO and the Free Trade Agreement of the Americas (FTAA). Now, why is this so? It is common sense and a matter of fact that close links do exist in the real world between trade and labour issues, just as they do between trade and environmental issues. Thus, a position that seemingly rejects such a linkage appears on the surface as quite unreasonable. How is it justified? I will answer that question in four steps.

The first section of this chapter describes the main trade negotiating objectives from an LAC perspective and places the trade/labour issue in that context. The second section clarifies what is not entailed in the region's positions on labour issues. Section three then provides an overview of the Latin American and Caribbean (LAC) countries' main arguments and concerns for opposing a linkage of these issues in trade agreements. Finally, section four sets out some questions and suggestions for further research and a constructive dialogue.

NEGOTIATING OBJECTIVES OF LAC COUNTRIES

As countries prepare to launch a new round of multilateral trade negotiations, developing countries have expressed strong concerns about what
they perceive as uneven results in the balance of concessions from the
Uruguay Round. There is some truth to this and it is partly related to the
time frames for the implementation of the commitments that were negotiated. A recent evaluation of market access results from the Uruguay Round
concluded that

> The major part of what developing countries gave is due now, the major
> part of what they receive will not be delivered until 2005, or is yet to be
> negotiated. What they gave (apart from the exchange of tariff cuts) was
> mainly acceptance of 'codes' on major areas of domestic as well as
> import regulations/institutions (such as intellectual property, technical
> and sanitary standards, customs valuation, import licensing procedures).
> What they got in return from the developed economies is MFA elimina-
> tion – not due until 2005 – trade liberalization and reduction of domes-
> tic support on agricultural products – yet to be negotiated.

Given this situation, a new round would have provided an opportunity for
developing countries to advance their objectives. Generally speaking, what
developing countries, including LAC, want in trade negotiations is
enhanced and secure access to large markets. This is seen as a necessary,
but clearly not sufficient condition for growth, employment generation and
poverty reduction.

Latin America priorities in market access include, mainly:

- elimination of high tariffs and of non-tariff barriers in sectors where
  they have comparative advantage (textiles, clothing, footwear, leather,
  food, agriculture);
- elimination of tariff escalation;
- tougher disciplines in the application of trade remedies by developed
  countries;
- further strengthening of dispute resolution mechanisms; and
- enlarged access for their skilled labour to global markets for services.

They are also very interested in more access to international investment
flows, but recognize that this is fundamentally a matter for domestic
policies to improve the investment climate: from macro-disciplines, to
normative frameworks for investment protection, to the core factors of
competitiveness.

Latin America, and particularly the smaller economies, are clear that trade and investment are the engines of economic growth and, in conjunction with appropriate social policies, offer the best chance for creating employment and reducing poverty. And this is why their priority is expanding trade and obtaining larger and more secure access to the markets of developed countries and to each other's markets. The introduction of other issues that threaten to complicate, delay or even derail the negotiations, is seen as a diversion from the main objectives in terms of growth and development.

WHAT IS NOT ENTAILED?

It is important to note what is *not* entailed in the opposition of developing countries, particularly in LAC, to the linking of labour issues to trade. Firstly, LAC countries are not saying that trade and labour issues are unrelated. They recognize that there are important relationships between trade and labour as well as trade and environmental issues. What they do not want is to link them in trade agreements or trade negotiations, and particularly not to link them to market access and trade sanctions, for reasons that will be discussed below.

Secondly, LAC countries do not reject the linkage because they have a policy of violating workers' rights, or because these countries see themselves as having a competitive strategy based on exploitative conditions. LAC countries have signed an important number of ILO conventions protecting core labour rights. There are problems of enforcement and compliance. Yet, it is one thing to find cases of violations and a quite different one to suggest that this is something promoted by governments as a matter of policy.

Thirdly, LACs are not declining to cooperate. In the Inter-American system there is cooperation at two levels: regional and hemispheric. At the regional level, Central America is a good example, where Ministers of Labour, including those of Panama and the Dominican Republic, meet regularly to undertake joint actions under the auspices of the regional ILO office. The main initiative, however, is hemispheric. Ministers of Labour of the hemisphere meet every two years. At their meeting in Viña del Mar, Chile, the ministers agreed on a Plan of Action, and established two working groups: one on Globalization of the Economy and its Social and Labour Dimensions; and another on Modernization of the State and Labour Administration. They identified priority areas and have a number of initiatives to make progress in each area, including: the role of the

Ministries of Labour, employment and the labour market, vocational training, labour relations and basic workers' rights, social security, health and safety, enforcement of national labour laws and administration of justice in the labour area, and social dialogue. The last meeting of Ministers of Labour of the Americas took place in Washington D.C. in February 2000.

It should be stressed that LAC countries are quite engaged in cooperation and committed to work together among themselves with the United States, the European Union and others on a broad range of issues. There are some funding problems for these cooperation programmes but there is political will and an ambitious agreed-upon agenda. Strengthening this hemispheric initiative on Labour Cooperation could be a major way of achieving progress in legal frameworks and enforcement of core labour rights, as well as in other critical areas.

OVERVIEW OF ARGUMENTS AND CONCERNS

To provide a better understanding of why the majority of LAC countries have been refusing to address labour issues in trade negotiations, the relevant arguments are grouped into five categories: first, arguments relating to political economy; second, those concerning the stage of development; third, questions concerning the logic of trade negotiation; fourth considerations of efficiency in achieving negotiating objectives; and finally, arguments related to the global architecture of the trading system.

Political Economy Arguments

The first political economy argument is related to how LAC countries perceive the political landscape in developed countries. LAC countries understand that pressures in developed countries to include labour issues in trade negotiations emanate from two major constituencies, sometimes acting in alliance: (a) politically powerful lobbying groups interested in defending protection and privileges, who want to limit international competition from developing countries by raising their production costs and deterring investment flows to them; and (b) morality-driven human rights and other groups that want to see higher standards abroad and have no protectionist agendas. The first group is perceived as not genuinely interested in improving the well-being in developing countries but rather motivated by *competitiveness* concerns and *perceptions* that they will be losers from freer trade.

Hence, true or not, many developing countries are concerned that motivations for including labour issues in trade negotiations are at best mixed, and at worst not really humanitarian at all, but rather expressions of protectionist interests. One aspect that reinforces the perception that this is an issue where pressure group politics is paramount, is the often-quoted statistic that only 12 per cent of the US labour force is unionized; but well organized.

A second political economy issue, closely related to the first, is the perception that self-interest or protectionist intent is clear from the selective focus on certain labour issues. Thus, the refusal to include clauses on issues of importance to some developing countries, such as the rights of migrant labourers or enhanced access for skilled labour in services contracts, is taken as a signal that even if labour issues were included in negotiations, the playing field would not be level. A third point relates to fears that by including labour issues in trade negotiations, developing countries might have imposed upon them models of labour/management relations that are inappropriate, be it because of their stage of development, or because changes in labour processes induced by globalization and the technological revolution are rendering such models increasingly obsolete. This serious concern, with potentially profound consequences, is shared by some developed countries as well.

Stage of Development Arguments

That last point is closely linked to stage-of-development considerations. They take various forms. To mention only one, there is the argument that since poverty, informality and labour market conditions in developing countries are quite different from those of an advanced industrial economy, the strict importation of rules and models of labour–management relations from advanced countries is questionable. A variation of the above focuses on comparisons between labour rights and models of participation in Europe and the United States and raises questions as to whether developed countries ought to undertake far greater commitments in the labour rights area than developing countries that are at a much lower stage of development.

Logic of Trade Negotiations

A further object of analysis should be the logic and realities of trade and trade negotiations. Here, three observations can be made.

The first relates to the fundamental asymmetry in market size and relative importance as trading partners between the US on the one hand,

and developing countries (LAC in particular), on the other. In reality, the US is the only country that can threaten with credibility and actually produce damage, in many cases disproportionately so, by closing its market to the other trading partners. Accepting the link between market access or trade sanctions and labour issues, as suggested by the previous US President Clinton in Seattle is, in practice, a way of institutionalizing unilateralism in a multilateral context, either in the WTO or in the FTAA. No win–win situation is perceived in this.

A second argument that explains not so much the opposition to linkage, as the strong feelings and inflexible positions on this issue by some countries, is the fear that any concession made to establish a Working Group on Trade and Labour as proposed by the US or a joint ILO/WTO Standing Working Forum on Trade, Globalization and Labour Issues as suggested by the EU and several other Members, is a slippery slope. Countries see no end to it. For instance: At which point are trade unions or NGOs in the US going to support fast-track? Will this support be delivered upon *establishment* of the Working Group on Trade and Labour in the WTO? Probably not. Countries will have to wait for the recommendations of the Working Group. But what if the recommendations of the Group are not acceptable for trade unions and NGOs? Thus, every solution engenders its own problems and some of those seem even worse than the current difficulties.

The third observation has to do with negotiating priorities and trade-offs. As already mentioned, developing countries' priorities include market access including agriculture and services, disciplining trade remedy laws and strengthening dispute resolution mechanisms. Inclusion of labour and environmental issues entails the risk of overloading negotiations and making them extremely complex, to the point of at best delaying or at worst impeding the achievement of results.

Efficiency in Achieving Objectives

A fourth category of arguments questions the effectiveness of trade sanctions as an instrument to achieve labour or environmental results. Are trade sanctions the best way to achieve results in improving labour and environmental standards? Are there superior ways of achieving these objectives and agendas?

A majority of countries favour a context of *cooperation* rather than one of *negotiation*, not only because of the economic and social damage that limitations to market access could inflict on them, but also because they are convinced that, to an important extent, the source of the problem lies in the lack of capacity to implement core labour rights, linked to limitations in institutional infrastructure and human and financial resources. From this perspective, technical assistance and capacity building are seen as first best instruments to achieve results. In other words, this is not a problem that can be overcome merely by using trade measures as a mechanism to bring governments into line.

The difficulties that many developing countries including LAC are facing in implementing Uruguay Round commitments in areas such as Technical Standards, Intellectual Property and Customs Valuation illustrate this point. It is not merely a matter of getting provisions and rules into the WTO, but of actual institutional and administrative capacity to implement them.

Some also think that insisting on linkage creates a confrontational and divisive agenda that undermines the objectives, instead of promoting good-will and creative solutions and cooperation on labour issues. In this view, linkage should be replaced by appropriate governance at the international level, where each agenda is pursued at the appropriate fora. This does not mean that there could not be cooperation and coordination between responsible agencies, such as the WTO and the ILO, given the overlapping of issues. But this is not the same as bringing labour issues into the WTO.

Shaping the Global Architecture of the Trading System

Finally, there are more fundamental questions to be considered: What is the appropriate governance at the international level? What is the appropriate architecture for the global trading system?

A first rather technical but important point concerns the architecture of the GATT/WTO system. Trade negotiators, in particular – and this is not only a developing country concern – worry about overloading the WTO with issues that the WTO was not designed to deal with and which could ultimately lead to the destruction of the multilateral, rules-based trading system.

This can be clearly illustrated with the debate around the proposals to accommodate in the WTO unilateral trade measures based on process and production methods (PPMs) in the country of export. The concern is that discriminating against products on the basis of the method by which they are produced, rather than their intrinsic qualities, amounts to the extra-territorial or extra-jurisdictional application of domestic regulations, per-verting the long-established GATT/WTO principle of national treatment of goods in the country of import. The crux of the argument is that the princi-ples of 'national treatment' and 'most-favoured nation' are intimately linked to the notion of 'like product'. These are the cornerstones of a multilateral trade regime that works well and has fostered a predictable and stable global trade regime. Allowing discriminatory treatment based on production methods, labour standards or human rights would destroy the predictability and undermine the fundamentals of the system. So there is a widespread agreement among trade experts that it is not advisable to amend WTO rules to accommodate unilateral discriminatory treatment.

In the environmental field, arguments like this triggered the proposal to create a World Environment Organization to provide a focal point for Multilateral Environmental Agreements and other environment-related issues and disputes. Originally suggested by Daniel Esty, this proposal was adopted by Renato Ruggiero, Director General of the WTO in early 1999. The parallel with labour issues is clear. These discussions further underpin the view that linkage in general is not feasible, and that it should be replaced by appropriate governance at the international level, where each agenda is pursued by a separate responsible agency, with appropriate coordination between them.

QUESTIONS AND ISSUES FOR FURTHER RESEARCH

A number of important specific issues need clarification. The following six areas singled out by the US proposal to the WTO as terms of reference for the Working Group on Trade and Labour, might be a good starting point:

- Trade and Employment
- Trade and Social Safety Nets and Protections
- Trade and Core Labour Standards
- Positive Trade Policy Incentives and Core Labour Standards
- Trade and Child Labour
- Trade and derogation from national labour standards (for instance in Export Processing Zones)

In addition, a better understanding of the links between Trade and Wages would help to dissipate many concerns and misunderstandings. Yet, also more fundamental issues need to be addressed. One is the globalization debate. Many are concerned that the present model of trade liberalization is exacerbating developmental inequalities, environmental degradation, workers' exploitation and gender imbalances, and demand that it should receive careful consideration based on solid evidence. These concerns will not go away. It is essential to discern the causes of inequalities and poverty. Attributing them to trade (whether in the United States, the European Union or in developing countries) is highly contentious and likely misguided. Are they due to trade, technological trends or lack of adequate social policies and safety-nets, or a combination of these factors? Likewise, the present portrayal of the WTO as the culprit of all that is wrong with globalization and as beholden to multinational corporate interests to the detriment of labour and developing countries is seriously flawed. We need a balanced and well-informed understanding of the real dynamics of trade negotiations, as well as the relationships between trade and development, trade and jobs, and trade and living standards.

The second area where more research and better understanding is needed is global governance. It is important to understand the concerns of trade negotiators about the risks for the GATT/WTO system to be overloaded with labour and environmental issues. The global trading system is a major achievement and needs to be protected. Any change of rules has to be carefully thought out. In particular, further dialogue and research on the advantages and disadvantages of a separate track approach for global governance by having labour issues dealt with in the ILO is essential.

Note

1.   The content of this material drew most of its input from a previous publication in the *Journal of International Economics Law*, vol. 3, Oxford University Press, June (2000), with permission.

13 Beyond Seattle, Davos and Porto Alegre: World Trade and Second Generation Reforms in Latin America

Dieter W. Benecke

INTRODUCTION

Since the beginning of the 1990s, most countries in Latin America, abandoning import substitution policies of the past decades, have opened their economies to foreign trade for a large quantity of products. Mexico, Brazil and Chile in particular, as well as Argentina for a certain time, have benefited in terms of greater growth and innovation from this policy. However, the days of the *windfall profits* of globalization seem to be over and limitations to growth arising from both external obstacles and internal social problems are becoming increasingly apparent.

Given that in addition, the other instruments of the *Washington Consumus*[1] are now no longer as effective as at the beginning of the 1990s, it seems appropriate to rethink national economic policies, embarking in this way on a programme of 'second generation reforms' focused on institutional change and the creation of an 'economic order' which introduces a longer-term perspective.

In a world climate which was even more unfavourable and in a national context at least as difficult as the current one in Latin America, Germany, by introducing the Social Market Economy model, took a decision which, though tough, was sure to bring about substantial reform.

This economic order, applied successfully since 1949, has enabled the country to emerge from almost total destruction to become one of the world economic leaders, reaping full advantage of world trade as regulated by the General Agreement on Tariffs and Trade (GATT), the precursor of the World Trade Organization (WTO).

The Social Market Economy is still very much the system in Germany today, even though it has undergone and will continue to undergo changes,[2] all the time retaining its fundamental characteristics. Certainly, this model cannot be applied in the same form in Latin America. However in light of the first generation reforms in Latin America, reforms which were necessary but insufficient to consolidate and accelerate development in the emerging countries, a wider dialogue on the economic order in Latin America is timely.

ECONOMIC ORDER AND ECONOMIC PROCESS

In Latin America, politicians tend to concern themselves primarily with the *economic process* and, since the decline of socialism and dependence theory, place less emphasis on the *economic order*. Here I outline the difference between policies relating to economic order and those relating to economic process.

The economic order is a system whose elements establish a clear and reliable frame of reference for the four economic agents: individuals, enterprises, civic associations (NGOs) and the state. The Social Market Economy is based on civil liberty and combines a regime of competition as free as possible with social solidarity as wide-ranging as possible. It establishes fundamental principles for behaviour, such as the protection of private property, consumer protection, personal responsibility of the individual and social solidarity, state subsidiarity, among others. It is the responsibility of the state to implement this order on the footing of a democratically taken decision; that is to say, it is for the government to determine and establish an appropriate economic order policy. Within this order, a number of economic processes operate, relating to pricing, taxation, deposit and credit interest, foreign trade policy and so forth. The daily economic policy or the economic process policy is aimed at adjusting these elements of the system to the current needs and challenges of the economy.[3] Can the Social Market Economy serve as a frame of reference, albeit in an adjusted form, for the emerging countries of Latin America? Which elements should be examined for their possible usefulness as a means of consolidating first generation reforms and guiding those of the second generation? As an ultimate aim, economic policy seeks to achieve dynamic and socially-just economic development, thus establishing a democratic society with *universal welfare*.[4]

As already noted, since the end of the 1980s, Latin America has carried out various reforms which may be characterized as the implementation of measures aimed at influencing the economic process, meanwhile neglecting the conceptual design of the economic order. It is true that elements of the liberal or neoliberal agenda served to orient the economic process policy: privatizations, the opening up of foreign trade, the contraction of public administration. However, these measures were taken more out of the urgent need to change macroeconomic factors, such as, for example, to reduce the inflation rate, correct fiscal imbalance and reduce the deficit in the balance of payments. While necessary, they do not constitute a sufficient definition of an economic order which will achieve dynamic, socially-just and sustainable development. In a system – and without doubt, an economic order is a system – the whole is always more than the sum of its parts.

Obviously, a certain economic vision is also expressed in the objectives and instruments of the past reform process. This might be summarized as less state and more private initiative. However, given the *political* character of the design of all economic models, this motto does not constitute an adequate economic model. In the few attempts which have been made to justify the position adopted, it has been argued that the priority was to solve current problems; in other words, to sweep the house before painting it. From this perspective, first generation reforms, fundamentally marked by monetarist theory, deserve a positive appraisal on the whole. But, the euphoria that usually accompanies the liberalization of an economy has now passed. The lack of a coherent economic order is increasingly apparent, all the more so as socio-political problems manifest themselves. The gap is widening: between rich and poor, between people with good and those with inadequate education, between qualified and unqualified labour force, between the well-informed and the ill-informed, between those who have good social security (increasingly meaning private insurance) and those who do not. This gives rise to growing problems in the labour market and in social and educational policy.

The situation is aggravated by globalization which increases the competitive advantage of the rich, the educated, the qualified, and those with insurance, and marginalizes the underprivileged even more. At the same time, globalization has rendered the discussion about national economic models more complex, supposedly because it reduces the space for autonomous action in economic policy at the national and regional level. How can the social security system be maintained or even expanded, if its costs become a comparative disadvantage that lessens the margin for social security or the preservation of jobs? Such is the frequent response of politicians and entrepreneurs. In effect, the design of an appropriate economic model becomes more difficult as international economic interdependency increases.

However this is not a reason to despair of the design of an economic order or to reduce economic policy to economic process measures, however important these may be. If the political responsibility to set down a clear framework of orientation for the economy is neglected, there is a danger that reforms will not take root and that internal tensions will increase. To get the best possible economic results for society, different factors must come together: growth and social justice must go hand in hand, employment and price stability, individual responsibility and solidarity, individual effort and subsidiarity, private property and social responsibility, competition and state intervention to reduce economic concentration. In this context, education policy by which is meant schooling as well as technical and professional training is the key to establishing greater equality of opportunity for its citizens.

Finding a balance between individual initiative, solidarity and subsidiarity is the real and constant challenge and therein resides the art of designing an economic model. It is doubtful if the more recent approach encapsulated in the *Third Way*[5] has sufficient definition to chart a clear compromise between individual liberty of action and social solidarity. Despite this lack of definition, it is worth paying attention to the future development of the concept and its efforts in this direction. Before turning to the requirements for future dialogue on economic models in Latin America, I briefly summarize the results of the *first generation reforms*.

Results of First Generation Reforms

For Latin America, 1999 was not a good year. For the second successive year, exogenous influences such as the Asian and Russian crises, a reduced inflow of credits from the industrialized countries, as well as the depression in the prices of petrol and other primary materials all affected economic development and left the countries of the region with 'zero growth'. The growth rate of Gross National Product (GNP) fell from 5.4 per cent in 1997 back to 2.1 per cent in 1998 and to zero per cent in 1999, based on 1995 prices.[6] The per capita GNP also decreased to 1.6 per cent in 1999. The rate of regional unemployment increased by 0.7 per cent over the previous year to a level of 8.7 per cent,[7] the highest unemployment rate since the registration of unemployment statistics in most Latin American countries.

Real salaries showed better results than the unemployment figures, due mainly to the reduction of inflation rates. In 1999 the rate of regional inflation was of the order of 10 per cent p.a. thus keeping to the same level as the previous year, in spite of the fact that certain currencies were devalued, thanks to their efforts at stabilization. The trade deficit also came down, due mainly to the reduction of imports as a result of lower internal demand. The lowering of the trade deficit also brought down the deficit in the balance of payments (4.5 per cent of GNP in 1998 and 3.2 per cent in 1999).[8]

Nonetheless an analysis of the period 1990–99 – in spite of the zero growth in 1999 – reveals an average annual growth rate of 3.45 of real GNP. This is significant by comparison with the European Union (EU) that achieved only 2.0 per cent and the US at 2.2 per cent,[9] and seems to confirm the success of the 'first generation reforms'. However, these economic figures obscure the fundamental problem, that of poverty in Latin America. The President of the World Bank, James Wolfensohn, underlined that 175 million people, or 36 per cent of the population of Latin America lives below the poverty line,[10] including 15 per cent in conditions of extreme poverty. According to Wolfensohn, the major problem is the extremely unequal distribution of income in Latin America. The poorest 20 per cent of the population of Latin America earns less than 4.5 per cent of the national income.[11] The gap between rich and poor in the region is widening all the time, remarked Wolfensohn.[12] This is supposed to be a 'natural' phenomenon in the first phase of the transition to an open market economy which, as is the case in Latin America, is not sufficiently accompanied by social measures. This deficit must be compensated for in a second phase of reforms, in the interest of political stability and if the first phase is not to lose its strength.

In 1990, a systematic debate was opened on the first stage of the reforms. On this occasion a group of Latin American and Caribbean 'policy makers' assessed progress in economic policy. They arrived at an agreement on ten instruments.[13] The *Washington Consensus* did not however take account of the distribution of income and wealth. Its instruments were aimed fundamentally at outlining simple ways of achieving greater macroeconomic stability, eliminating the extreme protectionism of the Latin American governments, and better exploiting the potential of growing world trade, as well as the flow of foreign capital. The Washington experts still hoped that globalization and the agreed reforms, afterwards called 'first generation reforms', would not only permit greater economic growth, but also bring about a significant reduction in poverty and, almost automatically, an improvement in the distribution of income.[14] The instruments of the Washington Consensus have proved inadequate to this objective or are not used for the purposes they were intended. It is likely that poverty which has been slightly reduced in some countries, is more a consequence of a lower level of inflation and a moderate economic growth than of the distributive effect which is supposed to arise from the liberalization of trade and the free circulation of capital. The high level of structural unemployment which became apparent once the economy opened suggests that the lower middle class and the lower class will continue getting poorer.

The objectives of the 'second generation reforms' in Latin America are multiple. On the one hand, they should achieve greater and more sustainable growth; this is a necessary, but an insufficient condition for development. The other great challenge is the duty to significantly reduce poverty. To realize this, measures must be taken to distribute the increment of welfare in a more effective way, as well as to integrate the marginalized sectors of the population in the modernization process. This will require major efforts in the area of training, not only among the young but also in the active professional population. Profound institutional reforms are necessary to reduce debt, establish a capital market which encourages national and international investment, improve judicial conditions, introduce severe sanctions for corruption,[15] intensify competition in an economy which is partly 'monopolized' by 'personal relations',[16] continue strengthening the competitiveness of the private sector and consolidating measures for macroeconomic stability through fiscal discipline.

The creation of conditions which favour the birth of modern companies and as far as possible small to medium-sized enterprises (SMEs), especially in the communication and information sector, is also a priority. To facilitate this, infrastructure needs improvement, in particular in the modern computer science networks sector. Responsibility must be decentralized in the 'think global, act local' sense. To do this, an appropriate *economic order* must be designed while sustaining the positive gains via the *economic process* policy of the past decade.

DESIGN OF AN ECONOMIC ORDER FOR THE TWENTY-FIRST CENTURY

The growing poverty in most Latin American countries constitutes not only a danger for the economic reforms of the first generation but also for the stability of democracy. Faced with this danger, the (neo) liberal focus of the 1990s is an inadequate response. Politicians frequently explain current problems by referring to exogenous factors, such as the volatility of foreign capital and barriers to international trade, especially of agricultural products, a problem which the WTO has still not resolved. These factors certainly make it more difficult to carve out a national stand-alone path, but for all that, they do not obviate the design of a model which takes account of national resources and takes advantage of the positive challenges of globalization. 'Blaming' foreign factors is in effect a regression to dependence theory, thrusting responsibility for the slump on the 'centre', in other words, on industrial countries and multinational corporations. Latin America, like Europe and Asia, is subject to certain limitations in its attempts to design an economic order. These are concentrated in three main factors:

- *Globalization* offers major opportunities to exploit comparative advantages arising from the free circulation of goods[17] and capital and from more intense and flexible communications systems. However it also entails difficulties such as those arising from greater migration, environmental problems, drug traffic and international crime, as well as social problems.[18]
- *Regional integration* entails, of necessity, harmonization of economic and social policies, abandonment of special protective norms and acquiescence to international forms of arbitration, thus delegating part of national sovereignty.
- *Value system* that requires and promotes different attitudes, such as:
    - (a) greater respect for the law and the implementation of necessary legal reform;
    - (b) a more analytic and self-critical approach which does not place the blame for one's own problems on third parties;
    - (c) a widening of individual responsibility instead of a dependence on the state, the unions or other organizations to solve one's problems;
    - (d) an acceptance of the challenge of competition instead of trusting to arrangements arrived at through personal relations;
    - (e) a respect for political institutions, this obviously entailing a change of attitude among politicians;
    - (f) a resistance to active and passive forms of corruption.

In order to participate actively in the global world, traditional attitudes towards the political, economic, social and cultural system must be adapted. In addition, the change in the structure of the demographic pyramid[19] forces a rethinking of the design of the political-economic order. Greater life expectancy requires an overall reorientation of economic policy generally and, in particular, of the forecasting system, the flexibility of the labour market, education policy and tax policy. Nothing less than a profound *change of mentality among politicians* is called for.

Principles of the Social Market Economy

Despite these limitations, there is sufficient flexibility at a national level to design a consistent economic order and corresponding economic policies.

It is not suggested here that the German model of the Social Market Economy in its different manifestations and developments over the years – in 1949, 1969, 1982 or 1999 – should be imitated. The intention is rather to discuss the elements which form the basis of its success:

1. Private property and social responsibility;
2. Free competition and control of concentration;
3. Individual responsibility, solidarity and subsidiarity;
4. Contractual liberty and juridical security;
5. Trustworthiness of the frame of reference established by the state and reliability of government behaviour;
6. Free flow of communication and media independence.

These principles will bear the desired fruit of a development which is both dynamic and socially-just, only in a democratic environment which guarantees civil liberty. The success of the model depends on the use of its instruments. None of the above-mentioned elements is absolute in character. There is room to shape them according to national specificities. The German system, influenced by the ideas of *ordoliberalism*[20] as well as by the Catholic social doctrine and the Protestant ethic, has proved sufficiently open and flexible to respond to the different challenges which impacted on Germany.

The market economy system, applied in the majority of Latin American countries in the 1990s, shows parts of these elements. However, in its social dimension – by 'social' we mean 'of society' – there are basic differences arising from inadequate distribution and the behaviour of some politicians who are not subject to sufficient control or rarely sanctioned for antisocial or corrupt behaviour. The same can be said of many entrepreneurs. Their risks are reduced not only legally but also because free competition is not accompanied by concentration controls or sanctions for underhand dealings. If there were greater transparency and stronger sanctions for anti-competitive behaviour, the 'market' would more easily regulate several of the existing problems.

The Economic Order and Fields of Political Action

The elements which make up the economic order seem generally acceptable. The political art is to realize them in such a way that individual liberty goes hand in hand with social responsibility, given the circumstances of time and place.[21] Those responsible for the design of the economic order and for its practical realization – that is, the state and politicians, civic associations and social institutions, scientists and individuals – can take action in the following areas:[22]

- *The planning and coordination system*: Here it is necessary to establish who is responsible for what type of planning and how the plans of the different economic agents may be coordinated. For example, the activities of the state in relation to public and private goods must be determined as well as those activities better handled by the private sector, thus allowing the state to concentrate on the essential aspects of its operation.[23]

- *The property regime*: The property rights of goods and production factors is a material condition for planning. The social responsibilities of ownership have particular relevance: for example, worker participation, health and hygiene, the environment and other aspects of public interest.

- *Fiscal order*: The budget should be balanced. A deficit and the indebtedness which it entails may be acceptable or even temporarily necessary. However a maximum rate of indebtedness should be established in relation to the national budget or to GNP, to avoid the risk of an overflow and its serious economic and political consequences.[24] Furthermore, the fiscal regime should comprise regulations to coordinate the budgets of the different levels of the state, ensuring the fiscal competence of the national, regional and municipal authorities.

- *The business regime*: The action radius of the different types of enterprises such as limited companies, cooperatives and so forth, is dependent on national regulations governing the individual and the public interest, worker participation and their right to form associations. In this instance SMEs are deserving of special attention given their social and innovatory role.

- *The competition system*: Interacting with the business sector, the competitive order establishes the rules of the game for: forces at play in the market of goods and production factors; market transparency; free access to markets; consumer protection;[25] safeguards against ruinous or disloyal competition and against abuse of a dominant position by an enterprise. Without doubt the economic future of Latin America will be determined by the competitiveness of its enterprises.

- *The monetary and financial regime*: This political field regulates the supply of national and international resources,[26] the position of the Central Bank and forms of payment. It guarantees solid commercial practice in the financial and insurance sector. This is usually done via an autonomous entity which is responsible for supervising credit institutions, insurance companies and the stock-exchange. Many Latin

American countries will have to be especially attentive in the control and sanction of corruption.

- *The foreign trade regime*: Once the economy has been opened in order to improve national competitiveness and participate in the global economy it is important that the international division of labour and the principle of comparative advantages are not undermined by politicians who engage in dumping and unfair subsidies. Nevertheless, a temporary system of selected promotion can be implemented with a view to strengthening certain type of production or business forms, such as SMEs. Dollarization presents a new challenge for foreign trade as well as for the monetary order.[27] Its implementation will affect not only Latin American economies but also those of the US and Europe.[28]
- *The social security system*: A solid social security system must take as its starting point the principles of self-help and personal responsibility of its citizens. Since the chances of individuals to participate in economic life vary significantly, partly for reasons outside their control, an element of solidarity must be introduced. Therefore the state must take measures to avoid social marginalization. Preventive action through education[29] is preferable while social loans as compensation should be regarded only as temporary measures, applying the principle of subsidiarity.

A much more profound dialogue on 'second generation reforms' in the eight fields listed above is necessary. Partial aspects have already received some discussion. Now a combination of these points in a coherent and sustainable system is necessary to increase the chances of greater growth and social justice in Latin America.

PRIORITIES FOR A POLITICAL DIALOGUE ON THE DESIGN OF AN ECONOMIC ORDER

The basic principles of the Social Market Economy require permanent discussion especially with regard to their implementation and effective realization. Nevertheless, it offers a more concrete system than the chimera of the so-called Third Way. Scientists and technicians constitute one of the primary target groups of this dialogue which then spread to those responsible for policy decisions. To this end, it will often be necessary to incorporate support of the media, for a broader dissemination to society regardless of the ideological or political position of the audience.

Naturally, while the dialogue on the design of the economy will vary from one country to another, it must take place at three levels: the state, the market, the individual.

To the state falls the direction, though not the sole responsibility, for policy planning and coordination, for fiscal, monetary and budgetary policy and the foreign trade regime. Market forces are the decisive element in determining business policy and the competitive regime, leaving to the state the responsibility for control of concentration so as to avoid abuse of power. In relation to property and social security, the prime responsibility should lie with the individual in interaction with the state and with business.

Action at these three levels has specific requirements according to the country. However, Latin American countries share certain characteristics. Here, priority should be assigned to (a) competition policy at the national and international level; (b) decentralization; (c) taxation instruments; (d) fight against poverty, social redistribution, education policy, modernization attempts; (e) culture as social identity; and (f) foreign trade policy. The following section takes as its basis the acceptability of the above-mentioned principles of the Social Market Economy.

(a) Working Competition[30]

Almost all the countries of Latin America have taken correct steps from the macroeconomic point of view in reducing the size of the state through privatization of public services. This has frequently created quasi-monopolies: with special tax and credit privileges that are not in accordance with a competitive economic order. However, private monopolies are usually as inefficient as state ones, if not in terms of productivity then in pricing policy and consumer services. It is doubtful if privatization would have been possible without offering guarantees to entrepreneurs, given that the economic situation in Latin America in the 1980s was not very promising. Today, by contrast, the situation lends itself more to attracting several competing enterprises. From the point of view of a more competitive economic order, it would be preferable where technically possible to divide the monopolies, thus allowing small and medium-sized enterprises (SMEs) to participate in bids for the privatization of state enterprises.

By modifying the process of privatization through setting time limits and on the range of privileges, it would be easier to open (partially) monopolized markets, thus attracting new competitors (spontaneous imitators)[31] by virtue of more effective communication. Currently, competitive behaviour in Latin America is still determined by agreements and the weave of personal relations. This situation cannot be changed from one day to the next. However, the present environment for discussion is more fertile than that of the 1960s and 1970s. The argument that markets are too small to be opened to competition has lost its force. Globalization, regional integration and, partially, as in the telecommunications sector, the activities of privatized enterprises have allowed for a considerable widening of markets.

Competition is also encouraged by direct foreign investment[32] which depends on the market dimension, although this is not the decisive factor. For the investor the macroeconomic conditions and the openness of the national markets in Latin America are equally important and access to these should not be obstructed by bureaucratic barriers or bribery.[33]

Competition policy has many elements which are also located in the institutional, social and psychological ambits. From the point of view of the discussion on the economic order in Latin America, the design of competition policy is the key issue for the future international competitiveness of Latin American enterprises. Studies on the openness of markets, the role of SMEs, industrial innovation, the abuse of power by the dominant market players, and the degrees of concentration and control of wealth, are key factors in determining the extent to which Latin America can insert itself in the process of globalization, as a passive victim or an active agent, being 'globalized' or as a 'globalizer'.[34]

(b) Decentralization

First generation reforms have established the base for economic decentralization. However, up to now, there has been a political counterweight to this process: the strong position of the President within a presidential democratic system which is still predominant in Latin America. An inherent aspect of this system and one which is difficult to change is a resistance by Presidents to delegate functions. The more the latter espouse personalism, the less they trust the political parties and the legislative branch and the more they fear regional leaders as potential successors or direct competitors. Despite this, the dialogue on the advantages of decentralization in the course of the debate on second generation reforms will have to be intensified. Special emphasis should be placed on the multipolarity of development drivers and the need to take full advantage of the development potential of the country, without losing sight of democratic consolidation at the different levels (national, regional, municipal). The decentralization discussion as an element of the *economic order* is usually facilitated if the debate centres on specific issues: communication between the different regional levels of the country; budgetary control; resource distribution between the central budget and the regional or municipal budgets and planning capacity.[35]

(c) Tax Policy

Tax policy affects *economic processes* as much as it does the design of the *economic order*. In relation to the latter, the alternatives of direct and indirect taxation must be fully considered: the consequences of direct taxes which can encourage or inhibit monetary returns; the effects of indirect taxes which can lead to regressive redistribution ('bottom up') – as is the case of VAT in relation to consumption rates. It is important to simplify the tax system. Probably in the majority of Latin American countries – Chile is an exception because of its clearly effective control system – the complex system and the consequent difficulty in controlling payments account partially for the high level of tax evasion. Certainly here, too, waste of public funds and corruption have a significant role. Many people ask themselves why they should pay taxes if these are not used for the production of public goods.

For the government, indirect taxes, since they do not directly affect income or property, are the most 'comfortable' instrument. However, from the point of view of social justice, by taking this less conflictive route government is neglecting an important instrument for *redistribution*. Systematic dialogue on tax policy which goes beyond mere ideological convictions should be based on a comparative analysis of tax collection, types of taxes, the tax burden and possiblities of control and sanction. If estimates on tax evasion were accurate, proper behaviour on the part of the taxpayers would reduce public indebtedness in the majority of the countries of Latin America at the stroke of a pen. Thus there is a strong argument in favour of a more intensive debate on the tax system, taking into account the requirement for *social justice*,[36] the appropiate use of tax revenues and their investment in a preventive and remedial social policy. A wider discussion on the economic order therefore would be engendered, a discussion with considerable relevance to the stabilization of a democracy.

(d) The Fight Against Poverty

In almost all Latin American countries, concern for the high or growing poverty rate goes far beyond mere lip-service. In the majority of cases, governments undertake actions and expenditure on this front, action which is justified but which does not get at the root of the problem. The extensive poverty of the population constitutes a 'legacy' from the past but the increase in poverty is a result of the 'present'. This problem is exacerbated by globalization, a process in which only those sectors that have access to greater economic and intellectual resources can participate. For the poor and for those with little education the 'poverty trap' has become more apparent. Through lack of knowledge and economic resources they cannot participate in the process of globalization or share in its positive consequences, and thus, in terms of knowledge and income are increasingly left behind by comparison with the more privileged.

In the fight against poverty, remedial social policy is necessary to improve redistribution. However, an appropriate educational, taxation and credit policy are more effective instruments of poverty prevention. Distribution policy should continue addressing absolute poverty while relative poverty should figure more and more prominently in the debate on the economic order.

The success of the struggle against poverty will determine not only the level of future economic development but also the degree of democratic stability. A growth in the percentage of poor in the population as a whole prepares the seedbed for populist leaders and even for dictators.

Misery and the struggle against poverty is not usually an attractive issue for the political, intellectual and economic élites of Latin America. While they are obviously aware of the existence of poverty and willing to make charitable gestures, the analysis of such themes as high technology, modernization, regional integration, and globalization offers greater prestige than does the perennial discussion of the struggle against poverty. For this reason, a debate on the economic order in which preventive rather than remedial policy prevails, is more promising. Such elements as educational policy, individual responsibility for social security, and the full integration of the population in a participative democracy usually constitute more attractive themes than the imminence of a 'March of the Lumpenproletariat' (B. Brecht). Some socialists who were intellectually active and at times leading the political discussion in Latin America in the 1960s and 1970s have given up their ideas. After the economic success of the (neo)liberals in the early 1990s, they seemed to have lost the battle and turned into market economists. Others maintained their position and feel themselves confirmed in their ideas, seeing the growing gap between rich and poor.

If their thesis in favour of intensive state activity in the economy and the adoption of protectionist measures against globalization were to prevail again, the successes of first generation reforms would be at risk. For many people, growing poverty, unemployment and regressive income distribution places doubt over the efficiency of the present democratically elected political leaders and even over democracy as such. If those who want to return to a closed and state-managed economy return to power or if populist politicians simply take advantage of the present economic dissatisfaction, then the economic order dialogue of the Social Market Economy type – as happened in the 1970s – will become once more a 'conversation of the deaf'.[37]

(e) Culture as an Element of Social Identification

Latin America has a rich cultural heritage. Identification with this constitutes an important tool insofar as the population has access to its riches. The relationship between politics *and* culture *and* between economy *and* culture has not received much attention so far in Latin American debates on the economic order. (Neo)liberal technocrats have ignored the fact that the cultural sphere may have great importance for employment policy in many regions, that it needs, finds and attracts considerable investment, and that it can influence sustainable tourism development and therefore regional policy. In addition it has been shown that culture has an important multiplier effect.[38]

Culture too has a place in the debate on economic models. On the one hand, philosophical ideas influence economy theory, on the other, artists and institutions can contribute to overcoming marginalization in parts of the population.[39] In general, culture has a considerable influence on the form of political dialogue, which is itself part of the political culture and important to participation in democracy. Culture is expressed in the concepts of the political parties and the national and international profile of political leaders. Considering increasing discrimination of minorities in many countries – also arising from social factors – more weight should be assigned to promotion of the cultural element of active tolerance as part of the economic debate. Certainly the economic consequences of cultural activity constitutes only one side of the phenomenon. But it is well established that the economy and its development are much more than a mere question of investment, consumption, savings and jobs; that they depend heavily on factors among which culture unquestionably plays an outstanding role. Creativity is of significant importance; without it no development process will work fully – and much less so in the case of an economy marked by globalization.

(f) Foreign Trade Policy: WTO

Except for some sentimentalists, the return towards a policy of closed economies is no longer a viable option for Latin America. Instead the challenge is to participate actively in the design of the future world economic order. As a result of the opening of their economies, Latin American countries contributed considerably to the success of the Uruguay Round. The great shortfall of this agreement, that of not having achieved an arrangement on the agricultural and services sectors, now has become the task of the WTO, established as the 'successor' to GATT in 1995. Latin American countries had placed high hopes on a successful outcome during the third round of the WTO ministers in Seattle in December, 1999, anticipating the opening of European and North American markets, especially for agricultural products.[40]

The Seattle talks failed not only because of inadequate preparation on the part of the WTO, but also by virtue of the intransigence of the United States with respect to the aspirations of developing countries, an attitude behind which the Europeans and in particular the French could hide their own agricultural interests. After Seattle it is obvious that the WTO is under review and – in spite of intense negotiations on the freedom of markets for services and agricultural products – the representatives of the member countries achieved no more than the receipt of national position papers and an agreement on the procedures for future negotiations. Furthermore international commentators have observed that the positions of the United States and Europe, as well as those of industrialized and developing countries, have moved even further apart since Seattle. It goes without saying that a solution to the current problems in those two sectors will be made all the more difficult by the inclusion of China in the group of 140 member countries of the WTO. For this reason, and also given the change of Director General, 2001 may be a decisive year for the future of the WTO.

The Seattle protests continued in Davos in January 2001, to the extent that they provoked a social counter-forum against globalization and (neo)liberalism in Porto Alegre, Brazil, where the 'Seattle Man' fought the 'Davos Man' (or Woman).[41] Seattle, Davos and Porto Alegre have clearly shown once more that a country must above all get its own house in order and formulate a convincing economic policy to solve its problems. One cannot expect globalization to solve them. If governments establish a clear sense of direction for their own agents it will be easier to combine the interests of entrepreneurs, consumers, workers and the state. A unilateral orientation towards foreign markets will not provide a solution to economic problems, and much less so to the social difficulties of the Latin American states. However a policy which neglects international markets will drag its country backwards.

Therefore the challenge for politicians in Latin America is to achieve an optimal combination of second generation reforms and the opening of the economy to the forces of globalization. The creation of free trade areas like FTAA or regional integration like the Andean Community or Mercosur constitute one of the more promising signs in this direction.

Since the times of ECLAC-policies,[42] not to mention the fruitless efforts of politicians since Simón Bolívar, Latin American governments have tried to strengthen their position by regional integration. It is not worth repeating here the (small) successes of the Latin American Free Trade

Association (LAFTA), and the more positive, though still unsatisfactory results, of CARICOM, the Central American Common Market (CACM), the Andean Community, and the Latin American Integration Association (LAIA). It will be more interesting to see if cooperation will develop in future between the areas of free trade and integration as a result of the efforts of President Fox (cooperation between Mexico, Brazil, Chile and Argentina) and President Cardoso (rapprochement of the Mercosur and the Andean Community).[43] The hemispheric triangle of cooperation between NAFTA, the Andean Community and Mercosur will take on a special importance in the negotiations for a Free Trade Area of the Americas (FTAA). The same is true for the political and economic association, proposed by the EU to the Mercosur (in its amplified version).

There are still discrepancies about whether regional integration agreements 'compete' with worldwide regulations of the WTO[44] or push the states to wider international agreements about opening their markets. If the negotiations for an FTAA prosper, giving a satisfactory result at the latest by 2005, Latin American countries will have less interest in negotiations within the WTO. The same may be said of negotiations between the EU and the (amplified) Mercosur.

Given the difficulties in reaching agreement on critical points, a 'two-speed' model is being proposed in the WTO – as was discussed in the EU. That is, that the wider arrangements for the liberalization of foreign trade will be valid only for those countries who wish to adopt them. If this happens, it seems clear that the WTO will weaken its position by comparison with regional agreements.[45] In such a case, it is likely that 'marginalization' will again overtake several Latin American countries. Independently of any progress with WTO, FTAA or the EU, it will be necessary to rethink economic policy in different Latin American countries. After the successful reforms in respect of short-term macroeconomic change, second generation reforms need to focus on institutional reform and a long-term 'national economic order'. With success on this front, the WTO and FTAA negotiations will prove easier, given a greater flexibility of national or regionally integrated economies.

CONCLUDING COMMENTS

The debate on the requirements set forth for a dialogue on economic models goes beyond the strictly economic ambit. To reach lastingly stable, socially sustainable, dynamic and democratically legitimized development, a close linkage between politics, economics and culture is vital.

It is likely that the reform policies of the first generation will diminish in their positive effect, given that economic reform, which is not widened or deepened, usually wears away after a certain time. One cannot rule out the possibility of increased structural unemployment and poverty, along with the flight of capital and inflation. To judge by the experience up to now, in a second generation reform greater efforts will go into addressing the symptoms than attacking the root of problems of the economic model. There is a chance that this attitude can be avoided if an effective dialogue is established on the deficits of current economic models and on the diffusion of possible solutions by comparative analysis of countries who have successfully negotiated the change process, such as Holland, Ireland, Denmark, Sweden, Portugal, New Zealand and others. The design of an economic model is a political task and thus depends on political viability.[46] The development of a political concept of the economy is the business of the political parties in conjunction with the sciences. If political parties continue to act more as instruments designed to assure presidential power, then another civic institutional place or space should be created to allow for conceptual reflection on communication between the needs of the people, and the government's possibilities.[47]

This debate on economic policies in Latin America, until now more characterized by pragmatism than by systemic ideas, should be transformed into a wider political and scientific dialogue. If the best intellectual forces could be engaged in this process, there is hope for faster and more sustainable economic and social development, one which can consolidate first generation reforms institutionally and structurally, while at the same time diminishing their negative effects bit by bit. The positive results will be more evident if a package of measures can be designed which combines the political, economic, social and cultural aspects of the national economic model.

Notes

1. These ten instruments are: fiscal discipline, priority in public spending for education and health, fiscal reform, positive and market generated rates of interest, competitive exchange rates, liberal trade policy, openness for direct foreign investment, privatization, deregulation and defence of private property. See Shahid Javed Burki and Guillermo E. Perry, *Más allá del consenso de Washington, La hora de la reforma institucional* (Beyond the Washington Consensus, Time for Institutional Reform), World Bank, Washington, D.C., 1998, p. 8.

2. An analysis of these elements and their application to the globalization of the German economy, entitled *Das Konzept der sozialen Marktwirtschaft, Grundlagen, Erfahrungen und neue Aufgaben* (The Concept of Social Market Economy, Principles, Experiences and New Challenges), St. Augustin, 1999, has been carried out by a working party of the Konrad Adenauer Foundation, chaired by the German ex-Federal Minister for Finance, Gerhard Stoltenberg.
3. Two practical examples serve to illustrate the difference between the policy of *economic order* and the policy of *economic process*. The decision to give autonomy to the Central Bank is part of the *economic order* policy. If a Central Bank changes the interest-rate of reimbursement, thus influencing capital markets, this is regarded as an *economic process* measure. Similarly if the government decides to change the tax system, this is an economic order measure given its impact on such fundamental aspects of the economy as business competition, social justice, overall attractiveness for economic activity, and distribution of taxes between central and regional government. If on the other hand, the government decides to change the tax rate or the method of collection, if it accords taxation advantages for certain activities for a certain period, then we are referring to measures which are part of the economic process policy.
4. Ludwig Erhard, *Wohlstand für alle* (Welfare for All), Düsseldorf, 1957.
5. When Ricardo Lagos took over as President of Chile, the then Prime Minister of Italy, D'Alema, together with Lagos and the Presidents Cardoso of Brazil and De la Rúa of Argentina, commended the *Third Way* as a means of future orientation of economic policy. It remains to be seen if this alternative to capitalism and socialism might develop into something more concrete. The *Social Market Economy*, by virtue of being a precise model, has defined individual freedom of action and social responsibility more satisfactorily. The former President of Chile, Patricio Aylwin, took this economic model as the basis for a dialogue on Human Development in Latin America – Challenges for Christian Democracy (*Desarrollo Humano en América Latina, Desafíos para la Democracia Cristiana*; the contributions were published under this title in December 1996 in Santiago de Chile).
6. Economic Commission for Latin America and the Caribbean (ECLAC) 1999, *Balance preliminary de las economías latinoaméricanas*, Santiago, Chile, 2000, page A-1 of the statistical appendix; the calculation was based on 1995 prices.
7. ECLAC, *Balance preliminar de las economías latinoaméricanas*, Santiago, Chile, 2000, page A-4 shows a difference in urban unemployment ranging from 19.8 per cent for Colombia to 2.6 per cent for Mexico.
8. ECLAC, *Balance preliminar de las economías latinoaméricanas*, Santiago, Chile, 2000, pp. 1–18.
9. IMF, *World Economic Outlook*, Washington, D.C., May 1998, pp. 145–6.
10. An ECLAC study ratifies Wolfensohn's data; approximately 35 per cent of the population of Latin America lives in poverty. This figure has been reduced since the beginning of the 1990s, but recently is returning to the 1980s level, the beginnning of what was characterized as the 'lost decade'. (ECLAC, *Panorama social de América Latina* (Social Panorama of Latin America), Santiago/Chile, 1999, p. 17.) This means that over the last 20 years the poverty situation has not improved in Latin America.

11. According to the same source, the corresponding figure for Africa is 5.2 per cent and 8.8 per cent for Eastern Europe.

12. IMF, *World Economic Outlook*, Washington, D.C., May 1998, pp. 145–6. ECLAC agrees, confirming that the distribution of income in some countries, especially in South America, has deteriorated. The Gini coefficient which measures income distribution has increased slightly in Costa Rica, Argentina, Brazil and Panama in comparison with seven years ago, and more notably in Venezuela and Paraguay. Other countries show improvements in the distribution of income, particularly Ecuador and Honduras, countries who have not improved their economy in the last seven years. See ECLAC, *Panorama social, de América Latina*, Santiago/Chile, 1999, pp. 57–67.

13. These ten instruments are listed in note 1.

14. This illusion is based on the belief in the role of an 'invisible hand' (Adam Smith) in economic activity and ignores the power structures and interdependencies relevant to the design of an economic policy.

15. A Transparency International study in Berlin characterizes most Latin American countries as highly corrupt states. Latin American countries are ranked in 69th place out of a total of 99, far below the position of industrialized countries which occupy the first 18 places. See Transparency International, *Corruption Perception Index (CPI)*, 1999, http/www.transparency.de/documents/cpi/index.html#cpi.

16. In Latin America, even more than in Southern Europe, personal relations play a greater role in social life and in business circles than in the US or Northern Europe. This phenomenon is evident in the labour market and in 'competitive' relations. Potential competitors agree on market conditions, on product differentiation, on regional division of markets, thus creating a *de facto* concentration and giving rise to 'substitution gaps' which are normally not sanctioned by the Monopoly Commission, if such exists.

17. Unfortunately protectionism still inhibits the movement of agricultural goods. Norms of hygiene and animal protection also contribute to the issue. The same is true for the services sector. Problems in these two areas could not be resolved in the Uruguay Round.

18. The study, *Die vielen Gesichter der Globalisierung – Perspektiven einer menschengerechten Weltordnung* (The Many Faces of Globalization – Perspectives on a World Human Order), carried out by a group of experts, 'Weltwirtschaft und Sozialethik' ('World Economy and Social Ethics'), and by institutions including church-related groups like Adveniat, Caritas Internacional, Misereor, Missio Aachen, Missio München y Renovabis (edited by the group for scientific studies on challenges for the world church of the German Episcopal Conference, Bonn, November 1999), refers to these problems which up to now have received little consideration at the micro level.

19. See Hans-Günther Schlotter (ed.), *Ordnungspolitik an der Schwelle des 21 Jahrhunderts* (Economic Order Policy on the Threshold of the Twenty-First Century), Baden Baden, 1997, pp. 7–8.

20. This concept has its origins in the Economic School (of the University) of Freiburg, Germany, where scientists like Hayek, Eucken, Röpke and others have developed a concept which combines maximum individual liberty with

an order which is acceptable for the majority in society. See Baldur Wagner, 'La Economía Social de Mercado: orígenes históricos, principios básicos y reformas necesarias' (The Social Market Economy: History, Basic Principles and Necessary Reforms), in *Contribuciones*, no. 4/2000, pp. 67–8.

21.   On the experience in Latin America, see the analysis of Dieter W. Benecke, 'El modelo de la Economía Social de Mercado – Semejanzas y diferencias con otros modelos en el mundo' (The Model of the German Social Market Economy – Similarities to and Differences from Other Models in Operation in the World), in *Desarrollo Humano en América Latina …* , pp. 149–56. See also Klaus Weigelt (ed.), *Soziale Marktwirtschaft im Aufwind* (The Social Market Economy on the Rise), Herford, 1989, pp. 9–90. The subsidiarity element has an added dimension by virtue of the European Union experience; see Frank Ronge, *Legitimität durch Subsidiarität, Der Beitrag des Subsidiaritätsprinzips zur Legitimation einer überstaatlichen politischen Ordnung in Europa* (Legitimacy on the Basis of Subsidiarity, the Contribution of the Principle of Subsidiarity to the Legitimization of a Supranational Political Order), Baden-Baden, 1998.

22.   See Dieter Cassel, 'Wirtschaftspolitik als Ordnungspolitik' (Political Economy and Policy for the Design of an Economic Order), in Dieter Cassel, Bernd-Thomas Ramb and H. Jörg Thieme (eds), *Ordnungspolitik* (Policy for the Design of an Economic Order), Munich, 1988, p. 315.

23.   Joseph Stiglitz, 'More Instruments and Broader Goals: Moving Towards the Post-Washington Consensus', speeches of the then chief economist of the World Bank, 7 January 1998 in Helsinki on the occasion of the annual Wider Lecture, p. 28, http://www.worldbank.org/html/extdr/extme/js-010798/wider.htm.

24.   Indebtedness has dogged the policies of various Latin American countries since the 1980s. In 2000 its gravity was such that it precipitated the fall of the President of Ecuador. See Osvaldo Hurtado, 'La deuda externa del Ecuador y sus efectos económicos y sociales en la segunda mitad del siglo XX' (The External Debt of Ecuador and Its Economic and Social Effects in the Second Half of the Twentieth Century), in Dieter W. Benecke and Alexander Loschky (eds), *Deuda externa, ¿Obstáculo para el desarrollo?* (External Debt – an Obstacle to Development?), CIEDLA-Buenos Aires, 2001.

25.   In the majority of Latin American countries, organizations for consumer protection have little scope for action. They are rarely consulted in the legislative process. Also at the supranational level, as for example in the Mercosur, consumer rights have been relegated with respect to producers' rights. It would be timely to introduce the discussion of consumer interests to the regular consultations of the Social and Economic Commission of the Mercosur.

26.   International financial institutions, globalized banks and international speculators also intervene in these cases, a factor which does not always facilitate the task of politicians. In Brazil the free circulation of capital was limited by a ceiling for export of capital, so as to stabilize the exchange rate between the Real and the dollar. Finally the Central Bank of Brazil could not resist the pressure to devalue, and ceased intervening in the foreign currency market. The Chilean government also temporarily limited the flow of foreign capital, introducing a provision which required that foreign

investment resources be deposited for six months in the central bank before being invested effectively. The 'speculative mobility' of international capital, which has increased within the framework of globalization, was discussed in a CIEDLA seminar on 'Fluctuación del capital extranjero y diseño de las políticas económicas nacionales en América Latina' (Fluctuation of Foreign Capital and the Design of National Economic Policies in Latin America) in October 1999. See http://www.kas-ciedla.org.ar/seminarios/info_fluc_cap_extr.htm.

27. The first attempt at dollarization in Ecuador resulted in the fall of President Mahuad. His successor Noboa insisted on the same plan, also giving rise to social disturbances. In Argentina, dollarization, fixed in April 1991 by law (no. 23.928) as convertibility of the Argentinian peso with the dollar in a 1:1 relationship, was accepted by the population with relief, although the 1:1 relationship has caused controversial discussions since 1999. In Central America, especially El Salvador and Guatemala, the experience has been similar to that of Ecuador, although less problematic

28. Many issues are still unclear. What role will the Federal Reserve Bank play in the future? Will the Euro compete on equal terms with the dollar? Will the US react more positively to dollarization if the Euro gets stronger?

29. On this, see Dieter W. Benecke, Rolando Franco, Martín Krause and Mikel de Viana in *Contribuciones*, no. 4/1999, CIEDLA-Buenos Aires. See also *Efectividad del sistema educacional en América Latina* (Effectiveness of the Educational System in Latin America), the results of a CIEDLA seminar in November 1999 in Costa Rica, http://www.kas-ciedla.org.ar/seminarios/info_edu_cosricas.htm

30. Here the more practicable political concept of Erhard Kantzenbach (*Die Funktionsfähigkeit des Wettbewerbs* (Functionality of Competition), Göttingen, 1966) is preferred to the concept of 'free', 'perfect' or 'regulated' competition. It is worth also noting the role of the SMEs and non-profit organization in competition (Dieter W. Benecke, *Kooperation und Wachstum in Entwicklungsländern* (Competition and Growth in Developing Countries), Tübingen, 1972, esp. pp. 133–84.

31. Ernst Heuss, *Allgemeine Markttheorie* (General Market Theory), Tübingen-Zürich, 1965, p. 9, places the entrepreneur who is a 'spontaneous imitator' and the entrepreneur who is a 'conservative' between the pioneer and the administrator types as described by Schumpeter.

32. In Latin America the discussion turns almost exclusively on direct investment by foreign enterprises, but not so much on the possibility that Latin American enterprises might invest in other regions like Central and Eastern Europe as part of joint ventures.

33. The main reasons for corruption are the absence of severe controls, the low salaries of government employees in comparison with the private sector and the change of civil servants with a change of government.

34. Here the case of the Brazilian enterprise Sucocítrico Cutrale Ltda. is worthy of mention. This company controls 80 per cent of the world market for citric juices. (See *Neue Zürcher Zeitung*, 7 August 2000). On the Mercosur, see Félix Peña, 'Una política de competencia económica en el MERCOSUR' (Economic Competition Policy in the Mercosur), in Dieter W. Benecke and Alexander Loschky (eds), *MERCOSUR – Desafío político* (Mercosur – a Political Challenge), *CIEDLA-Buenos Aires, 2001.*

35. At present an interesting experiment is taking place in Córdoba, Argentina, where the provincial governor has reduced taxes (while the national government has increased taxation on salaries), launching at the same time a regional and non-urban development programme.

36. On this, see Oscar Godoy Arcaya, Alberto Benegas Lynch, Carlos Sabino and Rolando Franco in *Contribuciones*, no. 3/2000, CIEDLA-Buenos Aires.

37. This phenomenon has become apparent in the debate between the participants in the World Economic Forum at Davos in Switzerland and the 'Social World Forum' in Porto Alegre, Brazil, in January 2001. Approximately 10,000 people, mostly representatives of NGOs from 122 countries, congregated in Porto Alegre to protest the negative effects of globalization and (neo)liberalism.

38. There are a number of studies on this issue in Europe, for example that of the Ifo-Institut on *Entwicklungstrends von Kunst und Kultur* (Tendencies in the Development of Art and Culture), by Marlies Hummel and Cornelia Waldkircher, Munich, 1991, especially, p. 12 on the question of the added value of culture; or Joe Durkan's study, *The Economics of the Arts in Ireland*, Dublin, 1994, which was carried out as part of a strategic programme of the Arts Council of Ireland (The Arts Plan 1995–1997, Dublin 1994). Similar studies have been carried out in Sweden, Finland and Holland.

39. It should be remembered that many pop groups come from economically marginalized areas.

40. Neither the arrangements on services GATS nor on brand protection rights TRIPS were modified in a way which would improve the Latin American position. Without a harmonization of competition laws, it will be difficult to reach satisfactory solutions at a global level. On the other hand, the existence of a system of arbitration to which the member states of the WTO are subject is a positive step towards greater justice in international free trade.

41. Simon Heusser *Wiederkehr der Deterministen* (Return of the Determinists), Tagesanzeiger, Zürich, 2 August 2000.

42. The UN Economic Commission for Latin America and the Caribbean, (ECLAC) has had a very strong influence in the 1960s and 1970s through its advice to governments on import substitution policies and regional integration.

43. See Dieter W. Benecke and Alexander Loschky, 'Mexiko sucht die enge Kooperation mit Argentinien, Brasilien und Chile' (Mexico Looks for a Closer Cooperation with Argentina, Brazil and Chile), in *Welt Report* (World Report), October/2000, Konrad Adenauer Foundation, St Augustin, pp. 13–16.

44. More than 170 regional or bilateral free trade agreements have been reached without the WTO and another 70 are in negotiation (see *Neue Zürcher Zeitung,* 13/14 January 2001), a fact which contradicts the globalization tendency and shows the reduced confidence in world-level agreements, arrived at previously through the GATT and now by the WTO.

45. The EU submitted its position to the WTO at the end of 2000. According to this, the EU is against a piecemeal negotiation of agricultural policy. It demands a packet of measures, for example that there should be equal treatment as regards export subsidy, official credits on exports (frequently used by the US); it proposes regulations on environment and animal protection (the case of the tortoises, for example), consumer protection to create more transparency about food products, among others.

46. If in 1949, the leader of the Christian Democrats, Konrad Adenauer, had failed to achieve a majority and if his opponent in the Social Democrats, Kurt Schumacher, had become the first Chancellor of West Germany, it is very possible that the Social Market Economy would not have been applied or would have been applied much later.

47. This is without doubt a fundamental reason for the low public prestige of politicians in Latin America. On this topic see various articles in *Contribuciones*, the journal of CIEDLA-Buenos Aires. Among others, see Marta Lagos, 'Quó vadis, América Latina? El estudio de la opinión pública regional en el Latinobarómetro' (Where to, Latin America? The Study of Regional Public Opinion in the Latinobarométer), in *Contribuciones*, no. 2/1999, pp. 31–53; Martínez O Gutenberg, 'Los partidos políticos en la lucha por la confianza – Problemas de representación y participación en América Latina y el resto del mundo' (Political Parties in the Struggle for Confidence – Problems of Representation and Participation in Latin America and in the Rest of the World), in *Contribuciones*, no. 1/2000, pp. 7–22; as well as the debates of a CIEDLA seminar on 'Participación en la Democracia' (Participation in Democracy), November 1999, Buenos Aires, final report, in http://www.kas-ciedla.org.ar/seminarios/info_san_ceferino..htm

Bibliography

ADVENIAT, Caritas Internacional, MISEREOR, *et al.* (ed.) (1999) *Die vielen Gesichter der Globalisierung – Perspektiven einer menschengerechten Weltordnung* (The Many Faces of Globalization – Perspectives on a World Human Order), November, Bonn.

ARTS COUNCIL OF IRELAND (1994), *The Arts Plan 1995–1997*, Dublin.

AYLWIN, PATRICIO (ed.) (1996) *Desarrollo Humano en América Latina, Desafíos para la Democracia Cristiana* (Human Development in Latin America, Challenges for Christian Democracy), Santiago/Chile.

BAUER RICHARD (2000) '*Optimistische Prognosen für Lateinamerika – Sorge um Armutsreduktion und soziale Stabilität*' (Optimistic Perspectives for Latin America – Preoccupation about the Reduction of Poverty and Social Stability) in *Neue Zürcher Zeitung*, 5 February.

BENECKE, DIETER W. (1972) *Kooperation und Wachstum in Entwicklungsländern* (Competition and Growth in Developing Countries), Tübingen.

BENECKE, DIETER W. (1996) '*El modelo de la Economía Social de Mercado en Alemania, sus similitudes y diferencias con otros modelos en el mundo*' (The model of the German Social Market Economy, its similarities to and differences from other models in operation in the world), in Patricio Aylwin (ed.) *Desarrollo Humano en America Latina, Desafios para la Democracia Cristiana* Santiago/Chile.

BENECKE, DIETER W., ROLANDO, FRANCO, MARTÍN, KRAUSE and MIKEL DE VIANA (1999) '*Efectividad del sistema educacional en América Latina*' (Effectiveness of the Educational System in Latin America), in *Contribuciones*, no. 4, Buenos Aires.

BENECKE, DIETER W. and ALEXANDER LOSCHKY (eds) (2001) '*Mercosur – Desafío político (Mercosur – A political challenge), Buenos Aires.*

272   *World Trade and Second Generation Reforms*

BENECKE, DIETER W. and ALEXANDER LOSCHKY (eds) (2001) *'Descentralización y coparticipación'* (Decentralization and fiscal participation), Buenos Aires.
BENECKE, DIETER W. and ALEXANDER LOSCHKY (eds) (2001) *'Deuda externa – ¿Obstáculo para el desarrollo?'* (External debt – An obstacle to development?), Buenos Aires.
BURKI, SHAHID JAVED, and GUILLERMO, E. PERRY (1998) *'Más allá del consenso de Washington – La hora de la reforma institucional'* (Beyond the Consensus of Washington – Time for Institutional Reforms), Washington, D.C.: World Bank.
CASSEL, DIETER (1998) 'Wirtschaftspolitik als Ordnungspolitik' (Political Economy and Policy for the Design of an Economic Order), in Dieter Cassel, Bernd- Thomas Ramb and H. Jörg Thieme (eds), *Ordnungspolitik* (Policy for the Design of an Economic Order), Munich.
CHOUDHRI, EHSAN U. and, DALIA S HAKURA (2000) *'Internacional Trade and Productivity Growth: Exploring the Sectoral Effects for Developing Countries'* in IMF staff papers, vol. 47, no. 1.
CIEDLA (1999) Centro Interdisciplinario de Estudios sobre el Desarrollo Latinoamericano (Interdisciplinary Center of Studies about the Latin American Development), Konrad Adenauer Foundation, *Fluctuación del capital extranjero y diseño de las políticas económicas nacionales en América Latina* (Fluctuation of Foreign Capital and the Design of National Economic Policies in Latin America), October, http://www.kas-ciedla.org.ar/seminarios/info_fluc_cap_extr.htm.
CIEDLA (1999) 'Participación en la Democracia' (Participation in Democracy), final report, November, Buenos Aires, http://www.kas-ciedla.org.ar/seminarios/info_san_ceferino..htm.
DURKAN, JOE (1994) *The Economics of the Arts in Ireland*, Dublin.
ECLAC (1999) (Economic Commission for Latin America and the Caribbean) *Balance preliminar de las economías latinoamericanas* (Preliminary Balance of the Economies in Latin America), Santiago/Chile.
ECLAC (1999) *Panorama social de América Latina* (Social Panorama of Latin America), Santiago/Chile.
ECLAC (2000) *Balance preliminar de las economías latinoamericanas*, Santiago/Chile.
ERHARD, LUDWIG (1957) *Wohlstand für alle* (Welfare for All), Düsseldorf.
GODOY ARCAYA, OSCAR, ALBERTO BENEGAS LYNCH, CARLOS SABINO and ROLANDO FRANCO, (2000) *'Responsabilidad, solidaridad y justicia social'* (Responsibility, Solidarity and Social Justice) in: *Contribuciones*, no. 3, Buenos Aires.
GUTENBERG, MARTÍNEZ O (2000) *'Los partidos políticos en la lucha por la confianza – Problemas de representación y participación en América Latina y el resto del mundo'* (Political Parties in the Struggle for Confidence – Problems of representation and participation in Latin America and in the rest of the world) in *Contribuciones*, no. 1, Buenos Aires.
HEUSS, ERNST (1965) *Allgemeine Markttheorie* (General Market Theory), Tübingen-Zürich.
HEUSSER, SIMON (2000) *Wiederkehr der Deterministen* (Return of the Determinists), Tagesanzeiger, Zürich.

HUMMEL, MARLIES and CORNELIA, WALDKIRCHER (1991) *Entwicklungstrends von Kunst und Kultur* (Tendencies in the Development of Art and Culture), Ifo – Institut, Munich.

HURTADO, OSVALDO (2001) '*La deuda externa del Ecuador y sus efectos económicos y socials en la segunda mitad del siglo XX*' (The External Debt of Ecuador and its Economic and Social Effects in the Second Half of the Twentieth Century) in Dieter W. Benecke and Alexander Loschky (eds) *Deuda externa, ¿Obstáculo para el desarollo?*, (External debt – An obstacle to development?), Buenos Aires, 2001.

INTERNATIONAL MONETARY FUND (IMF) (1998) *World Economic Outlook*, May, Washington, D.C.

KANTZENBACH, ERHARD (1966) *Die Funktionsfähigkeit des Wettbewerbs* (Working Competition), Göttingen.

Konrad Adenauer Stiftung (Foundation) (1999) '*Das Konzept der sozialen Marktwirtschaft, Grundlagen, Erfahrungen und neue Aufgaben*' (The concept of Social Market Economy, Principles, Experiences and new Challenges), St Augustin.

LAGOS, MARTA (1999) '*Quó vadis, América Latina? El estudio de la opinión pública regional en el Latinobarómetro*' (Where To Go, Latin America? The study of regional public opinion in the Latinobarómeter) in *Contribuciones*, no. 2, Buenos Aires.

PEÑA, FÉLIX (2001) '*Una política de competencia económica en el Mercosur*' (Economic Competition Policy in the Mercosur) in Dieter W. Benecke and Alexander Loschky (eds) Mercosur – *Desafío político* (The Political Challenge), Buenos Aires.

RONGE, FRANK (1998) '*Legitimität durch Subsidiarität – Der beitrag des Subsidiaritätsprinzips zur Legitimation einer überstaatlichen politischen Ordnung in Europa*' (Legitimacy on the Basis of Subsidiarity: the Contribution of the Principle of Subsidiarity to the Legitimization of a Supranational Political Order), Baden Baden.

SCHLOTTER, HANS-GÜNTHER (ed.) (1997) *Ordnungspolitik an der Schwelle des 21. Jahrhunderts* (Economic Order Policy on the Threshold of the Twenty-First century), Baden Baden.

STIGLITZ, JOSEPH (1998) '*More Instruments and Broader Goals: moving towards the Post-Washington consensus*', speeches of the then chief economist of the World Bank, 7 January in Helsinki on the occasion of the annual Wider Lecture, http://www.worldbank.org/html/extdr/extme/js-010798/wider.htm.

Transparency International (1999) *Corruption Perception Index (CPI)*, http://www.transparency.de/documents/cpi/index.html#cpi.

WAGNER, BALDUR (2000) '*La Economía Social de Mercado – Orígenes históricos, principios básicos y reformas necesarias*' (The Social Market Economy: History, Basic Principles and Necessary Reforms) in *Contribuciones*, no. 4, Buenos Aires.

WEIGELT, KLAUS (ed.) (1989) *Soziale Marktwirtschaft im Aufwind* (The Social Market Economy on the Rise), Herford.

Index